RAINY RIVER LIVES

RAINY RIVER LIVES

STORIES TOLD BY MAGGIE WILSON

Compiled, edited, and with
an introduction by Sally Cole

University of Nebraska Press
Lincoln and London

Library of Congress
Cataloging-in-Publication Data

Wilson, Maggie, 1879–1940.
Rainy River lives : stories told by
Maggie Wilson / Maggie Wilson;
compiled, edited, and with an
introduction by Sally Cole.
p. cm.
Includes bibliographical references
and index.
ISBN 978-0-8032-2062-1 (pbk. :
alk. paper)
1. Ojibwa Indians—Anecdotes.
2. Ojibwa Indians—Social life and
customs—Anecdotes. 3. Ojibwa Indians—Folklore. 4. Tales—North
America. I. Cole, Sally C. II. Title.
E99.C6W64 2009
398.2089'97333—dc22
2008047613

Set in Sabon by Kim Essman.
Designed by Ashley Muehlbauer.

For my daughter,
Isabella,
in memory of
our women's winter

CONTENTS

ILLUSTRATIONS

FIGURES

In the basement of the National Museum of Natural History in Washington DC, one late summer afternoon in 1994, I stumbled on a packet of yellowed, handwritten letters. Intrigued by this unexpected find, I picked up the accompanying envelopes, postmarked 1933 and 1934. They were addressed to "Miss Ruth Landes, Department of Anthropology, Columbia University, New York City." The sender was Maggie Wilson from Emo, Ontario.

I began to read the letters. Once I started, I could not stop. Through the words of Maggie Wilson, I passed the next several days immersed in the lives of Ojibwe people living along the Rainy River on the Ontario-Minnesota border during the last decades of the nineteenth century and the first decades of the twentieth century. A few of the letters recounted *adusokan*, the oft-told traditional tales. By far the majority were accounts of individual lives. The letters began, "Dear Ruth, This is the story of . . ." and were signed, "Mrs. John Wilson" or "Your Mam, Maggie Wilson."

I was stunned. Here, rotting in a basement far from the Rainy River, was a firsthand insider's account of those years of disruption and dislocation as Ojibwes were moved onto reserves, missionized, and taken into residential schools. The stories told of increasing turmoil in the intimate lives of individuals and families. They also told of marvelous feats of survival, of parents' efforts to care for their children, of bonds among siblings, of love and companionship between men and women. Maggie Wilson, the storyteller, set universal themes of loyalty and love, of jealousy and revenge, on the historical stage of the Ojibwe world on the Rainy River.

If these letters crumbled without seeing the light of day, it would be, I felt, yet another tragedy.

That summer of 1994, I was thinking about writing a book on the life and work of anthropologist Ruth Landes. I had made my first trip to the National Anthropological Archives (held at the National Museum of Natural History in Washington DC) to look at Landes's papers—her diaries, letters, and field notes—which she had bequeathed to the archives on her death in 1991. James Glenn, then-chief archivist, had recently cataloged her papers, and I was the first scholar to consult them.

I went to James Glenn's office to ask him what he knew about Maggie Wilson and the letters. He told me that Wilson had been one of the key people who had helped Landes when, as a young graduate student at Columbia University, she had been sent to the Manitou Rapids Reserve in northwestern Ontario, Canada, by her supervisor, Ruth Benedict, to study Ojibwe belief in the guardian spirit. During the summer and fall of 1932, Ruth Landes lived on the reserve, where she boarded with the government farm instructor and his family and lived frugally on a small research grant provided by Benedict. Landes found Maggie Wilson to be a wonderful storyteller, and she undertook the research with Wilson as her chief consultant. From her daily budget Landes had paid Wilson one dollar for each day's work—a contract guided by Ojibwe principles of payment for knowledge. "The times were desperately poor," Landes later wrote, "so I made a point of paying her one dollar at the close of each day, besides small extras. She respected this punctilio, which happened to coincide with Ojibwe requirements surrounding the relationship of teacher and learner."[1] When it came time to return to New York, Landes had encouraged Wilson to continue to tell her stories by writing them down and mailing them to New York. And Landes persuaded Ruth Benedict to continue to pay Maggie Wilson from university funds: fifteen cents per double-sided page of a stenographer's pad. This explained why, at the end of letters, Wilson often totaled up the number of pages she was sending. Through this arrangement, Maggie Wilson sent more than one hundred stories in forty letter-packages to Columbia University.

As I later discovered, Ruth Landes had searched in vain for the story-letters during the last decade of her life. Years after her death, James Glenn finally located them among the papers of another Columbia University anthropologist, William Duncan Strong, and realized that they belonged in Ruth Landes's papers. Glenn surmised that, because Maggie Wilson had been paid by the university, Ruth Benedict had stored the handwritten pages in the office files of the Department of Anthropology. The letters had later inadvertently been filed with Duncan Strong's papers when he had assumed the position of chair of the department. From there they had made their way to the National Anthropological Archives.

The saga of the letters preoccupied me over the years after that summer day in 1994 as I researched and wrote my book *Ruth Landes: A Life in Anthropology*. I discovered that meeting Maggie Wilson, a skilled observer and storyteller of women's lives, was the key factor in redirecting Landes's research at Manitou Rapids. Landes would write a standard ethnographic report on Ojibwe culture for her doctoral dissertation—published in 1937 as *Ojibwa Sociology*—and would eventually publish her research on the guardian spirit concept in *Ojibwa Religion and the Midéwiwin* (1968). But Landes's research career changed irreversibly when she found that her own interests in women's lives and in the creative agency of the individual overlapped with the prevailing themes in the stories told by Maggie Wilson. Their collaboration is perhaps the first "team" of a woman anthropology student and a native woman consultant in the history of anthropology and resulted in the publication in 1938 of *The Ojibwa Woman*, one of the first critical studies of gender in the discipline.[2] Landes considered Maggie Wilson one of her "three great teachers of anthropology" along with Franz Boas and Ruth Benedict.[3]

Ruth Landes: A Life in Anthropology was published in 2003, but the packet of letters continued to nag at my conscience. They were irreplaceable: a native voice telling the story of colonization as experienced by the colonized. This rich and unique source of information was in danger of disappearing. Many pages were already illegible or incomplete due to fading ink and disintegrating paper. How could the stories be preserved? They were too important to abandon to their fate in the archives. They needed to be transcribed and copied on CD-ROM and returned to the Rainy River, where the people at Manitou Rapids did not even know of this vital piece of their history.

As I was deciding to begin the task, out of the blue in January 2005 I received an e-mail from Cheryl Copenace, who worked at the Kay-Nah-Chi-Wah-Nung Historical Centre, operated by the Rainy River First Nations at an ancient summer fishing village and burial mound site at Long Sault near Manitou Rapids on the Rainy River. She wrote: "While researching family history (Maggie was my great-grandmother), I came across your name and current project re: writing my Kokum's stories as told to Ruth Landes. I would like to invite you to view our Web site and perhaps visit our facility and local elders in the summer months. It would be an honor to meet the person who has taken an interest in the history of Rainy River First Nations, as well as offer you a tour of our community." This was the spark I needed to begin working on this compilation of Maggie Wilson's stories.

In the summer of 2005, I again visited the archives in Washington. This time I photocopied all of the still-existing stories Maggie Wilson had sent to Ruth Landes. Over the winter of 2005–6, aided by graduate student Jordan Davidson, who typed verbatim transcriptions of the handwritten letters, I began the process of editing the stories. In the spring of 2006, I arranged to visit the Kay-Nah-Chi-Wah-Nung Historical Centre to discuss the book project. Cheryl Copenace no longer worked at the center, but another of Maggie Wilson's great-granddaughters, Sherry Wilson, did. In May I traveled to Manitou Rapids bringing with me samples of the photocopies of the handwritten stories, of the typed verbatim transcriptions, and of the first drafts of my edited versions. I also brought copies of photographs I had found in the National Anthropological Archives and at the Minnesota Historical Society Archives that I thought might illustrate a book of Maggie Wilson's stories.

Sherry Wilson was thrilled with the idea of the book. She provided me with a space to work at the center and arranged for me to meet with the elder coordinator, Dorothy Medicine, to discuss the translation of the Ojibwe words and placenames mentioned in the stories. On that visit I also benefited from discussions with former chief Sonny McGinnis, who was developing programs at the center, seconded by the Department of Indian and Northern Affairs, where he now worked. On a return visit in September, Sherry Wilson arranged for me to meet with the elder Gladys De-Bungee, who also helped me with the translation of Ojibwe terms and names of places mentioned in the stories.

The keen interest and generous assistance I received at Manitou Rapids reinforced, indeed legitimized and validated, my devotion to this project. I am honored to have been able to work on this collection and to present these stories to future readers. The younger generation of Ojibwes may find in them a renewed source of pride in their heritage. The general public will, I hope, be informed and moved by stories about Ojibwe lives a century ago and Ojibwe spirituality, which survived centuries of assault.

Sally Cole

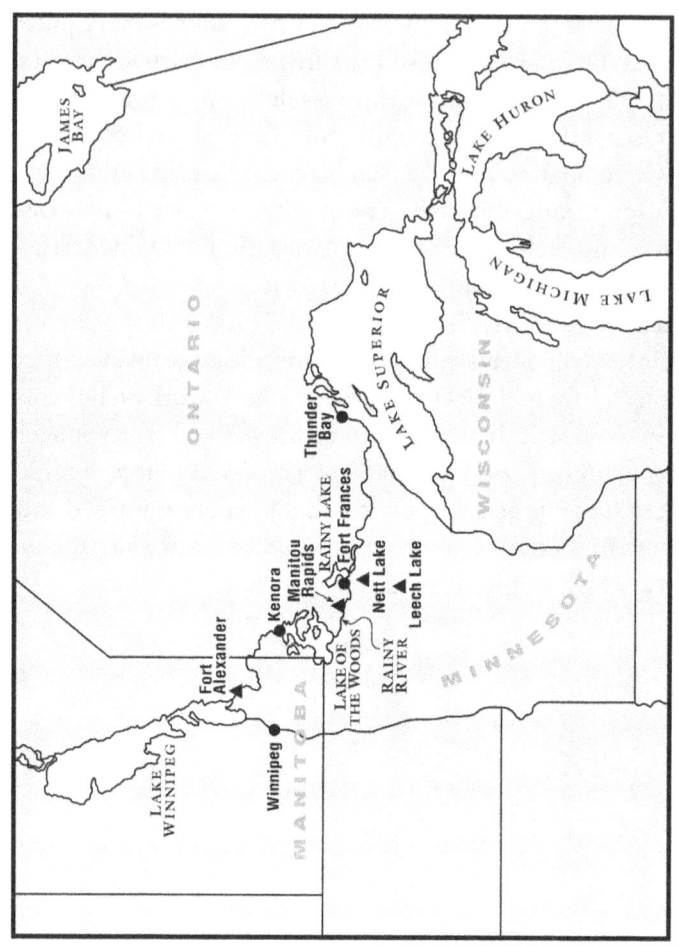

Map 1. Location of the territory of the Rainy River Ojibwes, northwestern Ontario and northern Minnesota.

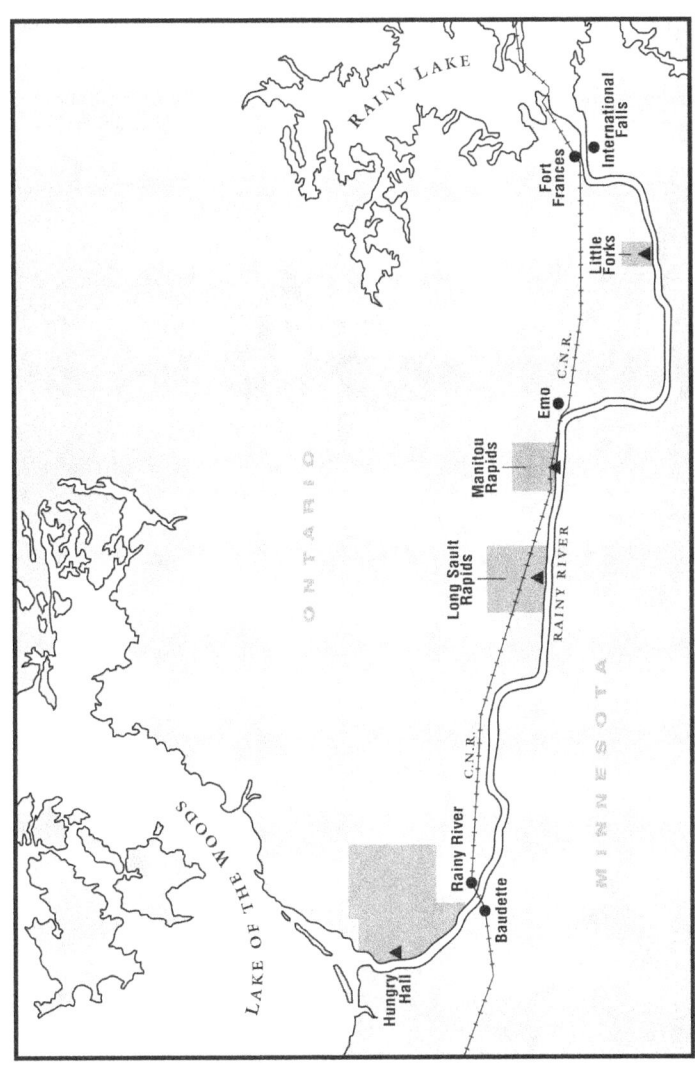

Map 2. The Rainy River.

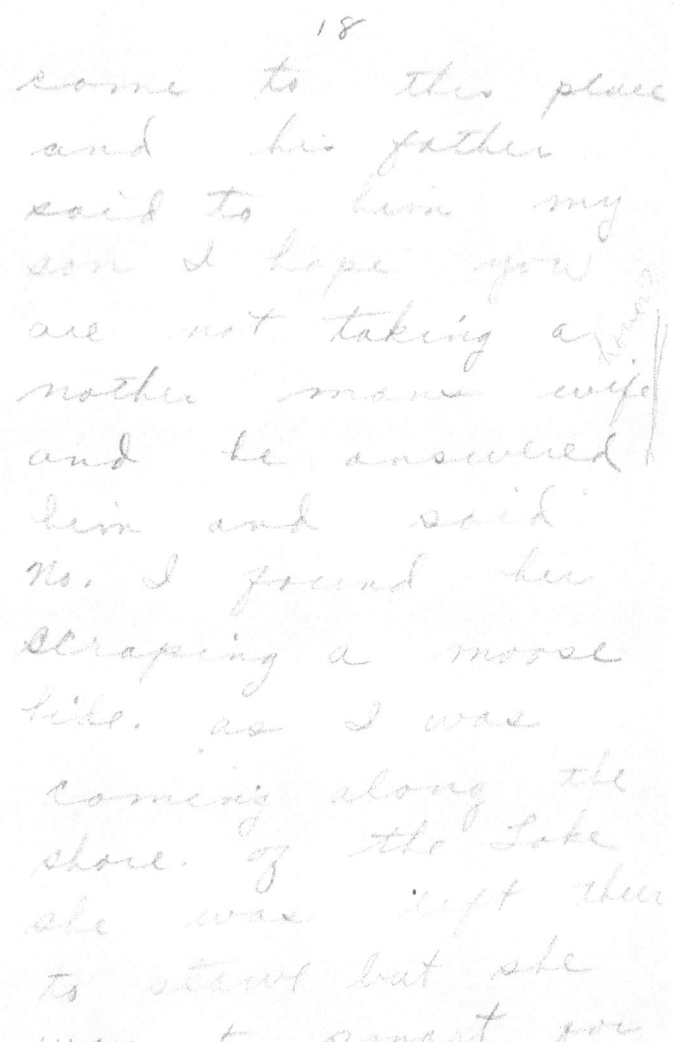

come to this place
and his father
said to him my
son I hope you
are not taking a
nother mans wife
and he answered
him and said
No, I found her
scraping a moose
hide, as I was
coming along the
shore of the Lake
she was left there
to starve but she
was to smart you

Fig. 1. Sample of handwritten story (see story 17 this volume, "She Was Left There to Starve, but She Was Too Smart for That"). Reprinted by permission from Ruth Landes Papers, story 13, box 37, National Anthropological Archives, Smithsonian Institution.

come to this place
and his father
said to him my
son I hope you
are not taking a
nother mans wife
and he answered
him and said
No. I found her
scraping a moose
hide. as I was
coming along the
shore. of the Lake
she was left their
to starve but she
was to smart for

Fig. 2. Sample of editor's verbatim transcription prior to editing, p. 18, story 13 (see story 17, "She Was Left There to Starve, but She Was Too Smart for That").

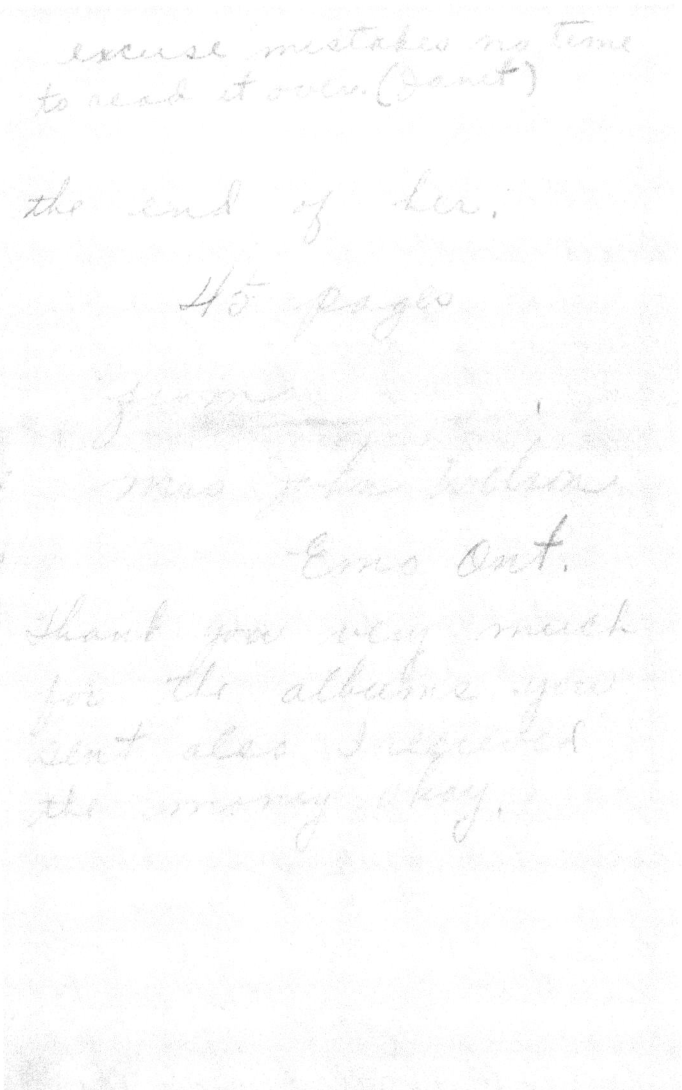

excuse mistakes no time
to read it over. (Janet)

the end of her.

45 pages

from

Mrs John Wilson

Emo Ont.

Thank you very much
for the albums you
sent also I received
the money okay.

Fig. 3. Sample of last page and postscript of letter containing story 28. Reprinted by permission from Ruth Landes Papers, story 110, box 38, National Anthropological Archives, Smithsonian Institution.

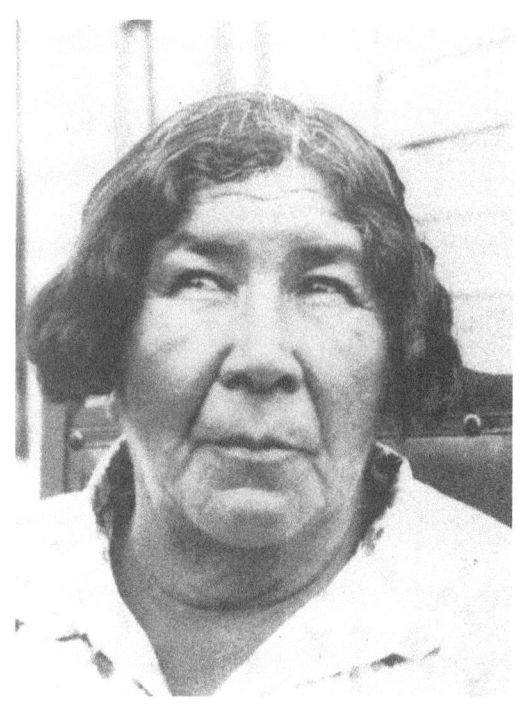

Fig. 4. Maggie Wilson, 1932.
Photo by Ruth Landes.
Reprinted by permission of
Research Institute for the
Study of Man.

Fig. 5. Manitou Rapids, 1920.
Photo by Frances Densmore.
Reprinted by permission of
Minnesota Historical Society.

Fig. 6. Maggie Wilson (on right) and daughter Christina, standing in beaded dress, 1920. Photo by Frances Densmore. Reprinted by permission of Minnesota Historical Society.

Fig. 7. Maggie Wilson's daughter Christina, in beaded dress with birch-bark basket, 1920. Photo by Frances Densmore. Reprinted by permission of Minnesota Historical Society.

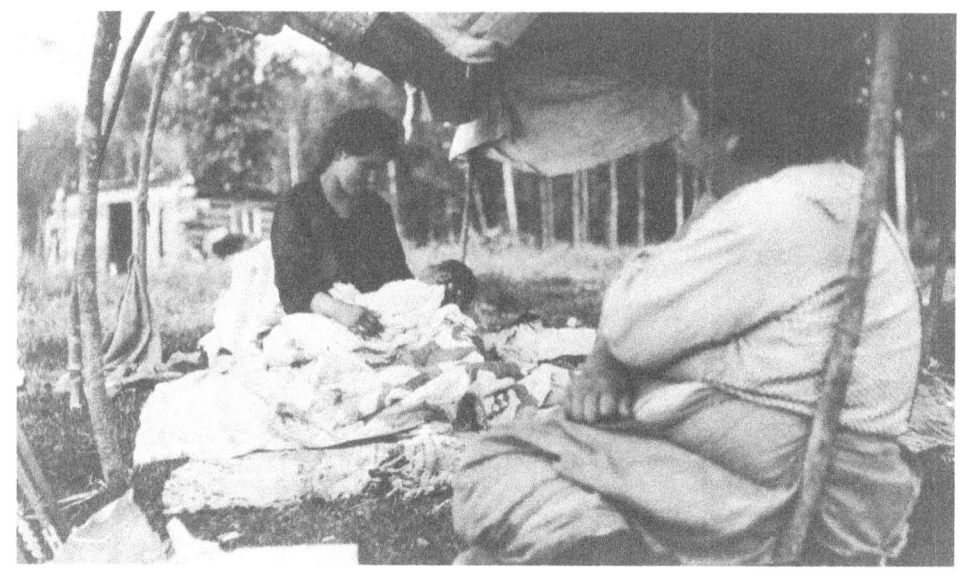

Fig. 8. Maggie Wilson (on right), daughter Christina, and baby, 1920. Photo by Frances Densmore. Reprinted by permission of Minnesota Historical Society.

Fig. 9. Maggie Wilson's son Leonard and daughter Janet, in powwow dress, 1932. Reprinted by permission from Ruth Landes Papers, neg. 99-10468, National Anthropological Archives, Smithsonian Institution.

Fig. 10. Maggie Wilson's daughter Janet in powwow dress, 1932. Reprinted by permission from Ruth Landes Papers, neg. 99-10465, National Anthropological Archives, Smithsonian Institution.

Fig. 11. Maggie Wilson's daughter Christina (standing at left), with her husband, children, and mother-in-law, 1932. Reprinted by permission from Ruth Landes Papers, neg. 99-10463, National Anthropological Archives, Smithsonian Institution.

Fig. 12. Maggie Wilson, sitting in front of her house at Manitou Rapids, 1932. Reprinted by permission from Ruth Landes Papers, neg. 99-10467, National Anthropological Archives, Smithsonian Institution.

Fig. 13. Birch-bark wigwam at Manitou Rapids, 1920. Photo by Frances Densmore. Reprinted by permission of Minnesota Historical Society.

Fig. 14. Cooking fire at Manitou Rapids, 1920. Photo by Frances Densmore. Reprinted by permission of Minnesota Historical Society.

I used to think we told these stories
To learn to survive winter
But now I know that winter comes
So that we tell stories
And learn to survive life.
—Kimberly Blaeser, *Trailing You*

Somewhere a woman lights her pipe.
Tobacco is sprinkled on the water and
lights sparkle across her face. A small
whirlwind prayer brushes over the
ripples. *Please remember me. Please
remember me.*
—Al Hunter, *Spirit Horses*

The family was the heart of Ojibwe society. Here children modeled adult roles as they followed elders in the performance of daily tasks and learned Ojibwe history, tradition, and values. The grandparents, the nominal heads of the group, were revered by all but especially by the young, who listened to their stories. Indeed, the grandparents were the guardians and repository of Ojibwe cultural knowledge. Their stories were imbued with spirituality. Stories educated about the past and the present, inspired the future, and entertained during the long winter nights.

Traditional social positions and roles played by men and women in Ojibwe society emerged over millennia in the patterned seasonal quest for subsistence in hunting, fishing, and gathering. Roles of women and men were reciprocal. Balance between the tasks performed by women and men created a harmonious society (Klein and Ackerman 1995; Leacock 1978). At the same time, the seasonal and annual fluctuations in the resources on which the Ojibwes depended for subsistence required role flexibility. If the cultural ideal was that men were hunters and women processed the rewards of the hunt to make food, clothing, and shelter, it was also accepted that both men and women performed whatever tasks needed to be done to ensure the survival of their families. This flexibility in gender roles was combined with the fundamental Ojibwe respect for the personal autonomy of the individual. Women, like men, were considered autonomous persons who possessed decision-making authority over their time, their labor, and the fruits of their labor (Albers 1989; Landes 1938; Leacock 1978). Thus the roles individual women assumed were not contested but were respected as personal choice.

The absences of men while hunting and the ever-present possibility of sickness, injury, or early death of a father or husband required that women have the independence, resourcefulness, skills, and strength to provide food for their families. As male absences lengthened due to their participation as trappers and traders in the fur trade over the course of the eighteenth and nineteenth centuries, women were often left on their own to tend gardens, hunt and fish, and entertain and educate children.

In letters and journals European traders and explorers remarked on the autonomy and leadership of Ojibwe women. Ethnohistorian Theresa Schenck has written a set of historical portraits of Ojibwe women who were recognized political leaders, courageous warriors, powerful visionaries, or shrewd traders. She underscores that Ojibwe gender roles were flexible and complementary: "There was a recognized role for women in warfare, in hunting and in government while men participated in such activities as gathering wild rice, producing maple sugar and making the cradle board" (1995, 2). British writer Anna Jameson, after spending the summer of 1838 among the Ojibwes at Sault Ste. Marie, was so impressed with the autonomy of the women that she described the Ojibwe woman as "despotic in her lodge," noting, "Everything it contains is hers; even of the game her husband kills, she has the uncontrolled disposal. If her husband does not please her, she scolds and even cuffs him and it is in the highest degree unmanly to answer or strike her" (1923, 286–87). Louise Erdrich provides a portrait of the archetypal woman in her description of the extraordinary woman who adopted and raised the white boy John Tanner in Rainy River country in the eighteenth century: "Net-no-kwa is a stereotype-busting powermonger. When she approached the fort . . . with her flag flying from her boat (it was probably a flag that described her personal dream vision), she was saluted by the fort's gun. She was a shrewd trader, an observant hunter, and a medicine woman who also got smashed on whiskey from time to time. She saved her family many times by her resourcefulness in times of crisis" (2003, 44).

After the treaty signings and the people's forced settlement on reserves in the late nineteenth century, some Ojibwe men took seasonal wage work in logging camps and mines, on steamboats, and in railroad construction. Women typically remained on the reserves to raise children and care for the elderly. Destitution, sickness, alcohol, and the intrusions of Indian agents and missionaries were all features of daily life on the reserves. Storytelling became the foundation of women's efforts to pass on cultural values and knowledge to their children and to maintain continuity in the face of social rupture.

Ojibwe writers Louise Erdrich, Gerald Vizenor, and Kimberly Blaeser all revere the role that women's storytelling has played in Ojibwe communities. For Erdrich storytelling is renewal for the soul in the face of what she calls "soul theft": "the systematic hard work of inventive humiliations and abuse by government and . . . nuns and priests" (2003, 5). "Telling stories through and in spite of immense hardship, dispossession and anguish" she says, has provided Ojibwe women with the medium through which to explore and grapple with the conflict and pain they endure. In turn Erdrich finds that "Ojibwa narrative has grown rich and subtle on the ironies of conflict" (2001a).

For Vizenor telling stories is "liberation by imagination" (Vizenor and Lee 1999, 91). Through storytelling, he says, women gain the courage they need to keep their families together in the face of poverty and racism (Vizenor 2000, 51–64). Women's stories honor the humor and "tragic wisdom" of their situation, and "tragic wisdom is our best chance in a dangerous world" (Vizenor and Lee 1999, 21).

Blaeser finds a special "storytelling aesthetic" in Ojibwe women's stories, "a particular world view that attributes to words and sounds a spiritual aspect" (1997, 555). Their stories weave the spiritual and the mundane, "the sacred and the daily." According to Blaeser, in Ojibwe stories, as in life, there is "a sacred center from which ripples of power and connection emanate. The center (or centers) is always dynamic, never static, and thus invokes responses which might include return, forgiveness, healing, vision" (558). Stories are about intricately linked relationships, about intersections: "Spatial, temporal and spiritual realities of Native people reflect a fluidity that disallows complete segregation between experiences of life and death, physical and spiritual, past and present, human and nonhuman. Thus they are reflected in cycles that involve return, reconnection and relationship" (557).

Maggie Wilson was a storyteller in this ancestral Ojibwe tradition. Her stories tell of the lives of Ojibwe people living along the Rainy River during the last half of the nineteenth century and the first decades of the twentieth century. The stories are full of strong women characters. They document the resourcefulness of women as they overcome starvation, abandonment, abuse, and loss. Wilson's stories illuminate the devastating impacts of colonialism and forced assimilation on Ojibwe women and families. She is full of love and admiration for her characters as they struggle to protect their children and keep their families intact. She tells stories to champion their lives. Through the examples of individual women's lives, she teaches lessons in autonomy and the importance of practical skills. The stories are both cautionary and inspiring.

When the young American anthropology student Ruth Landes arrived on the Rainy River in the summer of 1932 and began to ask Maggie Wilson standard anthropological questions about "marriage and residence patterns" and "the guardian spirit concept," Wilson chose to reply by telling stories of lives lived by people along the Rainy River. She constructed stories from the orally transmitted details of people's lives that circulate daily in all societies. The events of the lives portrayed in these stories were undoubtedly well known up and down the Rainy River. Wilson had known many of the people herself. In this sense, in writing the stories Wilson may be seen as the chronicler or archivist of these lives. Her stories honor their memory.

Remarkably, she had the rare ability to be reflexive and introspective about her own cultural setting. She documents in her stories the intimate social world of a particular time and place—the Rainy River at the turn of the twentieth century—the seasonal round of subsistence activities, the presence of Europeans, the mixed marriages. She names and illustrates Ojibwe customs and characteristics. At the same time, she recognizes the universal in Ojibwe experience. In Maggie Wilson's stories the Rainy River Ojibwes, like people everywhere, are faced with ethical dilemmas; experience shame, jealousy, and conflict; and long for everlasting love. Through compassionate storytelling she presents Ojibwe people in their special particularity and their universal humanity.

Wilson applied immense creativity, intellect, and keen observation skills in her storytelling. She gave the same careful attention to color and detail in her stories as she did in the intricate beadwork for which she was locally renowned. She employed a mixture of description, reconstructed dialogue, and invented internal monologues to craft stories of suspense, drama, and resolution. In her stories she recorded the minutiae of everyday family life, drawing together the threads of individual lives in narrative plots that often reached epic scale. In conventional written history of North America, Native people are "people without history" (Wolf 1984). They are cardboard figures with walk-on parts. In Maggie Wilson's stories the people and places of the Rainy River are at center stage.

Maggie Wilson told stories in the ancient Ojibwe tradition for courage, connection, and renewal, and in that sense her craft may be understood in Vizenor's terms as "liberation by imagination." Her imagination was rooted in experience. Her own life was the foundation of her practice as a storyteller.

Born in 1879 on the Little Forks Reserve, Maggie Wilson was the first child of Elizabeth and Benjamin Spence. Elizabeth's father was a Scottish trader with the Hudson's Bay Company. Her mother, in Maggie Wilson's words, was a "Cree half-breed woman." In one of her letters to the anthropologist Ruth Landes, Maggie recounts her mother's life.[1]

When Elizabeth was about five years old (ca. 1865), her father returned to Scotland, and she never saw him again. Soon afterward Elizabeth's mother married a Cree man, and the new family camped near Fort Alexander on the Winnipeg River north of Kenora. The stepfather was an abusive man. Following Native custom that extended family members adopt and care for orphans and children needing protection, Elizabeth was taken away by one of her mother's sisters. She spent two peaceful years with her aunt. Then a cousin who was married to a Hudson's Bay Company employee took the seven-year old girl to live with her and to work as a domestic servant. Elizabeth was regularly beaten, deprived of food, and locked alone in the company warehouse. When the cousin's husband was transferred to Fort Frances, Elizabeth had to go along. At the age of fourteen, after years of abuse, she finally ran away and found work at an Anglican minister's house. There she met Ben Spence, who worked as a driver for the minister taking him by dog team throughout the Rainy River district.

Elizabeth and Ben married in the summer of 1878 and moved to Little Forks Reserve, where Ben's father, Peter Spence, an English-speaking Cree from Fort Alexander, taught at the Anglican Church Missionary Society school. The year after they married and the year Maggie was born, Ben and Elizabeth began to receive annual treaty payments under the terms of Treaty no. 3 as members of the Little Forks band of Rainy River Ojibwes.

In the early years of their marriage, Ben took a succession of seasonal jobs, working for land surveyors and on the steamers that plied the Rainy River between Fort Frances and Kenora. Maggie recalled frequent conflicts between Elizabeth and her mother-in-law over the rights to the wages and purchased goods such as food and calico cloth ("print") that Ben sent home.

In 1881 Peter Spence was moved by the Church Missionary Society to teach at the Anglican mission at Long Sault Reserve. Ben Spence rented a house in Fort Frances and brought Elizabeth and Maggie there to live for the winter. In the spring, at Peter Spence's request, the family moved to Long Sault. After building a house there, Ben again went to work on the riverboats for the summer, and Elizabeth worked breaking the soil for a garden to plant potatoes and corn. Maggie reported that she and her mother nearly starved that summer until Ben returned bringing with him tea, flour, other groceries, and "things that were nice to eat," along with blankets, a shawl, and cotton yard goods. For several years they farmed at Long Sault, and Ben worked on the riverboats. In March 1885, when Maggie was six years old, Ben and Elizabeth's second child, also a daughter, was born. That year the Anglican Church moved Peter Spence back to the Little Forks Reserve. Ben, Elizabeth, Maggie, and her baby sister relocated once again. And once again they cleared land for a new farm.

A few happy years followed during which her grandparents "were different people," doting on their new granddaughter and now being kind to Maggie and Elizabeth. Elizabeth became a skilled and respected midwife, receiving payment in food and animals—her first pay was a young calf given to her by a non-Native woman whose baby she had safely delivered at Little Forks. The Spences raised cows, pigs, and chickens and grew potatoes and corn. The small farm prospered. Maggie remembered paddling by canoe with her father and mother along the shores of the Rainy River in the summer to pick blueberries and to fish for sturgeon, which they smoked for winter food. In early fall the family camped for several weeks near the wild-rice beds on Rainy Lake, harvesting and preparing the rice for winter storage. In the late fall they joined friends, the McGinnis family, at fishing grounds at Whitefish Creek on the American side of the Rainy River. They would return to the summer village at Little Forks to harvest the gardens and then move north to camp in the bush, where Ben and his cousin hunted and trapped during the winter. As spring approached, like other families along the Rainy River, the Spence family gathered at sugarbush stands to collect the sap and make maple sugar. Maggie recalled that for several years she helped her parents along with her father's cousin to work a stand of about three hundred trees on the American side of the mouth of the Little Fork River. She told Ruth Landes: "The people had told my grandmother she could have the trees because they belonged to an old woman who had died and left no relatives" (Landes 1937, 97). After they made maple sugar, it was time to return to Little Forks to plant the gardens and spend the summer.[2]

Those happy years came to an abrupt end when Maggie was ten years old. Tragedy struck from which the family never recovered. Ben's brother became ill, and to be near the hospital, the entire Spence family moved into Kenora on the last steamboat before the winter freeze. He died in November. The family stayed on in Kenora during the winter, and in March Maggie's little sister contracted measles and also died. Her grandparents' world was destroyed. They both turned to alcohol. Maggie Wilson recollects, "And from that time my grandfather was out of his mind. . . . It was a hard time to get him to wash his face or change his clothes. It was only my mother who could get him to change his clothes. And he always tore the collars off his shirts." When the ice cleared in the spring, the shattered family returned by steamboat to Little Forks: "We came back to our old home. When we got there, they were crying and burning stuff. Well, then they started over again and farmed and started putting out gardens and raising poultry and cows and pigs."[3]

Her parents often quarreled, blaming each other for their younger daughter's death. In the summer when Maggie turned fourteen, her father abruptly left them and moved to Kenora. That September Maggie went alone on the boat to Kenora and convinced him to return home. When he died two years later, Maggie's mother married her husband's cousin, Thomas Spence. Maggie, aged sixteen, married Isaac McGinnis of the Little Forks Reserve. He died within the first year of their marriage, and the following year Maggie married Tom Wilson of the Hungry Hall band. The young couple moved to the Hungry Hall Reserve at the mouth of the Rainy River on Lake of the Woods. Tom Wilson died of appendicitis in 1911 leaving her again a widow, this time with three small children to support. Maggie and her children moved to the Manitou Rapids Reserve in 1914. There she married John Wilson, the chief's son. Like her mother, Maggie Wilson was now a respected midwife employed by local women, both Native and non-Native. She and John Wilson had two daughters, one of whom died shortly after birth. At Manitou Rapids, she also adopted and raised a non-Native baby boy who had been left in a basket at her door.[4]

At the time when Maggie Wilson moved to Manitou Rapids, the people faced many new challenges. The Canadian government was confiscating uncultivated reserve lands for distribution to non-Ojibwe settlers. The Rainy River Ojibwe were consolidated into one band and squeezed onto one reserve at Manitou. They had never lived in villages of more than forty or fifty people, typically a few related families. Little Forks Reserve, where Maggie was born, was a band of forty-nine people. When the bands were consolidated, the Manitou Rapids Reserve suddenly grew to a population of almost three hundred and now comprised several historically distinct political units. Traditionally, political organization had been family based, and most decisions were made by consensus. Marriage, divorce, inheritance, and adoption practices were all considered family matters. Now the government appointed chiefs, and the Indian agent intruded on the most intimate aspects of their lives.

It was clear to the people that this forced consolidation and the intrusion on their autonomy would disrupt their traditional patterns of social interaction. In February 1915 each band sent representatives to Ottawa to meet with the Canadian government. Together they requested that the bands retain their political structures rather than be amalgamated with the Manitou Rapids band under a single chief. The government refused. It did, however, accede to the people's request that a secular elementary day school be built at Manitou Rapids. Here their children could learn to read and write without being required to convert to Christianity, as had been the practice since the 1870s at the mission schools on the reserves and, after the 1890s, at the residential school in Fort Frances.

After the relocation and after the best farmlands had been appropriated for European Canadian settlers, the government instituted a farm instruction program at Manitou Rapids. Maggie Wilson describes the people's efforts to farm. Her husband, John, cleared a few acres, built a two-story frame house, and planted wheat, barley, oats, potatoes, and corn. When Maggie's elder daughter, Christina, married in 1916 at the age of fourteen, she and her husband cleared bush to farm on adjacent land. When their son Albert planned to marry, John and Maggie gave him land to clear for a farm and build a house. By the time their younger daughter, Janet, married, John was ill. He invited his new son-in-law into partnership. The farm produce was to be divided between the two households.

Like most Rainy River Ojibwes in the first decades of the twentieth century, the Wilsons lived in chronic poverty. Farm yields were poor. Should there have been any surplus, government legislation prevented them from selling produce off the reserve to obtain cash to purchase foods such as flour and sugar and other goods. Meanwhile, they could no longer rely on game and gathered foods. Access to hunted game was lost with the government's appropriation of their lands. Pollution from pulp and paper mills had destroyed the sturgeon fishery, and hydroelectric dams had flooded the wild-rice grounds. Some of the able-bodied men were seasonal migrant workers in mines and logging camps or worked as hunting and fishing guides at tourist lodges. Some of the women sold their bead and porcupine quillwork; a few worked as domestic servants for non-Natives. Destitution was the lot of most.

Shortly after she moved to Manitou Rapids in 1914, Maggie Wilson began to have a recurring dream in which spirit birds, thunderbirds, came to her:

> I heard them singing. I wakened, got out of bed, thought about the dream, returned to bed and dreamt again. They repeated that they wanted me to go with them to a big mountain. . . . Each time I had a dream, I awakened, then returned to sleep and dreamed the same dream. . . . The Thunders wanted me to bring this dance to the world. . . . They would teach me one song at a time. They brought me a drum and showed me how to make it and how to use it in the dance. . . . I dreamt so much that at last it seemed no longer like a dream but like a person talking to me. It was so plain!

In vivid dreams the thunderbirds taught her dance sequences, drum patterns, and songs and told her to teach the people. "The Birds were kind and friendly. All who came to me were kind, petting me with their paws and feathers. They even laid their heads on my arms. . . . They told me they were bringing joy to me and the others. They were giving a nice thing to amuse me."[5]

When Canada entered the First World War, Ojibwe men—among them her son-in-law, Christina's teenaged husband—had enlisted and gone overseas with the Canadian army. "I dreamt the soldiers would come back if their relatives danced. . . . This would be a new war dance. People were glad to help and join the dance," she recalled. So she began to teach the people the dance she called the Union Star Dance. "I would wake up singing. Everybody wanted to learn the dance." With the approval of the Indian agent, Maggie orchestrated the performance of the dance for several years in Fort Frances.[6] She recalled,

> During the seven or eight years that I gave the dance, other people had dreams about it. They would not understand their dreams and would talk to me about them. Several people dreamt

songs that I put into the dance—because that was why they were given. . . . All who danced and who came to the dance brought tobacco, food, [and] some print which we offered to the Thunderbirds, asking protection [and saying,] "We offer this food and tobacco, brought here to the one who owns this dance for her to teach others. We thank [the Thunders] for the dance. We enjoy this dance. Let us have a good time. May he [*Ginyu*, Eagle] bless us all."

Sadly, her young son-in-law was killed overseas. And people became angry with Maggie because they were still poor and sick and soldiers had died. "The missionary scared me, saying the devil was after me," Maggie recalled. "If anyone sickened or died, it was blamed on me. Then my leg became too sore to dance. And about four years ago [ca. 1928] we turned Christian. So we gave up the dance. We laid all the furnishings in the bush to rot. But I still dream of Thunders and I do not think they are angry at me for having quit."

Maggie Wilson's dreams are in the wondrous visionary tradition that has for centuries been at the heart of Ojibwe culture. Ojibwe artist Norval Morrisseau (1931–2007) brought this tradition forward to the contemporary art world and became a key interpreter of Ojibwe aesthetic expression. He recalled, as a boy, asking his grandfather where the people got those "images they put on the rock paintings" along the shores of the northern lakes. His grandfather replied, "They come from the spirit world" (Morrisseau and Robinson 1997, 20).

Dreams reveal the spiritual aspects of the interrelationships among humans, between humans and the natural world, and between humans and *manitos*, or spirit beings. Animals, humans, *pawahgun* (guardian spirits), and spirits of the dead share the world. Frequent offerings, gift exchanges, and rituals of respect recognize the fundamental reciprocity between them that forms the basis of Ojibwe life. All creation is imbued with spirit; under certain conditions an object such as a stone may possess a name and a spirit.

Images represented in the visual arts, songs, and dances thus come to individuals in dreams and are spiritual. The meanings of dreamed images are particular to each person, and from an early age everyone is encouraged to dream. The early twentieth-century Minnesota ethnologist Frances Densmore reported that when she once asked an Ojibwe man the significance of seeing a turtle in a dream, he replied, "It might mean many things; no one would know except the man who dreamed the dream" (1929, 80).

In the introduction to the catalog for the retrospective exhibition of the art of Norval Morrisseau held at the National Gallery of Canada in 2006, Native art historian Greg Hill describes Morrisseau as a "shaman artist." Morrisseau locates the roots of his art in dreams he had at moments of spiritual crisis in his life, when he was isolated and abused at residential school, when he suffered a severe illness and almost died as an adolescent, and when he was institutionalized in a sanitarium for tuberculosis. Morrisseau, like Maggie Wilson, described his visionary experience as a dream-state journey that he called "soul travel" (Morrisseau and Robinson 1997). Through "soul travel" the individual transcends the mundane and enters into contact with the spirit world. "Soul travel" also encompasses the idea of transformation, of moving out of a traumatic experience through a process of healing. The vision dream is an important form of communication by which the visionary may bring to light new insights, new notions of reality, and new aesthetic imagery. A shaman visionary may perform healing rites, act as an intermediary between the spirit world and the existential world, and provide answers to troubling questions. The shaman visionary embodies the deeply spiritual worldview of the Ojibwe people.

Like Morrisseau, Maggie Wilson was an individual who stood out in her community as a mystic visionary (Landes 1938). Her powerful dream travels with the thunderbirds came to her at a time of upheaval in her own life and of deep crises in the lives of the people at Manitou Rapids. The government's forced relocations and assimilative policies, the scourge of alcohol, the fears for the

Ojibwe soldiers fighting a war in an unknown, faraway place, the wrenching apart of families when children were placed in residential schools, and the rampant infectious diseases that brought sickness and death all constitute traumas that could be expected to bring on "soul travel" and visions.

Elders, such as Maggie Wilson, who had powerful dreams become recognized name givers. After Wilson had her dream, people began to come from great distances to ask her to dream a name for their baby or to rename a sick person with a new and more powerful name that would help that person evade death. Taking on the highly honorific position of name giver, Wilson would dream a name and formally bestow it on an individual in a speech at the feast that was part of the naming ceremony. As a name giver, she would give a feast of dried berries and receive gifts in exchange for dreaming and giving the name.[7]

In Ojibwe custom an elder dreams a name that gives a person an identity linked to the powers of an ancestor, animal or spirit. Such bonding between a living person and the spiritual realm is believed to guide and assist the individual in life's joys and troubles. Louise Erdrich relates how Tobasonakwut, a present-day healer on Lake of the Woods, received his name: "Just after he and his brother were born, Tobasonakwut's name was discovered by his father, who gazed out into the bay and saw a certain type of cloud cover, low and even. Tobasonakwut. His twin was named for a small bird that visited his mother shortly after the birth" (2003, 63). According to Densmore, "the bestowing of a name was not . . . the principal function of a namer. . . . The principal function was the transmission to the child of the benefit which he or she derived from their dream" (1929, 53). Naming thus incorporates the newborn within the spiritual realm of the Ojibwes. Names are given to newborns but also at other times during one's life to recognize a new skill or achievement or a change of status (Dorris 1989, 46–64). Kimberly Blaeser (1994, 3) in her poem "Speaking Those Names" describes the power of Ojibwe names and nicknames to bind people together in social relationships: "I hear myself in those names / being pulled back by those names / know again myself in relationship."[8]

Some names are so powerful that they can create a new identity for an individual. According to Norval Morrisseau, the naming tradition established his artistic identity. He became an artist, he said, when he was given the name Copper Thunderbird at the age of nineteen. He was very ill and expected to die when his mother called "a very good medicine-woman." Morrisseau recalled,

> She did something special. You see, this is the custom of the Ojibway Indians when everything is hopeless, when even the Indian medicine is hopeless. . . . This is the highest sort of power that can be given to any one that is sick: and that is to give him a new name, a powerful new name. . . . So at that special moment she gave me a new name, the name of Copper Thunderbird. That was a very, very powerful new name; and it cured me. From then on I changed, because that was a name whose power you could actually feel. (quoted in Hill 2006, 17)

The name Copper Thunderbird healed Morrisseau and transformed his illness into his artistic sensibility. He spent the rest of his life drawing and painting the spiritual world of the Ojibwes, signing his name as Copper Thunderbird. Maggie Wilson was a name giver in this ancient tradition.

Maggie also dreamed the patterns she worked into beadwork and porcupine-quill embroidery and bit into birch bark. Skill in these arts requires both the spirituality to "soul travel" in dreams and the technical ability to reproduce the dreamed images by imprinting teeth marks on birch bark and by sewing bead and porcupine-quill embroidery on cloth and leather. Images rendered by women in quill and beadwork also represent the many medicinal plants that grow in the northern bogs and the berries that are important ritual foods symbolizing birth, renewal, and food for the dead (Densmore 1928, 1929; Landes 1938). Women's arts play a central role as offerings and gifts in the relations of reciprocity—with the dead, with the spirit world, with healers, and with kin—that are intrinsic to Ojibwe life.

Over the course of the nineteenth century, floral and vegetation motifs in beadwork gradually replaced ancient geometric designs that had represented dreamed spirit figures, such as the thunderbird. This was in part due to missionary censure. It also revealed artists' entrepreneurial skills. European settlers desired flower-ornamented objects to decorate their homes, and Native women were quick to recognize this new market. As art historians Janet Berlo and Ruth Phillips note, "The new art styles and types of commodities were the result of a ferment of creativity and invention on the part of native makers, but they were also motivated by the extreme economic deprivation brought about by the taking of their land" (1998, 104).

Maggie Wilson's main source of income was the production of beadwork and birch-bark objects embroidered in porcupine quills for sale to settlers and tourists. A birch-bark wall hanging of hers that once decorated the walls of a tourist lodge on Lake of the Woods is now on display in the museum at Kay-Nah-Chi-Wah-Nung Historical Centre on the Rainy River.

Assemblages of clothing and body decoration are primary vehicles to depict the spiritual powers an individual acquired through vision experience. Thus the art of self-adornment is important to Ojibwe people. The rich dress and body decorations of the Ojibwes impressed early European travelers. Colorful cloth, ribbons, and beads became prized trade goods. These goods were much desired by Ojibwe women, who innovated new styles of clothing and accessories and techniques of ornamentation. Maggie Wilson was a master designer and seamstress in this traditional domain of women's artistic expression. She carefully crafted the elaborately beaded clothing and moccasins her sons and daughters wore on ceremonial occasions and the dance regalia such as the jingle dresses her daughters wore at summer powwows (see figs. 9 and 10). The elaboration of the arts of self-adornment became increasingly important over the course of the nineteenth century. They provided a means for preservation of the ancient worldview that was being destroyed through the undermining of seasonal rituals and forced assimilation. Through careful embroidery and appliqué work on clothes and accessories, Ojibwe women sought to reclaim and perpetuate spirit power to nurture the souls of their loved ones.

In her poem "Sewing Memories," Blaeser describes how she keeps a treasure trunk of clothing her mother and grandmother had lovingly sewed for her from remnants and hand-me-downs when she was growing up on the White Earth Reservation in Minnesota: "They are like the books in my library . . . these pieces of time . . . tell their own stories of life lived in loss and in longing and yet in fulfillment, too." Into cloth, she says, the women sewed stories, "bits of our bodies and bits of our dreams" (1994, 75–76). Artists like Maggie Wilson and Kimberly Blaeser's mother and grandmother who sewed stories and spirit power into clothing maintained the vitality of Ojibwe traditions.

Maggie Wilson's dreams and songs; her midwifery and healing knowledge; her bilingualism; her exquisite beadwork, porcupine-quill embroidery, and birch-bark crafts all contributed to her wide renown in the Rainy River area. When ethnologist Frances Densmore visited Manitou Rapids in 1920 to record songs and Ojibwe knowledge of medicinal plants, the government Indian agent introduced her to Wilson. A decade later when anthropology student Ruth Landes arrived in Manitou Rapids, Maggie Wilson was the person everyone recommended to work with her. That summer of 1932, Wilson and her husband were both ill. The farm was in decline. They were destitute, subsisting on what Maggie Wilson earned from the sale of her beadwork and birch-bark crafts and her occasional work as a midwife and as an interpreter for government agents. Living in the dire poverty of reserve life during the Depression, Wilson was glad for the work Landes offered her, and they embarked together on the storytelling project.

Despite her struggles and the harsh conditions under which she lived, Maggie Wilson was a person of immense creativity and discipline. She weathered the hard years of her life with courage and resourcefulness, raising five children to adulthood, including her adopted non-Native son. Despite adversity, she maintained a strong sense of self and a wry sense of humor. As a person who had powerful dreams, she accepted her responsibilities to pass on her knowledge, to give names that might heal the sick and the despondent, to bring joy to otherwise difficult lives. She had a rich, empathic understanding of life's joys and sorrows based on her own experience.

In the last decade of her life, Maggie Wilson drew on her experience and tapped even further into her well of creativity to produce what is now her lasting legacy. She recorded a remarkable treasure trove of stories that reveal her mastery of the Ojibwe art of storytelling and stand as testimony to the historical suffering and resilience of the Rainy River Ojibwes—men, women, and children.

THE STORIES

Maggie Wilson's stories chronicle the life of the Ojibwes prior to and during the reserve era of the late nineteenth and early twentieth centuries. The stories are told in the intimate voice of an insider, a voice the world has rarely heard, from a particular place about a particular people at a particular time in their history.

Wilson narrates her stories on the stage of the historical events of the Rainy River: fur trading with the Hudson's Bay Company; battles with the Dakotas; treaty signing in 1873 and subsequent "treaty days" each July when annuities ("treaty") were paid to each family; the building of the railway in the 1890s; and the consolidation of the Rainy River bands at the Manitou Rapids Reserve in 1915–16.

The ways in which Ojibwes maintained a strong connection to the land based in their dependence on migratory rounds of seasonal economic activity for subsistence are revealed in the settings for many of the dramas the stories relate. Because the land of the Rainy River Ojibwes was located on the ancient "highway" of rivers that Europeans traveled to the interior of the continent, their lives unfolded against the unyielding historical force of colonization.

Tragically, the people sometimes turned the violence that was bred in the crucible of European colonialism, social disruption, and the rampages of infectious diseases and alcohol inward to their own kin and kith. Indeed, the violence depicted in some of the stories is shocking. In doing so the stories relate difficult knowledge giving voice to what was, at the time, unspeakable.[9]

In counterpoint to this violence, Maggie Wilson tells us of tremendous compassion among people. We learn about the extraordinary efforts of individuals to keep their families together and to care for one another. We see such concern and tenderness extended especially to the most vulnerable members of the community: the children, the elderly, and the sick. Indeed, adoptions of relatives and strangers are featured in almost every story.

The stories also illustrate the attempts to maintain and promote Ojibwe institutions and values in the florescence of curing rituals, naming ceremonies, games, and dances. We learn about the increasingly frequent attribution of spiritual knowledge and healing powers (which Maggie Wilson calls *manitokaso*) to a wide variety of practitioners in the hope that these would help the people withstand the onslaught of troubles.

The question of the "truth" of her stories—the extent to which they are "fiction"—is hard to avoid. It has been widely recognized that there is no single "truth" in history. The meanings given to lives and events emerge from an interpreter's position relative to them. Maggie Wilson was not a historian or a scientist. She made no claims to objectivity. She elaborated stories of individual lives, not as "evidence" in a claim to "truth" but, in line with age-old tradition, to educate and to entertain. She told stories in an oral culture in which elders, through storytelling, teach younger people ethical behavior and the value of practical skills. There is no doubt that, in order to tell a good story, Maggie Wilson embellished dramatic details and created narrative twists in the plots. She may have created protagonists whose characters and biographical events actually represent composite portraits of several individuals. A great strength of Wilson's trove of stories is that they reveal the conflicts, dilemmas, and complexities of Ojibwe lives.[10]

Maggie Wilson's narration of Ojibwe lives is based in part on her own experience, in part on the lives of people she knew, and in part on the stories told to her by others. The themes that recur throughout the stories—death, sickness, remarriage, rescue, adoption—are the themes that interested her. They echo her own life. Like many of her characters, she too was left vulnerable by the loss of a child, of a spouse, and of a parent. And she too, through resourcefulness and "trickiness," confronted and overcame abandonment, sickness, poverty, and starvation. It may be that she herself is her greatest protagonist.

Gerald Vizenor relates that, when he was asked to write his autobiography, he resisted "the first person burden" (Vizenor and Lee 1999, 79–80). "I could not bring that much attention to myself," he says. Instead he told stories of his life through the voices of others. "My stories are not about me but about my experiences," he explains. The stories Maggie Wilson told suggest a similar autobiographical impulse in her storytelling.

Vizenor also reports that telling these autobiographical stories was a healing process. Storytelling created a sense of liberation. "The stories create me," he says (Vizenor and Lee 1999, 60). We can hope that, like Vizenor, Maggie Wilson also found storytelling healing and liberating. There is no doubt that, through her stories, she creates a strong sense of self. For in this oeuvre of stories, Maggie Wilson emerges as a key actor in history and as the author of her own life. This much is true.

Thus Maggie Wilson's stories blend personal and cultural history—part autobiography, part biography, part ethnography.[11] They tell not only of change and disruption but also of creativity and continuity. As the protagonists grapple with universal themes of love and jealousy, of loyalty and betrayal, of revenge and reconciliation, of loss and endurance, the stories reveal the particular texture of Ojibwe life.

Maggie Wilson's remembering brings into view much that has been invisible in previously written accounts of Ojibwe history. The stories offer rare firsthand testimony to the experiences of

colonization and disenfranchisement and to Ojibwe resourcefulness and resilience as the Ojibwes seek continually to reconstitute
their life worlds.

EDITING THE STORIES

I have selected thirty of Maggie Wilson's stories and present them
in five sections that explore what I consider to be Wilson's major
themes: "Men and Women," "Parents and Children," "Siblings,"
"Women Alone," and "Friends and Foes." I have given each story a
title drawn from a phrase that appears in the story and encapsulates
one of its main themes. In this I follow the practice in the compila-
tions of stories by Jim Clark (2002), Harry Robinson (1992), and
Gerald Vizenor (2000). The selection of the stories and titles as
well as the organization into five parts is arbitrary in that most of
the stories speak to multiple themes.[12]

The stories in parts 1, 2, and 3 show that the search for love is a
guiding force in the social lives of Ojibwe people. Love is found in
relations between men and women, between parents and children,
between brothers and sisters, and in the many cases of informal
adoption that Maggie Wilson relates. The stories tell, for example,
of old women who rescue and adopt younger women who have
been abandoned or abused, of a young man who adopts an elderly
couple as parents, of a married woman who heals and adopts a
young white man as her brother.

"Women Alone" presents sagas of women whose extraordinary
courage and resourcefulness enable them to overcome difficulties
in their lives. The solo journey away from adversity and misery
to begin a new life is often a motif in these stories. Stories tell of
women paddling long distances, hunting and butchering a moose,
and surviving alone in the wilderness. They describe women who
refuse to confine themselves to prescribed feminine roles and thus
are able to overcome starvation, abandonment, abuse, and loss.
The stories portray women making choices in their lives. They
report that, when widowed, some women choose to remarry and

preserve the conventional gendered division of labor, whereas others choose not to remarry and instead take on "masculine" skills and activities to preserve their independence. Stories tell how jealousy drives some women to leave polygynous marriages, whereas others choose to stay because they value the companionship and help of a co-wife. Wilson's stories are the cautionary tales of an older woman enjoining younger women to develop practical skills and autonomy to survive life's many challenges. The paradox is that, while the stories emphasize that personal autonomy is the key to women's survival, their telling creates a sense of community among women.[13]

"Friends and Foes" explores the inevitability of conflicts and the importance of drawing on the help of friends—often guardian spirits—in order to redress evil and surmount obstacles. On the one hand, they tell of the many battles with the Dakotas, the kidnappings of women, the meanesses of stepmothers, the dangers of wolves, and the threat of starvation. On the other hand, they relate kindnesses shown by Dakota kidnappers and aid received from bears, moose, and other *pawahgun*. They tell of visions and dreams during which an individual receives his or her *pawahgun* and illustrate proper protocol and relations of reciprocity with it. They describe naming practices, occasions for feasts and speeches, death and mourning rituals, and healing and divination practices—all of which reveal how spirits inhabit the everyday world and bring comfort and knowledge to Ojibwe people.

Speaking in the local syntax of rural northern Ontario English interspersed with occasional words in Ojibwe, Maggie Wilson narrated the stories to her daughter Janet, who wrote them down on a stenographer's pad. In editing I have attempted to preserve the flavor of the oral storytelling.

I have added punctuation, division into paragraphs, and standardized spellings to help smooth the flow for readers who face the written text and do not have the mediating presence of the person and voice of the storyteller. Where a word has been forgotten or left out, I have added it for ease of reading and indicate any additions in square brackets. I have also adjusted spellings that did not match the meaning (e.g., "to" when "too" was meant; "their" when "there" was meant).

I have kept local grammatical forms such as "youse" instead of "you." I have retained Maggie Wilson's variations in use of the past tense for certain verbs; the most common are "seen" instead of "saw," "come" instead of "came," "use" instead of "used," and "start" instead of "started." She was not consistent, however, in the use of these terms for the past tense, and I have retained this variability. Hence, both "use to" and "used to" appear in the stories. I retained Wilson's usage of "learned" for "taught": "She learned her daughter how to . . ." I have also retained Wilson's construction "her too" and "him too," which means "also," "too," or "as well": "She took her things from the canoe and went up the hill, her too."

In stories in which Wilson related Ojibwe encounters with other Native groups, she often described her own people as "Indians" and named the others as Crees or "Soos" (as she referred to the Dakotas). In some of the stories, she also used the terms "half-breed," "nigger," and "squaw," which were then in common usage in rural Ontario and which she had acquired from the English speakers around her. She used these terms without derogatory intent and without the negative connotations they now carry, and I have retained them in the stories.

As noted previously, names are very important in Ojibwe culture. However, because some of the stories treat difficult knowledge of incest or violence within families, I have deleted any personal names that Maggie Wilson had mentioned in the stories.

The use of Ojibwe words presented a challenge for me since I do not speak or write Ojibwe and Maggie Wilson and her daughter did not use a consistent spelling for the Ojibwe terms and place-names in the stories. Their spellings of words vary between, and even within, stories. In the preface to *A Concise Dictionary of Minnesota Ojibwe*, linguists John Nichols and Earl Nyholm write that Ojibwe "is not spoken in a single standard form but varies from place to place in sounds, vocabulary and grammar" (1995, vii). They acknowledge that the words in their dictionary represent the speech of a few individuals belonging to the Mille Lacs band in northern Minnesota and that "other forms of the same words used there and elsewhere are equally valid" (vii). As explained in the preface, over the summer of 2006, I consulted elders at Manitou Rapids and staff at the Kay-Nah-Chi-Wah-Nung Historical Centre to try to establish the local spelling of these words. The elders helped me to nuance the meanings of these words, but as Nichols and Nyholm found, they did not establish a consistent local system of spelling. I have decided to retain the variability that occurs in Maggie and Janet Wilson's spellings of Ojibwe words and have therefore reproduced Ojibwe words here as they were recorded by Maggie and her daughter-scribe. Because Maggie Wilson simply inserted Ojibwe words or concepts into a sentence that was otherwise spoken entirely in English, she usually did not conjugate a verb or pluralize a noun. I have followed her practice. In the glossary I list the Ojibwe terms that appear in the stories along with their diverse spellings.

RESIGNIFYING THE TRADITIONAL

In *Books and Islands in Ojibwe Country*, Louise Erdrich explores the Ojibwe literary tradition as she explores the islands of Lake of the Woods. She considers the various meanings that have been attributed to the word "Ojibwe" and picks her favorite: that "Ojibwe" comes from the verb *ozhibii'ige*, "to write," because, as she says, "Ojibwe people were great writers from way back and synthesized the oral and written tradition by keeping mnemonic scrolls of inscribed birchbark. The first paper, the first books" (2003, 10–11). "Books have been written around here ever since someone had the idea of biting or even writing on birchbark with a sharpened stick. Books are nothing all that new. People have probably been writing books in North America since at least 2000 B.C. Or painting islands. You could think of the lakes as libraries" (2003, 5).[14]

Erdrich marvels at the agglutinative quality of the Ojibwe language. Word roots provide for the endless incorporation of new concepts, technologies, and behaviors. She is fascinated that *mazina'igan*, the Ojibwe word for "book" (which is also the word for "letter," "paper," and "document") employs the same root, *mazina*, as the words for rock paintings (*mazinapikiniganan*), dental pictographs made on birch bark (*mazinibaganjigan*), movie theater (*mazinaatesewigamig*), television set (*mazinatesijigan*), and photograph (*mazinaakizo*). These words containing the root *mazina* are all concerned with images and their representation and indicate the long history and deep importance of communicating images—of writing—to the Ojibwes (2003, 5).

These time-honored adaptations of the *mazina* word root allow Erdrich to place painting pictographs, decorating birch bark, and writing books together as products of the same human impetus. She then frames the question that motivates her personal journey to visit the rock paintings on the islands and shores of Lake of the Woods. She asks, "Books. Why?" By the end of her very intimate peregrination, she has arrived at several answers: "Because our brains hurt" (6). "So we can talk to you even though we are dead" (55). "Because they are wealth, sobriety and hope" (99). "So that we will never be alone" (141). These are also my reasons for continuing the project Maggie Wilson began.

Reading Maggie Wilson's trove of stories at the beginning of the twenty-first century, one sees them as a testament both to one woman's mastery of the Ojibwe art of storytelling and to the Rainy River people's resilience in the face of history. Whether it was Wilson's intent to bear witness to her people's "survivance," we will never know.[15] But this is her legacy.

We know that the storytelling project with Ruth Landes was important as a commercial transaction for Maggie Wilson. She occasionally wrote postscripts to her letters, telling Landes what she planned to purchase with the money, anticipating an upcoming occasion. Yet this was also traditional: a request to a person to tell a story was accompanied by a gift and often preceded by a feast (Densmore 1929, 103).[16]

Moreover, Maggie Wilson had adopted Ruth Landes as a daughter, often signing her letters "Your Mam." Thus telling her stories to Landes can also be understood as following Ojibwe custom whereby older women told stories to younger women. Through characters and the narrative action of stories, elders instructed younger women in women's roles, taught them about the relations between men and women, and illustrated the ethical resolution of moral dilemmas. Significantly, Maggie Wilson was at the same time telling the stories to her younger daughter, Janet, who served as her scribe, writing down the oral stories to send to Landes in New York. So through her work with Landes, Maggie Wilson was able to recapture a traditional means by which cultural knowledge is passed from mother to daughter, a process that had been severed when Janet had gone to residential school.

We can also see that Maggie Wilson found pleasure in the work. She enjoyed her creativity. She embroidered her stories with attractive details and interesting plot twists. She told stories much as she embroidered the intricate designs in her beadwork.

Maggie Wilson had moved the stories from a traditional oral storytelling medium to the written form of letters. My effort to edit and publish the stories is a next step in their life, in the process that Faye Ginsburg has called "resignifying the traditional." Ginsburg (2002), Lucas Bessire (2003), Randolph Lewis (2006), and others have explored the cultural continuities in the work of contemporary Native artists working in new media. They highlight especially the bringing of the "storytelling aesthetic" to film.[17] Blaeser, Erdrich, Vizenor, and numerous other poets and writers acknowledge the sources of their creative inspiration in Ojibwe historical experience and spiritual worldview. Greg Hill (2006), Ruth Phillips (2006), and other art historians trace the inspiration for the visual art of Norval Morrisseau and the other "Woodland Artists" in millennia-old dreaming practices and the representation of dreamed images on rock and birch bark.

Retelling Maggie Wilson's stories in a twenty-first-century form is my contribution to the efforts of the many individuals who are working to maintain Ojibwe cultural traditions in a global world that is pressuring all peoples to relinquish their deep knowledge systems. Bringing her stories out of the archives and into the light recognizes the ongoing vitality and value of Ojibwe women's knowledge and is an expression of confidence in the future.

Maggie Wilson grew up on the Rainy River in the last quarter of the nineteenth century listening to stories the elders told. She spent her entire life along the river, where she "lived a rough life," as she would say. But she also cultivated her creativity and her compassion for the people around her. Her creative sensibility was, on the one hand, extraordinary but, on the other, rooted in the lived experience and patterned behavior of generations that had gone before her. She is one in a long line of storytellers whose dreams may be traced back to the images of the rock paintings on the Lake of the Woods and found in the present-day writings of Ojibwe poets, novelists, and scholars.

Maggie Wilson's stories describe a people who were highly mobile as they followed an annual seasonal round of economic activities over an open country but who had been recently confined to live on reserves along the Rainy River.

The seasonal round tapped a wide variety of nutritious resources. In the spring people congregated in maple groves to make the high-calorie maple sugar (more than 1,600 calories per pound). In May and June large groups gathered at the Manitou and Long Sault Rapids to capture the spawning giant sturgeon (one sturgeon averaged two hundred pounds in weight). Sturgeon was highly nutritious, providing more than seven hundred calories per pound. Smoked, dried, or processed into a pemmican-like cake, it was a staple food. In June families planted gardens along the shores of the Rainy River and on islands on Lake of the Woods. Corn was the major crop, but potatoes, pumpkins, onions, carrots, and beans were also grown. In summer months a variety of berries—blueberries, sand cherries, raspberries, black currants, and gooseberries—were harvested along the Rainy River. Blueberries were sun dried and compressed into cakes to be stored for winter use. In late August and early September everyone worked on the wild-rice harvest. Wild rice was key to the economy both as a subsistence food and as a commodity for trade. Dried rice boiled with a little fat, fish, berries, maple sugar, or meat was highly nutritious, supplying more than 1,600 calories per pound. Whitefish, which spawn in the fall, were also caught and smoked or dried. Whitefish was almost as nutritious as sturgeon. Garden crops were harvested, and corn was dried and stored as a reserve food for winter. In winter people dispersed into small family groups to hunt game (moose, caribou, bear) for food and trap a variety of fur-bearing animals (beaver, marten, lynx, fisher, bear, fox).

Along with mobility, social flexibility was key to the Ojibwe adaptation to the changing seasons, environmental conditions, and annual variability in the resources of the boreal forest. Essential to the survival of the Ojibwes were the practices of "switching" among different resources; seasonally relocating and dispersing people; nurturing a wide circle of kinship ties through adoption, visiting, and flexible residence and marriage patterns; and following the fundamental values of sharing and reciprocity (Densmore 1928, 1929; Hallowell 1992; Landes 1937, 1938; Quimby 1960, 1966; Waisberg 1984).

To contextualize the setting within which Maggie Wilson lived and told her stories, I provide a chronology of historical events and changes that were taking place in the way of life of the Rainy River Ojibwes in the late nineteenth and early twentieth centuries. In preparing this chronology I consulted the work of Michael Angel (2002); Jennifer Brown (1986); Derek Hayes (2002); Harold Hickerson (1988); William Noble (1984); Laura Peers (1994); G. I. Quimby (1960, 1966); Leo Waisberg (1984); and Leo Waisberg and Tim Holzkamm (1993).

6000 BC–AD 300: Intermittently, hunting and fishing peoples live along the shores of the Rainy River.

AD 300–1650: People camp during the summers at Manitou Rapids, Long Sault, and Hungry Hall on the Rainy River, where they fish sturgeon, hunt moose and beaver, and bury their dead in large mounds.

After 1650: Through Native trade networks, the people living along the Rainy River obtain European iron goods and glass beads.

1731: French trader-explorer Pierre Gaultier Lavérendrye establishes Fort St. Pierre at the western end of Rainy Lake at the head of the Rainy River. The Ojibwes are allied with the Crees (living north of Lake of the Woods) in frequent campaigns against the Dakotas to the south. Dakota-Ojibwe conflict intensifies with encroaching European settlement on Native lands.

1732: Lavérendrye establishes Fort St. Charles at the mouth of the Rainy River on Lake of the Woods. The Rainy River becomes an important transportation corridor in the French exploration and trade route from Lake Superior to Lake Winnipeg and the Northwest Territories. Ojibwes living in the Rainy River region begin direct trade with the French, exchanging local food and furs for European goods.

1756: The French abandon Fort St. Charles and Fort St. Pierre to battle the British at Quebec. The trade at Rainy River does not resume for several years.

1763: The British claim dominion over Canada. Ojibwe rights of occupancy and hunting and fishing rights are recognized in the Royal Proclamation of 1763. The proclamation establishes that any land for European settlement at Rainy River must first be purchased from the Ojibwes by the Crown. The proclamation places the people "under the protection" of the Crown, thereby beginning the paternalism that later characterizes Canadian federal government policy.

After 1763: Ojibwes trade with Montreal-based Northwest Company traders, who travel the Rainy River route to the Northwest Territories in rivalry with British Hudson's Bay Company traders, who control the maritime routes from Hudson Bay.

1775: The Ojibwes extract a toll from Europeans traveling the Rainy River. Northwest Company trader Alexander Henry reports that he must pay in presents and rum in order to travel the river corridor.

1780s: The Rainy River becomes an important transfer depot in the fur trade between Montreal and the Northwest Territories. The Northwest Company builds Fort Lac la Pluie at the head of the Rainy River on Rainy Lake near the former French Fort St. Pierre. The post operates until 1816. Here the Ojibwes trade furs, wild rice, dried sturgeon, sturgeon oil, maple sugar, canoes, and canoe components (bark, gum, and spruce root). The Northwest Company reportedly purchases 1,200–1,500 bushels of wild rice annually until 1821.

1790: The Ojibwes now also trade at Rainy Lake Fort, the new post that the Hudson's Bay Company builds near the present-day town of Fort Frances, Ontario. After a fire in 1820, the post is rebuilt. It is renamed Fort Frances around 1840. In 1898 it becomes a Hudson's Bay Company store. It operates until destroyed by fire in 1903.

After 1821: After the Northwest Company amalgamates with the Hudson's Bay Company in 1821, the fur posts in the Northwest Territories are now supplied from the north through the maritime routes from Hudson Bay, and fewer traders travel the Rainy River route. The Rainy River Ojibwes nonetheless continue to trade food, especially wild rice and fish, and furs at the Hudson's Bay Company post at Fort Frances and with free traders from the American side of the Rainy River.

1830s: The Hudson's Bay Company establishes trading posts at Fort Alexander near the mouth of the Winnipeg River at Lake Winnipeg in 1833 and at Rat Portage (later Kenora) on the northern shore of Lake of the Woods in 1836. The Rainy River Ojibwes travel to these posts to trade.

1857: The Province of Canada passes "An Act to Encourage the Gradual Civilization of the Indian Tribes." The act offers enfranchisement to Native men who are of "good moral character," able to read and write, and who renounce their Indian status. Scientists of the Red River Exploration Expedition, sponsored by the Province of Canada, travel through the area to establish its potential for agricultural settlements and determine the best route for the transport of settlers from Lake Superior to Red River (Lake Winnipeg). This is the first of many government expeditions through the Rainy River area.

1867: The British North America Act establishes the Dominion of Canada, a confederation of Ontario and Quebec (the former Province of Canada) and Nova Scotia and New Brunswick. Without consultation with the original inhabitants of these lands, the dominion's first prime minister, Sir John A. Macdonald, begins the process of acquiring Rupert's Land and the Northwest Territories from the Hudson's Bay Company and plans to build a railway to link the new nation and encourage immigration and settlement.

1868: The government surveys and begins construction on the pre-railway overland route, the Dawson Route, from Port Arthur (Thunder Bay) on Lake Superior to Red River (Winnipeg), Manitoba, passing through Ojibwe territory. Part land, part water, the route requires a month of travel and seventy loadings and unloadings of freight and baggage.

1869: The Rainy River Ojibwes meet Canadian government surveyors who travel the Dawson Route to the Red River to lay out land lots for new settlers in anticipation of the transfer of western lands from the Hudson's Bay Company to the Dominion of Canada. The Ojibwes later hear of the Métis resistance to the surveyors led by Louis Riel at Red River.

1870: In protest against the government land survey, Louis Riel establishes a government at Red River. En route to suppress Riel and his government, British and Canadian military troops take the Dawson Route through Ojibwe lands. Riel goes into exile in the United States. The Hudson's Bay Company relinquishes the Northwest Territories and Rupert's Land to the Dominion of Canada.

1871: The Canadian government authorizes the survey of the route for a transcontinental railway and begins to sign treaties with Ojibwes and Crees in anticipation of opening the West for European settlement, mineral exploration, and the building of the railway.

1873: The government establishes the Northwest Mounted Police to control conflicts arising over land acquisition between the Native residents and settlers moving west. The Rainy River Ojibwes sign Treaty no. 3 at Northwest Angle on Lake of the

Woods. The government promises them assistance to expand agricultural production, including training by a farm instructor; one yoke of oxen and one bull and four cows for each band; five harrows for every twenty families; one plow for every ten families; and sufficient barley and oats to plant on the available cleared lands. Each family is also promised two hoes, one spade, one scythe, and one ax and annuity payments of five dollars per adult to be paid each July. The government establishes seven reserves along the river—Hungry Hall 1 and 2, Long Sault 1 and 2, Manitou Rapids 1 and 2, and Little Forks—at traditional sites of sturgeon fishing, gardens, and summer villages. The Rainy River Ojibwes are relocated on reserves and pressured to give up their political autonomy and subsistence economy, which affects the annual gatherings and the performance of rituals based on seasonal mobility.

1876: The government passes the first Indian Act of Canada. On the one hand, the policy envisions that the Ojibwes will be assimilated into European Canadian society by abandoning their mobile lifestyle and seasonal economic and cultural activities and adopting settled life as farmers. The assimilationist policy also provides the legal framework for the establishment of residential schools. On the other hand, the policy is segregationist. It provides for the creation of the race-based reserve system, which inhibits the full participation of Native people in the wider Canadian society. The people are now "wards of the state," and their daily life on the reserves is to be overseen by a government representative, an Indian agent based in Fort Frances. The Indian agent is authorized to intervene in all aspects of Ojibwe life, including the education of children.

1876–81: The government authorizes the Anglican Church Missionary Society to build schools at Long Sault and Little Forks Indian reserves on the Rainy River. Many parents refuse to send their children to school when they discover that their children must convert to Christianity before they will be taught to read and write.

1880: Construction begins on the Canadian Pacific Railway (CPR) across the northern edge of Lake of the Woods at Rat Portage (Kenora).

1881: The Indian Act of 1881 prohibits Ojibwes from selling surplus garden produce off the reserve, thereby quashing any incentive the people have to expand agricultural production. To supplement the meager subsistence gained from farming, some Ojibwe men find wage work in logging camps and sawmills, on river steamers traveling between Fort Frances and Kenora, and in railway construction. During the absences of men, Ojibwe women, children, and the elderly are left to manage on their own. Some Ojibwe women work as domestic servants in non-Native households. Ojibwe values of sharing and reciprocity are challenged as families increasingly come to depend on wages and the goods that can be purchased with them.

1884: Pollution from sawmills upstream on the Rainy River begins to affect the sturgeon stocks.

1885: Louis Riel and Gabriel Dumont lead the Northwest Rebellion of the Métis and their allies. Three thousand federal military troops travel overland by the Dawson Route to Saskatchewan to quell the rebellion. They camp among the Ojibwes en route. The CPR railway is completed. Louis Riel and eight Cree and Assiniboine warriors are accused of sedition and hanged. The news reaches the Ojibwes on the Rainy River. The Northwest Rebellion is the climax of the federal government's military efforts to control the Native and settler populations of the West. The Indian Act becomes the instrument of administration of the Ojibwes, the Crees, and other Natives, who lose their political autonomy to the Canadian state but do not gain the full rights of Canadian citizens. They will not have the right to vote in federal elections in Canada until 1960. An amendment to the Indian Act introduces the Potlatch Ban in 1885. The legislation, in force until 1951, is first formulated to stop potlatch ceremonies in British Columbia but gradually comes to be applied to any Native religious or cultural expression throughout Canada unless sanctioned by government agents. By 1895, unless authorized by the Indian agent in Fort Frances, the Rainy River Ojibwes perform the healing ceremonies of the Midewiwin and other communal rituals as clandestine activities.

1886: The first CPR passenger train stops in Kenora on its way from Montreal to Vancouver. The Ontario and Rainy River Railway (O&RRR) begins construction of a railway from Port Arthur west along the Rainy River. Some Ojibwe men work on its construction.

1889: The government authorizes the Church Missionary Society to open a school on the Manitou Rapids Indian Reserve.

1890s: Many Ojibwe parents refuse to send their children to the mission day schools on the reserves because they do not want them to be converted to Christianity. The Canadian government authorizes Oblate Roman Catholic missionaries to build a residential school in Fort Frances. The Indian agent orders parents to send their children and takes children by force from parents who refuse. The children live ten months of the year away from their families, homes, and culture. At the residential school, the children's hair is cut, they are punished if they speak Ojibwe, not English, and many suffer physical, emotional, and sexual abuse from the very people the government has entrusted with their care.

1900: The sturgeon fishery is in terminal decline due to introduction of pound nets at the mouth of the Rainy River by non-Native commercial fishermen in the 1890s. The commercial fishermen trap the sturgeon in great numbers at the start of their spawning run upriver, which prevents reproduction and thus the fish from reaching the Ojibwe fishing grounds at Manitou Rapids and Long Sault.

1901: The O&RRR between Fort Frances and Rainy River is completed. The railway passes through the Manitou Rapids Indian Reserve.

1904: Rat Portage is renamed Kenora.

1905: The sturgeon spawning grounds are destroyed beyond recovery by wastes and pollution from the pulp and paper mill upstream in Fort Frances.

1908: The Duluth, Virginia and Rainy Lake Railway (DV&RL), which began construction in northern Minnesota in 1901, is extended to International Falls and by bridge across the international border to Fort Frances, Ontario, where it is connected to the O&RRR running between Port Arthur and Rainy River. The connection increases the annual arrivals of American tourists to the area and develops the market for beadwork and porcupine-quill embroidery and other crafts produced by Rainy River women.

1910: Hydroelectric dams built at Kenora and Fort Frances cause extensive flooding to the wild-rice grounds along the Rainy River, destroying this essential Ojibwe food source.

1915–16: The Canadian government relocates and consolidates the seven Rainy River bands at Manitou Rapids and appropriates most of their reserve lands on the premise that they are not being used for agriculture. The Ojibwes send representatives to Ottawa to petition the Canadian government to establish a political structure that will enable each band to retain its own chief and councilors. The government rejects the proposal and creates one administrative unit, the Manitou Rapids band. The government accepts the people's request that a secular elementary day school be opened on the Manitou Rapids Reserve.

1914–18: Rainy River Ojibwes, still without the right to vote in Canadian elections, serve with Canadian forces in the First World War.

RAINY RIVER LIVES

ONE

MEN AND WOMEN

Fig. 15. At the maple-sugar camp, Cass Lake, Minnesota, ca. 1930. Reprinted by permission from Koll Collection, Minnesota Historical Society.

Fig. 16. Canoes in the wild-rice beds, Lake of the Woods, ca. 1912. Photo by Carl Gustav Linde. Reprinted by permission of Minnesota Historical Society.

1

She Got In with Him Again

After They Were Widows

This is a story of an Indian woman. Before she grew up, her parents got in with some old people who had a son. And these two families were in good. And they planned when their children grew up for them to get married. And when she did grow up, she found that she did not care for this man. Also he was not so crazy for her though she was a nice-looking young girl and she was handy at doing all kinds of Indian fancy work and all the work an Indian woman does. Her parents were also afraid of the parents of this man. They could not refuse when these old people said that they wished for her very much because she was a good worker and was very quiet.

And there was another young man that cared for her a great deal. She also kind of cared for him too.

For three years she refused to go to the young man which her parents wanted her to marry. She use to go with this other young man secretly. And he use to often beg her to marry him. But she had to refuse him because she really belonged to this other young man. And she was also afraid that she would cause trouble on their parents.

And for three years, the young man waited. And one time, while all the Indians were camping in one place, their parents made them a wigwam and told them to live in there. And she had to do it because that meant she had to get married now. Their parents gave them blankets and a canoe and also other things to use.

She was very unhappy, as she liked this other young man. She hardly ever spoke to her husband, and he also never tried to make love to her either. They were both shy of each other because they never really got acquainted with each other. Sometimes the man's parents sent them to go someplace thinking that they might get acquainted that way. But they were more shy of each other on these trips. When they would get off anyplace to eat lunch, her husband would take his plate of food and go off someplace and eat alone. She too ate by herself. And then they would go back.

But after a while, they got acquainted. Her husband never said a wrong word to her. In fact, he was good to her. And she also never tried to hurt his feelings. The young man she used to go with felt very bad when she got married, but he never tried to see her again. And the next summer after that, he also got married. But he never ceased to care for her. But of course she did not know. And she tried to be a good wife to her husband, who was chosen by the old people.

And for five years she lived with him. He was a great man for traveling. He was out a great deal. She never paid no attention to what he was doing. He use to bring her a lot of things. In fact, she was always well dressed and had lots to eat. And her mother- and father-in-law were good to her. Also her sisters-in-law [were good to her too]. And one time, after she was there five years, her husband went away. He said he was going out trapping. And he also said that, if he found work anyplace, he would work and send her some money. So after he was gone for several months, she waited to hear some words from him. But she never got any word from him.

At last one whole winter went by. She never heard from him since he went away at blueberry-picking time. She heard some talk that her mother-in-law and sisters-in-law were saying that the reason why her husband went away is because she didn't have a child, that this man wanted to have children. This is what she heard. But she did not care what they said. She took notice too that her in-laws weren't the same to her anymore. They hardly ever spoke to her.

She went back to live with her parents, and when blueberry-picking time came again, all the Indians moved again to this same place to pick blueberries. She and her parents moved too. She use to pick berries every day and sell them, and she bought goods for her dresses. And one day, while she was sitting all by herself picking berries, she seen a man coming towards her. She recognized it was this young man she use to go with. He said, "So you are alone again. I wish I was still alone too. It was me that wanted to marry you very bad. I would have been very proud of you." And she smiled at him and said, "Well, it was not my fault. It was our parents that wanted us to get married." And the man said again, "Do you know what's keeping your husband away?" And she said, "No. I don't know." And he said, "He's married to another woman. I am not fooling you. Do you believe it?" And she said, "Yes. And I do not care." And the man said, "Yes. And the people where he is are coming here soon to pick blueberries, and he's coming too with his in-laws. You will see him here soon." She did not say anything again, and the man walked away. And she went home.

In the evening she was very quiet. She said nothing to anybody. She was just wishing she could go away someplace, for she hated to be there when her husband came there with another woman. She was ashamed to face her husband with another woman. Her mother asked her what was wrong, and she told her mother that her husband was getting married to another woman. She also said, "It is your fault why I have to face such shame. If it weren't for you two, I would be happily married to another man who cares for me." And her parents said, "Yes, it was our fault because we cared for you. We were afraid those old people would ruin you by some of their bad medicine, and that was why we couldn't refuse though we longed to keep you single." Then she said again, "I can't stay here to face such shame. I might as well be dead!" And her parents said, "Do not take it like that. Try and live for our sakes. You are still young, and it would be cowardly for you to destroy yourself." She never said anything again, and they never mentioned anything.

Then three or four days after, when they were coming home from picking blueberries, they seen a lot of Indians coming. She knew right away it was these people that this man told her about. She went right home and sat down. All the Indians were busy putting up wigwams, and as she was sitting there, she took notice of a man standing around where her in-laws had their wigwam. He had on a white shirt, red armbands, and a red silk handkerchief around his neck. He was standing with a woman that showed she was to become a mother soon. She knew right away it was her husband and his new wife. She felt very sorry again, although she tried not to care. But she was ashamed and mad. She went in the wigwam. She did not want anyone to see her.

And a couple of days after, she picked up her clothes that were dirty and went down to the lake to wash. And as she was sitting there washing, she seen a man coming in a canoe. She never paid no attention to him. She knew that the man was getting off close by—right where she was. And he would drop the paddle in the canoe. But she wouldn't look. But he dropped the paddle again, and she looked. It was her husband. And when he seen her looking, he called her by name, saying, "So this is where you are!" And she spoke right away, her too, saying, "Yes. This is where I am. And where have you been keeping yourself all this time? You said you were going out working and trapping." And he spoke to her again: "Why don't you get married, you too? Because I don't want you anymore. I have a wife now and she's got my child too. And don't never try to see me alone anyplace." And she said, "I don't care whether you are married or not." And then she asked him, "What's your wife's name?" And he said, "[Your name] is my real wife's name."

She jumped up and ran to where he was standing and grabbed his paddle. And as she was going to hit him, she seen that there was a lot of ducks in the canoe and then she let the paddle go and said to him, "I come pretty near breaking this paddle on your old head, but I won't. Instead, I'm going to take some of these ducks." And she picked out the biggest ducks there was and took them to where she was washing. And the man took the rest of the ducks home. They were small ones, and of course his new wife didn't know anything about it.

But there were some kids playing around near there, and they seen these ducks lying there beside her while she was washing. And they ran up and told their mother. And this woman came down for curiosity and seen these ducks. And she said, "Oh! I didn't know you were washing here. I'm coming for water." And the woman said, "Yes. This is where everybody gets water from. Over there." And the other woman went away and went along to this man's wigwam and told his new wife about these ducks she seen the woman having. And of course the new wife start quarreling with her husband.

And when the woman got through washing, she start cleaning the ducks. And when she was through, she seen an old woman coming. It was her old mother-in-law. She knew she was coming for the ducks, and she hid the ducks. The old woman said, "I am coming for those ducks because my daughter-in-law is fighting my son. She claims that he gave them to you. That woman that came here and seen you went along and told her." And she said, "No. I will not give the ducks to you. She can come for them herself. If she comes, I will give them to her." So the old woman went back without the ducks.

She stayed around there waiting for this woman. But when she didn't show up, she took the ducks and went up holding them so everybody would see them. She was not afraid of anybody now. She was just teasing this woman that took her husband away from her, although she didn't care for him. But she was ashamed. And when she got to her wigwam, she cooked the ducks. And her parents and herself had a nice meal over the ducks. Her parents never asked her where she got them from because they knew. This [other] woman told them that [she] seen the ducks beside their daughter while she was washing.

She picked blueberries every day and made good money and was dressed nice. She fixed herself up nice, for she was a nice-looking woman. And when blueberry-picking time was over, all the people moved away again. And she also moved away with her parents. They paddled all day and slept. And then paddled again all day. They were going along with some other [people]. And again that night they camped. And after everybody was asleep, she also went to sleep.

All at once, somebody shook her, and she wakened. It was dark, and she could not see who it was. But he spoke to her, saying, "Will you let me sleep with you?" She understood his voice. It was her old husband. But she pretend she didn't know him. And she said, "No. I will not let you sleep here. You must have some other place to sleep. You do not have to sleep here." And he said, "Don't say that to me because it's enough that I've been following you for a long time now." Then she said, "Why then are you following me? I have nothing of yours to follow. Why didn't you follow the one that has your child? Not me. I haven't got anything for you to come to me. I have nothing for you to be proud of me. Go back home to the woman who has your child. I am just as pleased to be alone. It wasn't our plans to get married. It was your own parents that wanted us to get married. Not us. So you might as well go back home and leave me alone. I wasn't jealous. [That's not] why I took those ducks. I just wanted to tease a little. That was all. I knew long ago that your people didn't care for me anymore because I didn't have a child." And the man said, "No. I am not going back. I'm going to stay here because my wife is always scolding me. She's jealous of you because you took those ducks. That's why she's always fighting me." Then she said, "I do not want you. I want you to go back to your wife and child and do what's right."

But the man sat there for a long time. And then he said, "You've always been like that. You've never cared for me. And that's why I went away to another woman. To have what every man wants from his wife: love. But my wife is too cranky. Remember this. I will always have you in my mind and will always be your husband."

But she said, "No. You've got another wife. You thought more of her than you did of me. So go now and forget that I ever married you." And he said, "All right, I will go. But please give me a lunch first, and I will go home." So she got up and gave him something to eat. And then away he went. And then her parents said to her that she did right by sending this man away.

And then they got to Kenora and sold their berries. And when they were there for a few days, some other people came to Kenora, and they brought the news that her husband was nearly killed—that all day they were just watching for him to draw his last breath. This is what she heard. She felt very bad for this man, and she was very quiet. Her parents took notice of her, but they did not say anything to her.

And one time a woman came and asked her to go and stay with her and help her. So she did go and work for this woman. And after she was there for quite a while, she use to see the man she use to go with before she was married, passing by there often. And one time he stopped and spoke to her, saying, "Do you hear the news that your old husband was brought two days ago to town? He nearly died because his wife nearly killed him." And she said, "No. Where is he staying?" And he named where the man was staying. "He was brought there to a doctor. His head was nearly breaking. The doctor had to cut him bald-headed because his hair was too thick. His head was cut all over." She did not say anything again, and the man walked away.

And that same evening after she got through with her work, she took a walk to where her husband was staying. When she came close there, she seen him sitting up on pillows, and his wife was sitting close by. She was going to pass right by, but he spoke to her, saying, "Come here." And she did. And he said to her, "Isn't it true that you sent me away when I followed you the time you moved away after blueberry-picking time?" And she said, "Yes. It's true." And he said again, pointing to his wife, "She would not believe me when I tried to tell her that. She said that you were glad to see me and that's why she gave me a good licking and nearly killed me." Then the woman said, "Well, who wouldn't be glad to see her husband coming back? I never did you any wrong. It's all your fault you went away and left me for this woman. And now look what you get! She nearly killed you! But I never done that to you." And she came away. The woman never said one word but just turned her back to her.

She never seen them again or tried to. But late in the fall, she heard that her husband was better now and that instead their baby died. And after the baby died, his wife went away and left him there. And after his wife was gone for many days, his parents told him to go after her. And he went because his parents were afraid of this woman's parents. They were bad people. They told their son that if his wife wanted to fight him again, to run away and leave her. When he got to his wife's home, she was already gone away with another man from the Ocean Shore [Lake Superior]. So he went back to Kenora without his wife.

While he was gone for his other wife, she [his first wife] got in with a man from Saging [Fort Alexander], and she married this man and he took her away to Saging. She left her parents in Kenora. As soon as she got over there, she learned that he was already married, and she didn't like it. So she made up her mind not to stay over there because this woman already had three or four children. She went with another woman to this little log store, and this was where she seen her husband's other wife. Also this woman told her that he wasn't any good and was very mean to his wife. So she told this woman that she was not going to stay there, and they told her that they would bring her as far as the horses could come and from there she could walk the rest of the way. So next morning, after her husband was gone, they took her as far as the road. They called it the Dawson Road. White men were already starting to work on the railroad and this was the road. She started walking on this road. And every time she came to where some white men were working, she would go off the road and go around these men.

She walked for many days. Soon she was out of moccasins, and her feet hurt her very much. She use to tie old sacks on her feet.

She use to be very tired because the nighttime was when she use to walk very fast. Then she walked again all night. And when morning was coming, she went off the road and slept. And at daylight she wakened but went right back to sleep again, for she was so tired. And when she wakened again, the sun was away up.

And when she got up, she seen two rough-looking men standing beside her. They were white men. She got awfully scared, for they were talking to her, but she could not understand them. They were handing her a bottle of whiskey. She turned around and away she ran, the two men right behind her. She ran on the railroad, and as she was running she seen another man coming. She would have to meet him. As she came near, he spoke to her in Indian, saying, "Don't run." And she stopped and looked back. The men that were running after her had already stopped. And the man asked her where she came from, and she said, "Saging." He looked at her feet and said, "Haven't you got any shoes to wear?" And she said, "No." He also asked her if she knew where she was now, and she said, "No." And he said, "You are only a half mile away from a town named Keewatin. I have a store there, and I understand Indian quite a bit." And he pointed, and she looked. She seen houses and smoke and a mill. And he told her to go to one of these houses, that there was a woman there that could talk Indian. So she went and sat down near there.

She took the old rags off her feet, and while she was sitting there, she heard someone whistling and she looked up and seen this same man coming. He was with a woman this time, and when they seen her, the woman asked her to go to their house. And she did. The woman gave her some water to wash, and then she had a good meal. She told this woman why she came to Saging and why she was going back so soon again and also about these men that scared her. And the man said that these men were very tough and were drunkards and didn't even have a home for themselves. Then, when she got through eating, the woman gave her some clothes to put on, and she did. And also there was a pair of shoes and stockings brought from the store. These she put on too. And she slept on a soft bed that night and had a good rest. Then the next day the storekeeper told her to come to the store, and she did. He told her to scrub the floor, and she did. Also, she washed [the clothes]. It took her all day to do this.

And when she got through, the man gave her a bundle of clothes and also some money, and he asked her where she intended to go. And she told them that her parents were in Kenora. And the man told her, "You will go home tomorrow, but you won't have to walk anymore. You will ride on the ferryboat and get off right at the Hudson's Bay dock in Kenora. You will start at seven o'clock in the morning, and it won't take more than a half hour to get there."

So she slept again that night at this half-breed woman's house, and next morning she was taken down to the dock, and she rode on the ferryboat. In half an hour's time she got off in Kenora. Her parents were surprised to see her. Very soon she told them about this man whom she married having another wife and four children. And also about this man that was so good to her when she was in trouble. Also this man told her to come to work every Monday to wash [the clothes] and scrub his store. And she stayed in Kenora, and she went to work for this man every Monday [in Keewatin]. He paid her good. He also use to pay her fare on the ferryboat.

And after she was there for quite a while, [her first husband] heard late in the fall that she was back in Kenora now. So he went to Kenora and looked for her. She felt very bad for him, and when he came there she said that she would marry him. "It wasn't my fault why we left each other, and it wasn't me that ruined your looks either." So she married him. And for a couple of years, they lived together. They learned to care for one another a great deal. He was very good to her then. And he always got a lot of nice things for her. Their parents were pleased to see them happily married to each other now. She never had no children, but his parents were just as glad because his other wife was so mean to him, and anyway his child didn't live.

And several years after, when all the people went to Kenora in the spring to take their muskrats and other furs to the Hudson's Bay

Company, she and her husband came to camp there too. They had brought a lot of muskrats and other kinds of fur. On the other side of town some other people were camping. They were from Eagle Lake, the place where her husband got his other wife from—the one that nearly killed him. But she did not know that the other woman and her parents were there too. This other woman [had come] back from the Ocean Shore, as her husband sent her away from there when she got too mean to him. And when she got to Eagle Lake, she heard that her [first] husband had gone back to his [first] wife, and she was very mad, for she was a bad woman. Some women heard her sharpening her knife that night, and she also said that she was going to go over to her husband's wigwam to kill him and his wife.

But he never knew that his other wife was there. So that night they went to bed as usual. He was lying on his stomach, and his wife had her arm around her husband while they were sleeping. They did not know that this other woman came in and stabbed him on the back. [The woman] also stabbed his wife on the arm; she had her arm around her husband's back. She jumped up right away, and as she was going to run out of the wigwam, the woman grabbed a stick of wood and hit her across the nose right on her eyes. And she fell back, for she was knocked cold. Her husband jumped up with the knife still in his back and shouted the brave Indian shout when being killed. He said, "Someone come here and pull this knife out of my back. Someone stabbed me. Also my wife is killed." Of course all the men that were sleeping there close in wigwams jumped and came into the wigwam and seen the woman lying there just as if she was dead.

The men pulled the knife out of his back, and great quantities of blood poured out. They were covering him with a white blanket, and it was soaked with blood. The women came in too and start to work on his wife for a long time. Then she come to. Her husband was dying from loss of blood. The woman that stabbed him ran home. And after the men ran over to tell the people on that side that the man and his wife were killed, this woman was very scared, for she was afraid of the Hudson's Bay man. And her parents took her away right away that night. Her mother was crying all the time.

The man's father tried to doctor him, but before daylight he died of loss of blood. But she was a little better the next day. She was very sorry her husband died, as she loved him now and she missed him very bad. Her husband was buried, and her in-laws and her parents were very good to her. They were always together most of the time. And for two years she gathered up a man's whole outfit, and she gave these clothes to her in-laws. This was what you call *keewainige*—paying for her husband's death so her in-laws would let her go. And her in-laws were very proud of her. They fixed her up and combed her hair and tied it up. Also washed her face and talked to her. They were glad because she was always good to her husband and he would have been still alive. But it was this other woman that killed him. They never seen this other woman either because she never came to where there was people. She was always in the woods hiding.

For another year she stayed single. At nearly the same time her husband died, the wife of the other man she use to go with [when she was young] also died. And she got in with him again after they were widows for three years. They married one another. Well, then she lived with him the rest of her life. He had two children. She took care of these children like as if they were her own children. He was a *nahdahwiiwe* and Indian doctor. Also other kinds of *manitokaso*. He was very good to her, and she also was good to him.

And his children, a boy and a girl, both grow up to big people. Her parents both died soon after that. So her bad luck never ended. But in spite of it all, she was happy. So they got to be very old. And the boy and girl got married. That's all I know about this.[1]

2

Why Didn't You

Take Good Care of

Her While I Was Away?

This is a story of an Indian woman who lived at Hungry Hall at the mouth of Rainy River. She had two husbands. The first husband she married; she stayed with him for quite a long time. She had a little boy with him. He took good care of her. He was a good old man. Never said a wrong word to anyone while he lived with her. And she had a baby girl with him. But the girl died when [she] was three years old. Her little boy was quite big now. And in the spring they went to Rapid River to see their bear traps. She also went along with her husband.

And one time when they went, as they were getting to one of their traps, they seen a big bear trying to get away from the trap. And it got away before he had time to shoot it. And the bear grabbed him and threw him about six feet away. He also threw the gun away. But she ran away with her boy to where their canoe was. And she waited there for her husband to come. At last she gave up and thought the bear killed him.

And as she was sitting there waiting for him, she heard someone yelling. She knew it was her husband. So she got out of her canoe and went back to the bush and start to yell, asking if he was living. And he yelled back, "Yes, but not very long." So they start to run. And when they got there, her husband was nearly crushed to pieces. And he said to her, "Run for the gun." And she did. And then she asked him where the bear went. He said it left him nearly dead. And then he tried to crawl. Both his arms were torn deep into the flesh. Also his body. And his hind part was torn open. Also on his side near the stomach he was really torn open. And that's what nearly killed him. The bear just throwed him all over. And then he pretend[ed] he was dead, and the bear smelled him and then left. And as the bear was walking, his claws dug deep into the ground. He was mad. When [her husband] tried to move, the blood would come out, and he lost an awful lot of blood.

So she made some kind of sling to carry her husband down to where their canoe was—like a baby on her back. And [she] put him in the canoe and paddled to the nearest place, where an old white man lived. She thought this old man would do something to stop the blood. And the old man came down after she pulled ashore. And sure enough, the old man helped her. He took the man out of the canoe, and he start to wash the wounds and put bandages on him all over his body.

And after they got through, the old man asked them this: "I will send you to Kenora to the hospital, and you will stay there 'til you're better. You won't get better if you stay here. And while you are gone, I want your wife to stay here. I will have her here as my wife and will pay her. So she will make a living here for your boy."

And about three hours after, the steamboat came, and the man took [her husband]. Before he went, [her husband] said to her: "You can stay here while I'm away and work for this man, and if he wants to marry you, you can marry him because I won't get better anyway—as long as youse are good to my boy. And if I do get better, it will be all right, as no Indian would make me better anyway." So they went to the hospital.

She stayed around there outside. She did not go in while the man was away. Her and the boy went around watching the cows and pigs and chickens. There was no one living close there. Only across the water some other farmers were staying. And about a mile away, on the same side, others were farming. And from over there came the one [who] came to milk the cows while the old man was gone.

And when he came [back], he told her that her husband was all tied up and put on a nice bed and also the Indian agent was going to look after him. And [he said], "If you want to see him sometime, you can get on the steamboat and go and see him. But I want you to stay right here and work for me while he's away." So she did not say anything.

And she start to cut poles to make a wigwam. And the man came over and asked her what she was going to do with these poles. She told him she was going to make a wigwam, and the man start to help her. So when she finished her wigwam, the man asked her if she was going to stay there. And she said, "Yes." But he would not let her, and he asked her to stay at his place. So she did. This was about four days after her husband left.

And then she told him that there were some more bear traps over there. So she went with him to see them, and they brought home two bears. And she skinned them and dried the hides and meat. She cooked it, and the old man ate the meat like any Indian would. He also helped her with everything. And when he went to town, he brought her shoes and print and some other nice things. She was now getting well acquainted with him, and he would always come and hug her when she was doing anything. And she knew now that he was after her. But she did not care, as her husband told her to do so.

And as she was living there with the white man, one day as the steamboat was going by, it stopped, and a man yelled, saying the man at the hospital died. He lost too much blood. So then they thought her husband died. She use to cry an awful lot. And the man use to always try to comfort her and tried to cheer her up. And then she at last made up her mind to marry this man. So he told her they would go to Fort Frances on the steamboat. And when the steamboat passed, they got on and went to Fort Frances.

Why Didn't You Take Good Care of Her?   17

And she got baptized, and they were married by the church. He also bought nice clothes for her. Also for her son. And her boy was also baptized.

When they got home, her husband asked her if she would like to go and visit her husband's grave. So again they went on the steamboat and went to Kenora. And she went to see the agent and asked him where her husband was buried. And the agent said, "He is not buried yet, and I don't think he will be buried because he will get better. He's still in the hospital. This was a different man you heard about. He shot himself and died with loss of blood."

So then she did not know what to do, as she was already married to the old man. Then she went to the hospital and seen her husband. She took her son, and the man thought it was nice to see his wife and son dressed like white people. The old man also bought nice clothes for him and also gave him some money and told him when he gets better that he was to come to his house and stay there with them. And the man was pleased to know that his wife and son were kept right.

But she did not have the heart to tell him she was married to the old man. Then they come back home. And she stayed there as his wife, for he thought a lot of her and loved her. But she was sorry and lonesome for her husband.

In the fall—about September—just when the boat was going for the last time, the man come back. He was not quite better, though he [had] stayed at the hospital all summer from May 'til September. And then he came there and stayed. No one ever made a fuss. And when spring came, he got better. He helped the old man put out his crop, and he helped him with everything. And she use to cook for the two men [and] washed for them. Also mended their clothes. She was good to both of them. And a year later, she had a little girl with the old man. The Indian slept upstairs, and they stayed downstairs. They use to have a nice time talking. Both men were good to her and liked her very much.

When next winter came, the man went away to the [logging]

camp. But the Indian stayed right there and took care of the cows and pigs and the horses and chickens. They stayed right there as man and wife. Then she had a little boy with him.

And when spring came, the man came home. He did not say anything when he knew that his wife was having a kid with the other husband. And again, they start plowing, and the Indian was the one that was sowing. Also the boy was now big enough to help too. And they made a fence—the man holding the fence post while the Indian was pounding it in. And the people that saw them use to make fun of them. But they did not care as long as they got along fine. And in the evenings they use to sit around on the hills watching the people passing by. The Indian use to go out moose hunting and duck hunting and fishing and brought it all home to his wife. And the other man would go out working, bringing home lots of money to his wife.

Then the next child she had was a little girl. So that's two little girls she had with the man and three boys with the Indian. But her children were all baptized and went by the name of the old man. He knew that the boys were the Indian's sons, but he did not care. He cared for all of them just the same as if they were his own. Also, the Indian never said any wrong word to him either [or to] his wife. And when the two girls got to be big, they start to tease this old Indian 'til at last he picked up and left them. And he took his oldest son with him. But he left the two younger boys.

When the man knew he was going away for good, he tried to coax him back. But he never did go back. He [only came] for a short visit. When the man went away to the [logging] camp to cook, he asked the Indian to come there and mind his farm. So he did come back and stayed there all winter. But as soon as the man came back, he went away again. And for years he went back and forth like that.

Soon after that, some people moved there close and were neighbors to them. And that winter when the man was away cooking at the camp again and the Indian came there again to stay, she use to go and visit the neighbor woman. And this woman forced her to drink. So she use to get drunk and go home that way. She got so's she came there often for a drink.

And one time she stayed nearly all night and went home. And as she was going to crawl under the fence to get through, she got caught all over on the barbed wire. It was very cold that night, and she could not get out. And her Indian husband was at home sleeping. Also all her children were sleeping. And she was so drunk she did not have sense enough to yell. So she froze to death right there. Only next morning she was found froze stiff. She had a bottle with her, which she was going to take home to her Indian husband. And so the man was called home. And only after he came, she was buried. So the two men were left widows.

And only after she was buried, the man said something to [her Indian husband]: "She was your wife just the same as mine and that's why I always left her with you. Why didn't you take good care of her while I was away? You could've stopped her from drinking if you wanted her. And if you [had] looked for her and brought her home that night, she wouldn't of frozed to death like that. And I'm very sorry to lose her, for I loved her very much and I sure will miss her an awful lot." But the Indian did not say anything. For he knew it was true. And also he felt sad himself.[1]

3

You Can Have Him
All to Yourself

This is a story of a man from Hungry Hall Reserve. This man was married to an Indian woman. When treaty was first given out at Nor'west Angle, he got in love with another girl there. So he married her, and he went back and forth to his two wives. He would go and stay with his new wife awhile. Then he would come back to his other wife. The women never seen one another. He went on like this for quite a while 'til the treaty changed. All the people from the Lake of the Woods and from Hungry Hall up the Rainy River now went to Fort Frances, and all the Indians met there in Fort Frances to get their treaty on the fifteenth of July. The blueberries were ripe already.

So the man went along up with [his first wife]. And his young wife was there at Fort Frances already. So they got there, and the man and his wife got off, and he took his things up. And of course she took her things up and went up, her too.

The Indians were gambling and playing moccasin game. So she sat there. But the man went on to look at the men gambling. She didn't know where they were going to camp. There were tents all over. And she got up and walked to the closest tent. And as she was looking through, this [young wife] splashed boiling blueberry jam on her face. She was badly burnt. She did not know that this woman was living in this tent. So her husband had to call an old woman to put medicine on her face. Her face, neck, and ear was all badly burnt.

You see, the man intended to keep his two wives if they could get along. But they didn't. This young girl was the one that was jealous of the main wife.

So after this woman was burnt, she got mean, her too. She didn't do anything to her that time. So she didn't enjoy herself that time 'cause she had a sore face. So after the Indian celebration was over, the man moved back to Hungry Hall with his wife that was burnt, and his other young wife went to Hungry Hall with some people that were from where she was from.

And in the fall at rice making, about the first part of September, the Indians had Indian dances at Hungry Hall. And of course all the men got dressed. And this man was getting dressed, and he scolded his wife 'cause she didn't make him a pair of new moccasins. And he went out to his other young wife and brought home a pair of new beaded moccasins. And of course she didn't like that. He promised her when she got burnt that he wouldn't go back to this other young woman if she wouldn't say anything to anyone. And he didn't keep his promise. So she got disappointed.

So after her husband went to the dance, she could see [his young wife] going into the dancing place. She was one of the women that helped the men singing. You see, there had to be eight women sitting outside the drum helping the men sing. So while the man was at the dance, [his first wife] packed her things and got her canoe ready. And after she was ready, she sharpened her butcher knife. People seen her doing this. And she walk[ed] to where they were dancing. Birch bark was all around. And [the young wife] was sitting with her back to the bark. So the woman lifted the birch bark up and spoke to her, saying, "My, you hurted me bad the time you burned me. Now it's my turn to hurt you." So she cut her face right from her nose to her ear. She cut her cheek right open and a piece of her nose and ear off. And she said to her, "I am leaving you with my husband. You can have him all to your own. I can go and get a husband—not some other woman's husband."

Then she went down the hill and got into her canoe, and away she went down the river. And she went to the Lake of the Woods, where they call Nâyawagashink. So she stayed there 'til winter, and she got married to a young man.

So that's all about her. We'll go back to [her husband].

So he was left there. He had to tend to this woman again with her sore face, and he had to marry her all the rest of his life. So they just lived like that. They didn't have no children. So she carried that scar on her face all her lifetime. But the other woman had no scar. And the man died before either of the two women he married. That's the end of this story.

4

He Made Up His Mind
to Look After Her

This is a story of a Cree woman. She came from Wahbuhsimong, Whitedog, north of Kenora. Her husband was a good hunter and also made a good living. They had only one child, a boy. They never had any more children after that. Her husband was good to her at that time.

Then the boy got sick one time. He was very sick for a long time. They did everything to try and make him better 'til at last she took up her own *manitokaso*. She doctored him with a rattle. But nothing seemed to help him out, and he died.

She use to wonder where her husband would go. Sometimes when the boy was still living, he used to stay out late. And then when the boy died, she was very sad. She missed her little boy. She was very lonely after her boy was gone. And the worst of all, her husband would go out in the night and stay out all night, and only in the morning he would come home. He never spoke to his wife, but he would just come in and lay down to sleep. She never asked him where he went to in the night, but she just simply kept right on working and paid no attention to him. But she used to often wonder where he went in the nighttimes. And then again the next night he was away all night.

Next morning he came in late, and he slept again all day. And towards evening he got up and ate. He never said a word to anyone. He took his sack and took an otter skin out and cut it in strips. Then he took a comb and start to comb his hair and braided it in two long braids. Then he took the strips of otter skin and wound it around the braids. And he also put on his clothes that were nice. Also he put on nice moccasins. But he did not put any kind of paint on his face. Then he took a new blanket, and out he went again.

She then made up her mind to follow him. So she went out behind him and followed him among the wigwams. All the Cree Indians were camping together there. And away at the end of the wigwams, this was where her husband went to this wigwam. Then she peeped in and saw two old people and a young girl. The old people were gone to bed already. Just the woman was sitting up. And the man sat down right beside her. Right away she start caressing his braids. She stood there for a long time and watched them. Then she came home and went to sleep.

Next morning her husband came home and slept all day. She did not say anything to him again. She use to cry an awful lot. And one time her mother-in-law spoke to her while she was crying. She told her to quit crying, that nothing or no one would have pity on her anyway. And anyway, people were beginning to think of them as no good on account of this man's carrying on. The people were beginning to take notice of him being dressed up all the time, while she was mourning heavy for her little boy. And for a couple of more nights he did that.

And then she made up her mind to do something. And after her husband went out again that night she went to bed and pretend[ed] she was asleep. Then she got up very quietly, and she washed up her face and combed her hair, and then she braid[ed] her hair into two long braids at the back and tied on bunches of ribbon. Then she put on new moccasins. Also she put on her good dress and waist. Then she took a shawl or blanket and covered up with it. And she took her leather strap she used for carrying wood. And then she went out very quietly.

She went to her little son's grave, and she cried very hard. Then she went along and came to some gray willow trees. And then she tied her leather strap onto these trees, and she said, "What is there left for me to live for? No one cares for me, and my boy is gone. So I will go too and join my boy." Then she put the leather around her neck.

And before she was ready to do this, someone grabbed her on the shoulders and said, "No! You can't do this to yourself! Because you are nice looking. I know what's been on your mind since you knew about your husband, but don't worry about him. I will take you away from here so you will not know what he's doing. I will take you to where your parents are, and you will never leave them again as long as you live. I've been watching you for a long time, and I know too what's been on your mind ever since." So he took her by the hand and led her away from there. He also said, "Get ready right away if you want to take anything along with you. And please hurry up."

She never said one word while he was talking. She did not know what to do. But anyway she went along with him, and he took her to her wigwam. "I will come here with my canoe. Be sure and hurry." So he went. And after he was gone, she stood there. And she was puzzled who he was. She could not understand his voice either. Then she went to this wigwam where her husband went. She peeped in again and seen her husband sleeping with this woman. She got very mad, and she was wondering what to do when this same man came up to her again and put his hands on her shoulders and said, "Come away from there and come with me. It will not do you any good to stand there and look at him. He's not good enough for you. But I will try and be good and make up to you all the misery you've been through."

So she went back with him to her own wigwam, and he told her to get her things which she liked best and to hurry. So she went into her wigwam and took some things. And she had a little pup and took him along too. And then the man took her down to the canoe. And away they went. She did not paddle but sat in the canoe. And then they went through a big portage. And after they got on the other side, the man stopped and made a fire and made some tea.

It was still night. She tried to see his face, but he had his head down and she could not tell who he was. And he gave her some good things to eat. He started playing with the little pup. Then she thought to herself, "Whoever he is must be very silly." And the man said to her without looking at her, "I know what you are thinking of me. You think I am silly because I'm playing with your little pup." Then she began to fear him. And after their lunch they went down again and started out with the canoe. And he said, "There is a rapids near here. We will not go over it 'til morning." So they stopped there close by, and he told her she could sleep in the canoe. And he got off and lay down on the grass, and they slept.

She woke up first. The sun was up, and she touched the man's feet and said to him, "Wake up! It's morning now." He jumped up and made another fire. And she cooked something, and they had breakfast. Only then she knew who he was: a young man who lived near them. She use to see him often sitting around there. And this was him. She did not say anything. So they went over the rapids, and he asked her to go into a bay first. And she said, "All right." He got out of the canoe and told her to wait for him there. He took his gun along, and she waited around there. She heard shots, and he came down again. He had some ducks, and he said to her, "If you are willing to have some meat, let's go and get some." And she said, "Sure! I'll be very glad to have some meat." So she went up with him, and they brought back some meat. Then he asked her if they would not stay there and dry this meat for a couple of days. She said it was all right.

Then they made a little wigwam. And he also told her that, all this time she lived with this other man, he never ceased to care for her. And when he heard the people talking about this man, he found out that he was flirting with this other woman. Also he heard people saying that she was blamed for her little son's death, and this was why her husband did not want her anymore. Then he made up his mind to look after her. And then he start spying on her. He loved her all that time, and that was why he never married anyone. But he never bothered her while she was married to this other man. And when he knew what this other man was doing, he knew now that he did not wait in vain for her. Only then she knew why her husband didn't care for her. And it was not true that she [caused] her little son's death. She had tried her best to save him, but she couldn't. And he told her that he was going to marry her. So they slept there that night.

They stayed there for about three or four days drying meat. And one time they seen two men coming on the lake in a canoe, and she ran and hid on them. She did not want them to see her. And the men came right up to the wigwam and said, "Oh! This is where youse are making meat!" And he said, "Yes." And they said again, "We are sent here by the people back there to look for youse. Your grandmother is worried about you because you are lost. And also one woman is lost." And he said, "We are not lost. We know where we are, and [we] also know what we are doing." Then he gave them some meat, and away they went.

So she came back to their wigwam again, and he told her what these men said, and she was very scared. But he said, "Please don't be scared like that. I will take care of you so that no harm will come to you. Don't you know that I love you an awful lot, and it hurts me to know you are like that?" He took her in his arms right there. She said she would care for him, her too. He told her to get ready, that they would go to her parents now. So they went.

And as they were getting closer, her mother seen them coming. She went in and told her old man, "Our daughter is coming but with another man." And her old man said, "I suppose she is doing something to make us ashame[d]." The old woman went down and met her daughter and kissed her. She also cried for her little grandson. But the old man did not go out at all. He was worried [and] ashamed of his daughter. She told her mother everything that her husband done to her. Also how she was blamed for the death of her little boy. Her mother was very glad to see her, and she went in to see her old man and told him all about it. The old man did not say anything

The [young] man made a wigwam close by there, and this is where they lived. She had a young brother, and he was very proud of his new brother-in-law because he knew he was good to his sister. She never missed anything [had everything she needed]. Her new husband was very good to her, and also he was a good hunter. The old man got over it. Soon he began to see he had a far better son-in-law this time. And then they all moved to Red River to go around buffalo hunting on the prairie. And they went around for a long time.

And when they came back from buffalo hunting, many of the people camped in one place for celebration before rice-making time. And [her first husband] happened to be there too with his wife. And of course the men use to play moccasin game and the women squaw hockey and all kinds of other Indian games and dancing. Her husband told her to join in anything that the women were playing.

So one time she was asked to play squaw hockey. Because she had nice clothes and she also wore nice shoes, people wished for her clothes. Then she played too. This other woman was playing too, the one who took her first husband away from her. She was poorly dressed, and her old moccasins were no good too. And as they were playing, this woman was in her way. She pushed her over, and [she] fell and her feet went up. And she said, laughing, "Look at her old moccasins! They look like lynx paws." She was playing against her. And the side she was on won. And after she went home, her husband said, "Don't do that. [Don't] tease anyone—especially that woman." So she never said anything because she always did what her husband told her.

Then the next day the men played moccasin game. Her husband went too and took a gun and blanket. His brother-in-law went with him. The [first husband] was to play against him. He also brought a gun, too. And before they start to play, he was working at the gun and the shell fell out. And this young man took the shell while this other man didn't know it fell out. And while they were playing, [the first husband] knew they were getting beat. He took the gun again and started playing with it. Of course [her young husband] was watching him. He knew what he was going to do. Sure enough! He pulled the trigger when the gun was pointed toward him. But there was nothing but gunpowder in it. And he started to shout. The young husband that was supposed to be shot laughed and said, "Here, man, here's your shell. You forgot to put it back in." And he said, "I also have a knife in my pocket." He drew his knife out, and as he was ready to stab this man, his brother-in-law took his hand and took the knife away from him and also pulled him up and took him home. The other man went home. And soon they seen him paddling away with his wife. And the men yelled after him saying he was a coward.

Her husband told her they would only stay there four days. Yet the people began to move away to make rice in different places. And they went too. And also her parents went along with them. And where they went, [her first husband] happened to be there again. And her husband told her not to go back in the bush to cut the wigwam poles, that his brother-in-law and he would cut them. He knew [the first husband] was intending to kill his wife with the ax she would use. So sure enough! [Her first husband] started to yell, saying for the women to cut the wigwam poles. But she did not go, as her husband told her not to go. And so [her first husband] failed to kill her again, and he moved away from there again.

And after rice-making time they moved back to their own place. The railroad was starting to be worked on now, and this is where her husband worked for about three years. Later one summer, while she was washing [the clothes], there was kind of a dock there, and this was where she was sitting. Her brother was inside the wigwam. He had a sore foot. He was now a grown-up man. And while she was washing, someone spoke to her, saying, "You make me mad when you are so happily married and also when you didn't care when our boy died. And the man you are married to now is very proud." She answered him, saying, "You didn't care either when our boy died. You were the first to marry a young girl."

He pushed her into the water. She could not swim. And when she would come up and grab the dock, he would step on her hand and kick it off. And she would also yell. And her brother that was in the tent heard her, and he came out. He could hardly walk. He seen this man standing there. He had a stick and came close behind him and started to hit him with this stick and knocked him into the water. His sister had time to come out of the water, and they both went up. And the man came out of the water too, and he skipped away from there as fast as he could. Her husband came home from work as she was putting on dry clothes, and her brother told him all about it how he saved his sister from nearly getting drowned by this man. Her husband was very mad, but he did not follow this man. He always worked on the railroad. The white men thought a lot of him because he was a good worker.

And the next summer again while they were living there, this [first husband] come there with two men in a canoe. And he told this man that he was coming for this woman—that she was his wife, and he didn't care whether he let her go or not, he was going to take her anyway. And this man said, "No. You will not take her away from me as long as I'm living. You cast her aside for another woman, and I saved her when she was going to take her life on account of you. And I care for her an awful lot, and I'm going to fight to hold her." And the man came right up to him and started to fight. He threw him down, and [the first husband] said, "All right, men, come and help me." But the men did not move. They kept right on fighting, and he was getting licked very badly because he was older. He said he was going to take this woman anyway. And this man said, "No. You're not going to take her away because I'm going to kill you because you are always bothering us. We never go and bother you, and you've done enough to us now and I cannot stand any more from you. That's twice now you nearly killed my wife. You did not care for her. You're just jealous because I'm proud of her. So I'm going to kill you now with my own hands so you will never bother us anymore." And he start to hit him harder, and one of his blows knocked him dead. The [other] men just stood there looking at them. After he knew he was dead, he told the men to take the body home. And they did.

The people tried to get him into trouble by telling the white men, but they couldn't because the white men believed his story and they also liked him. So he was free. Nobody ever bothered them then. They did not have any children.

5

The Wind Took the Canoe
Right Across the Lake

This is about Indians at Lake Saphiria in Manitoba. They're my relatives. The woman is my aunt. This happened about fifteen years ago.

One time when they were first married, they went out duck hunting late in the fall—just two of them, her and her husband. And they had a little pup along and their bedding and all their groceries, and as they were going along, there were no Indians or whites there close. As they were across the lake—like, this lake is a big lake, no one ever crosses the lake with a canoe—they had to go along the shore. So they went along the shore going into bays [and] creeks, hunting ducks along [the way].

And after they were gone for two or three days, they came to a place where there were a lot of ducks. And the man says to his wife, "We will land here and make a fire, and you can make some tea. And while you're getting our lunch ready, I will go and see if I can't get to the place where the ducks are." It was kind of a point, like, and he was going to walk to go and kill ducks there. It was kind of windy, and when the man got off, he took out his gun and ax and all his shells and put them on the ground. And he took just the gun with him. And the woman got off, and she took a blanket and all their cooking kettles and tea pail and a young moose-hide bag where they kept their tea and their matches and another bag where she kept all her sewing. But the little dog was still in the canoe.

So the man went to where the ducks were, and so she started gathering wood to make a fire. And as she was getting through and getting up, she seen her husband coming running. And when she looked out on the lake, she seen their canoe far out on the lake. The man took his clothes off and ran into the water and tried to swim after the canoe, but he couldn't get it so he quit and came back.

And she was sitting there crying when he come back. And he said to her to stop crying and not worry, as they would live [there] as long as they could 'til the lakes would freeze up as that would be the only way they could get home. And they walked back until they came to a wide river they couldn't cross, and they made a wigwam there out of cedar poles and brush. This was about in the last of October. And she was expecting to become a mother in November. So they stayed at this wigwam. It was on a point, like, where this river was. They made this wigwam real warm.

Well, they lived there. The man killed all kinds of caribous and moose. There were no deer at that time, only caribou and moose. And the man had a wide file, and he broke this file in half and made a leather scraper. So they set to work and scraped hides and tanned them. They even made one big moose hide as a mattress, and they made rabbit-skin robes to cover with. And she made a moose-hide coat and pants for her husband and a moose-hide dress for herself. She made all kinds of leather coats, mitts, pants and shirts and dresses and moccasins. She also made rabbit-skin coats, and she made a baby dress and blanket—she kept that for her baby. And she even took off her underskirt and made baby clothes with it because she didn't have anything else to use.

They were looking every day to see if anybody would look for them. But they never could see anyone. And their canoe was found about seven miles [up] the bay. The wind took the canoe right across the lake. And the people across the lake that were hunting ducks found the canoe full of water and a little pup tied in the canoe, drowned. And the parents of both thought them drowned. And the parents were all mourning and crying for them. They were taking it very hard.

And they were still living in this wigwam. They had lots to eat, living on wild food. And about the sixteenth of November, she got sick. She had everything ready as best she could. The man cut wild hay with the knife so she had this hay to lay on. So she got sick that night, and when the hard pains came, the man start to cry. And just when the baby was to [be] born, she said to him, "Shut up! And don't sit there crying. Come here and help me as much as you can. It's not you that's having the pains." So the man come there and was shivering and crying and would ask his wife, "Are you going to live?" So finally, the boy was born! He was a big boy. So everything come out fine.

So she got better and strong again. And the man made a cradle for their baby. And then he made toboggans. And she had caribou skin to lace the baby in. The man made deadfalls and killed fishers, martens, [and] mink. So they had lots of fur.

This was about in December now. The lakes were frozen now. But Lake Saphiria never freezes—only on the shore. But that big, wide river was frozen up now by that time. And then, about the twentieth of December, the man said to his wife that he would go and take a load of stuff such as meat and hides and go and see if the ice was strong enough for them to walk on. So she told him to go but to be very careful and come back: "What will become of us here if you go there and drowned?" So he went halfway and left his load there and went back to his wife. So he told his wife that it was good and said they would go if she could walk. And she said that she could walk anyplace. So they started off the next day.

And they went as far as where he left his load the day before. He made a little camp there, and they stayed there overnight. So the next day they started off again. They walked all day and late at night. And when they came to her mother's house, she could see her sister standing near the window washing the supper dishes. And she was all in black. Her husband had on a leather coat and pants and a beaver cap, and she was dressed in leather trimmed with fur, and she had a beaver cap. And the baby was laced in caribou leather and covered with a rabbit robe.

So her husband knocked on the door, and her sister opened the door, and she yelled back to the other room and said, "Who are these? Come on out and see these strangers!" And they all came out—her father, mother, brothers, and sisters. And they all got ahold of them and start to cry with gladness. They didn't know whether to believe their eyes or whether they were ghosts. And someone ran and told his father and mother.

So they arrived in Fort Alexander the twenty-third of December. And all the people in that village were so surprised that they didn't sleep all night. They were visited 'til daylight and all day the next day. People were laughing and crying at the same time. Nice things were brought for them to eat and clothes for them to put on. For all the people there thought them dead and were all surprised to see them alive again. Even the headman at the trading post came there and took their pictures in their clothes which the woman had made. And another merchant from Winnipeg came there and bought all their clothes. Nothing was sewed with thread. It was all sewed with sinew. That's what they call those things they get from the moose muscles. Their parents even gave all their things away thinking that they were dead. There even were some other people living in their house.

But they got all their things back from the people, and they got more too. And they sold all their furs such as minks, fishers, lynx, and martens—everything the man killed while they were in the wilderness. And they got a lot of money for them. And everybody was glad to see them because they were good people. They were all sorry when they thought them dead. And they had other children, and that boy that was born in the wilderness grew up to be a man and had children.

She use to tell us that she had no soup all this time while they were there, but she use to boil ashes in her cooking kettle and wash her towel after she would strain this ash water. Salt was the only thing she grieved for. She used to say that the meat didn't taste like food when she had no salt with it. She didn't mind very much [not having] sugar. Well, they had swamp leaves for tea. And they never let the fire go out. She use to say that they didn't mind living there, as they always had lots to eat. And fur and moose hides and caribou hides to work at. And she was always sewing leather and making moccasins.[1]

TWO

PARENTS AND CHILDREN

Fig. 17. Family traveling by canoe, Lake of the Woods, 1911. Photo by Carl Gustav Linde. Reprinted by permission of Minnesota Historical Society.

Fig. 18. Selling blueberries in Kenora, ca. 1912. Photo by Carl Gustav Linde. Reprinted by permission of Minnesota Historical Society.

6

We Will Take You
and Love You as Our
Very Own Daughter

This is a story of a woman. Her mother died when she was a little girl. Then she stayed on with her widowed father. And for a little while, her father stayed single. He was very good to his daughter. When he use to eat, she would also eat with him. Also, he gave her everything nice. And then he took a woman and married her. She felt very bad when she knew her father was married again. When her father seen her crying, he said to her, "Do not cry." And she said, "I am sorry to see another woman already taking my mother's place." And he answered her, "Don't cry. She will be a mother to you. And I will tell her to be good to you." So she quit crying and made up her mind that she would do the same.

But soon she found out that her stepmother was awfully mean. She no more got the best that her father brought. She even never ate with them. Her stepmother always gave her the worst of everything. And when her father would be away hunting, her stepmother never gave her anything to eat. [She] would always tell her to cook for herself and would always be scolding her and slapping her and everything. And when her father came home, her stepmother would be telling all kinds of lies to put her into trouble, and her father sometimes scolded her for nothing. When he would go to the Hudson's Bay Company, he always brought lots of calico. And her stepmother always took the most and the best. The girl always got the poorest and dullest color print and always hardly enough for a dress. She use to cry an awful lot.

This went on for a couple of years. Her father never made a fuss over her now, and she use to feel very bad. She missed her mother's love. Also her father's love.

Then she had a baby sister. She loved her baby sister very much. And yet her stepmother never let her hold her.

So when spring came again, they moved away to sugar making on an island, and they stayed there and made sugar. When her stepmother boiled the sugar water, she use to sit near there and eat the sugar which fell out of the pail. And when her stepmother seen her, she gave her a slap, and she start to cry but not hard. And as she was wiping her tears away, she got another slap. And her stepmother said to her, "Keep your dirty hands away from the sugar, you homely-looking thing." Then she said to her husband, "She's dipping the sugar out of the kettle." And her father spoke to her [and] told her to get away from there.

So she got up and went back into the bush crying. She climbed up a tree and start to cry. After she sat there for a long time, she heard someone yell, and she looked around. She knew it wasn't a human person. She also thought, "Let it kill me, whatever it is." And when she looked up, she seen a *pahguk* skeleton, and it was yelling hard. She listened, and she understood it saying, "*Noshis.* Don't cry. Soon we will laugh. You will laugh hard too."

She did not understand what this skeleton meant by saying that. So she came down from the tree and walked home. As soon as her stepmother seen her, she start to make fun of her saying that she went away mad and all kinds of other things. So after sugar-making time, they moved back to their own place. She never was given anything nice to wear or anything nice to eat. She was looked upon as an old dog or something very dirty. But she lived anyway. She was never happy. [She was] always grieving for her dead mother.

Then, when her little sister was three years old, they went out making sugar again at the same place. Her stepmother always use to tell her father on her. Then, one morning, her father scolded her again. He said, "You are always mad. What are you mad for? I'm told that you're mad because you want me to marry you instead of your stepmother." Then she answered him and said, "I suppose she would marry her father—whoever he is." Then he said, "What are you always mad for?" Then she answered again, "I'm not mad. I'm sorry, sad, and unhappy because she's so mean to me. And I also miss my mother because she was so good to me." Then her stepmother said, "Just listen to her! My, she knows what to say!" Then [the girl] said, "Yes. My mother told me she's going to take my father away from you soon." She did not know why she said this, but it came out of her mouth anyway.

So when they were just about through making sugar again, her father said one morning: "I had an awful bad dream last night. I dreamed that my dead wife was fighting me." There was a big fire on, and a large kettle of sugar boiling hard. And [her stepmother] said, "I wish she would fight me. I would soon fight her back." He got up and tripped over something. He fell right into this big kettle of boiling sugar and burned to death right there. She jumped up and ran to her father. He was already dead. She start to cry. Her stepmother came to her and gave her a good licking and told her it was all her fault. Then the rest of the people that were making sugar came running there and seen he was already dead. They took him and dressed him up. Then they dug a hole and buried him right on this island.

So they told this woman that they were moving away from there and also told her to move away from there. And she said she would. She waited for all the people to go. Then she got ready to move too. The girl also got her old things ready and put them in the canoe. Her stepmother took her things and throwed them out and told her, "I'm not taking you along. You can stay right here and marry your dead father. That was the reason why you were always mad. And also your old mother can take care of you. I'm going to get married right away again, and I don't want to be bothered with you anymore. You can stay here and starve."

So she watched her stepmother push the canoe out and get in. She said to her stepmother, "Take me along as far as to the mainland where there are some Indians, and you can leave me." But, no! She did not want her to get in at all. Then the girl spoke to her little sister, saying, "When you come to where there is some Indians, say that you left your sister on an island." Then she start to cry as hard as she could. Also her little sister was crying. She watched them 'til they were out of sight. She could hear her little sister crying along [the way].

So she went back to where their camp was. She sat there crying. Left alone. An unwanted orphan. She was about thirteen years old now.

There was nothing for her to do. She was on an island. No way of getting to the mainland. Nothing to do and nothing to eat. So when night came, she crept under some brush and cried herself to sleep. Next morning, she woke up and sat around crying. She walked around the shore of the island. Many times she watched to see if anyone would be passing by. The fourth day she got so hungry and weak. Then she thought of that little bundle that her stepmother hung on the grave of her father. So she went over and opened it. There was some sugar and matches and tobacco. She took a mouthful of this sugar, and she got over her weak spell. In the night times she use to be so scared. She would hear some kind of little funny noises. She cried an awful lot [so] that her cheeks begin [to be] raw and she had sores beneath her eyes. She picked up all the old birch bark and made a little wee wigwam just hardly big enough for her to sleep in.

Then the sixth day, just about noon, she climbed up a tree and sat there. She was crying and looking nowhere. All at once, she heard some people talking to one another. She looked up and saw a canoe coming with two people, a woman and [a] man. They were looking towards her, saying, "What is that over on that tree? It does not look to be a bear." Then she got scared. She stood up on this tree and said, "No. I have not become a bear yet. I'm still a human person." Then the man spoke to her, saying, "Are you sick with some bad disease? [Is that] why you are here?" And she said, "No. I'm not sick. I was left here by my stepmother because she does not want to be bothered with me. You must've heard about the man that burnt here. Well, he was my father. And my stepmother always hated me, so she left me here to die right here where my father was buried." So the woman told her to get down from the tree. So she did get down. The man said, "We will have our dinner here with you, and we will take you along for our very own daughter and love you. The reason why we are going around like this [is] we lost our only child, who was a boy, and we miss him very much. So we will take you and love and care for you as our very own."

She was very glad and happy to know that at last she would be taken and well cared for. She was all in rags, and the woman told her to take her old clothes off. She took out some print and soon made her a dress. Also nice moccasins and many other nice things were given to her. And so they had dinner. That was the first real meal she had for over six days. They were sitting in front of her father's grave, and the man gave a little speech as he was putting something in the fireplace.

So that night, they camped right there, and next morning they went, taking her along with them. They did not go near where there were Indians, but they camped along [the way] and at last they come to Kenora. And this is where they lived. Her adopted parents never told [anyone] that they found her on an island. They use to say that she was given to them. But she use to tell what had happened—when she got to be a woman.

Back to the stepmother:

Her little sister use to cry much for her. Her stepmother did not say anything about her. She did not go to the same place where the people went. She went to her own people, where they did not know anything of her stepdaughter, which she left on this island. The people took notice of this little girl crying. They understood her saying, "Come on. Let's go back for my sister." She never paid no attention to her little girl crying though, and after ten days was up, she got ready and said, "I'm going to the island to visit my husband's grave and also to go and see my stepdaughter. She would not leave her father's grave. I left her food and things to use, and I am afraid she will be short of food now. So that's why I'm going back to look for her."

So she came away. And when she got to the island, she could not find her stepdaughter anyplace although she looked everywhere. All she found was her old clothes. And she also found some pieces of new print. Then she had an idea that she was alive and must've been found by some people. But she was awfully scared. So she went right back and told the people that she could not find her anyplace. She was very scared. The Indians took notice that she was very quiet. She got married again soon. And after many years, when her own girl was a young girl, her husband wanted to marry her daughter. He scared his stepdaughter so much that she picked up and went away to Kenora. And she found her sister over there living in a nice place.

So then she had her young sister there with her now right in Kenora town. And then she use to hear white women singing in church, singing hymns. And she use to understand these hymns because they were the ones she use to hear when she was on this island. She married a half-breed.

And when [the stepmother] missed her daughter, she went to Kenora and said, "Wherever my daughter is I'm going to throw her out! Whether she is in the king's house or not!" And [when] someone told her she was living with her sister, she turned and came right home, as she was afraid of her stepdaughter.

So she never bothered them, and also her daughter never came to see her either. She also married a half-breed boy, and they were all baptized and lived like white people right in Kenora town. The end.[1]

7

Her Father Was Sitting
with His Head Down
with Tears in His Eyes

This is a story of an old woman, the old great Grand Medicine believer. She was a little girl when she took sick. And some Indian doctors did their *nanadawiiwa* to her, and another one dreamed of her and told her she had to go through the Grand Medicine. The Grand Medicine was not yet done in this part of the country, but the Indians heard of it at Ponemah [Minnesota]. And so someone told her parents to go through it; then she would get better.

And so, of course, her parents got ready. They cooked Indian rice and blueberries and sugar. And they asked the two old medicine men to come there, and they had a feast and smoked the tobacco they put there and they had a speech. So after she promised to go through the Grand Medicine, she got better right away. And awhile after, she did go through it. And then, as they were living [there], one of her brothers younger than her got sick. Then he was also told to go thru' the Grand Medicine, but the boy died before they were ready. And so she was told to go through the Grand Medicine for this boy that was dead. So she did. And later, after she was about sixteen years old, she got sick again. She never knew anything. She was that sick. And someone told her to go through the Grand

Medicine. That was the third time. And she got better again. So that same summer she got sick again and was told to do the same thing. And she did. So that was the fourth time. And each time, she had to give more than the last.

So at her fourth *midawi*, there were four old men as leaders 'cause that was the fourth time she went through it. And the head old man was old enough to be her grandfather. She was about eighteen years old at the time and was a nice-looking squaw. And this old man fell in love with her and wanted her to be his wife. And so after they were through, of course, she did not know how this old man felt towards her. Only after she was sleeping in their wigwam, she knew that there was someone after her. And several nights after, she knew it was this old man.

So when he use to come there at nights, she would crawl away from where she was laying, and she would go to where her parents were and crawl in between them. And her father would kick her, thinking it was a dog. She wouldn't speak to them either, and he would keep on kicking her 'til she nearly use to fall in the fireplace.

So at last, her father took notice that she was always crying and sad. She wouldn't eat, or they couldn't get her to do any work 'cause she was always kind of hiding. And when night came, she would sleep in a place where no one could find her. She was a smart girl. She [used to] always [be] getting birch bark, cutting wood, or making mats. But she didn't do [this now], and that was why her father took notice of her being so sad and quiet. So he told his old woman [wife] about this and told her that she should try to find out what was wrong with her.

So her mother told her that she wanted her to go with her to set nets. And they did. So [her mother] had a good chance then to ask her what was it that hurted her feelings and told her frankly to tell what it was. And so she said, "The reason why I'm like this is that I'm ashamed when an old man wants me for his wife. I'd sooner die than to marry him 'cause I hate him. And another thing, I'm afraid that he will use his bad medicine on us and have death on us." So the woman told her daughter that it was true what she said: "He might make you crazy or destroy your only brother through his bad medicines. And if we would marry you to a different man he would do the same."

So they come back. And when they came back to the wigwam, her father was sitting with his head down with tears in his eyes. And he looked up. And all he could say was, "Oh, my poor daughter!" And then she went into the tent, and she seen two brand new Hudson's Bay blankets and a new gun. While she and her ma were setting nets, this old man had come there and asked her father if he could marry this girl. But the man did not say anything to him. So he told his wife about it.

And so she start to cook their supper. And while she was sitting there, she made up her mind that she would kill this old man when he came there again that night. And she heard her parents talking, and she saw her father coming out with a big bundle on his back. He took it over to the old man's wigwam and tried to talk to him. But the old man shoved the bundle away. He didn't want it and didn't speak at all. He was sitting up. So [her father] just left the bundle there and came back to their own wigwam.

So that night, she sat up holding the ax just ready to kill him anytime he came. So she waited. At last she fell asleep. And when she woke, it was daylight. So she got up less sad 'cause she thought that the old man would not bother her anymore. And [for] about ten days after, she was happier and less afraid of this old man.

So one night after she went to bed and slept, she awoke and found that someone was sleeping beside her. She knew it was this old man. So she start to cry. She did not know how to move or how to get up. Every time she would move, she would faint. And so she fell asleep again. And in the morning she was crying. Her mother spoke to her and told her to get up and cook for the old man. So she got up and cooked and fed him. And all the while, she was crying her heart out. She never spoke to him or sat with him. She always had her back to him, and he never bothered her any.

So all his things were brought to their wigwam. He was well

off. He had lots of goods, blankets, guns, and everything 'cause he was a *nanadawiiwa* and Grand Medicine *midewiiwe* and *jisuki*. Oh! All kinds of *manitokaso* he did! And this was how he got everything—all the nice things he had.

He was never home. He was either *nanadawiiwe* doctoring or *jisuki* or *midewiiwe* Grand Medicine. So she was not with him very often. And she hated him with all her might. And the old man gave her father back the things he had given to him.

So at last, she stayed with him so long that she gave herself up to him and lived with him. Then he used her as a maid at all his *manitokasowin*. And so at last, she had a kid with him. It was a boy. That was five years after she was married. She always lived near where her parents were, and the old man was good to them all. He was a good hunter too. So they were always well off. But she never went anyplace where there were people 'cause she was so ashamed to be seen when she had an old man for a husband. She always stayed in their wigwam. But her parents got to like the old man 'cause he was good to them.

Her son was five years old when she had another baby with him. It was a little girl this time. And after the baby got a little older, her old man started to teach her how to put people through the Grand Medicine and to doctor people. He was learning her all the medicine and also the bad medicine. And then that was why she knew that he used medicine on her. He even had medicine so that anyone he went close to would not know how to move, and she knew this was the medicine he used on her.

So their two children grew up to be man and woman. And their daughter got married first. None of their children didn't look right. Their daughter was cross-eyed on one eye. And their son had a split on his upper lip. They had to stick it together 'cause the baby could not nurse with its split mouth. And as I said before, their daughter got married first and had four children. And her son married a widow woman that had two children. And he had four children with her.

So her mother and father were all dead by this time, and her son was about thirty years old, as she use to say. And herself [she] was about fifty years old. And one time [her old husband] got sick and was crazy and nearly killed her. He cut her or stabbed her on the chest. But it happened it was on kind of a thick place. And then she use to cry an awful lot 'cause she did not have any parents or friends to go to and her children were all married. And he got awfully mean with her. He use to beat her with the long stem on his pipe. He was jealous of another old man, but it wasn't true. Then this other old man heard that this old man was jealous of him, and it made him mad. And through his bad spirits and bad medicines and *powagunuh* [he] made him a *windigo*.

So that fall, he became a *windigo*. But it took a long time. He use to sit in one place, and he wouldn't eat anything the old woman gave him. And so he ran away from them. This was at Willow Creek, and he come to Cass Lake to a logging camp. And the white men took him in and tied him up and wrapped him in blankets and gave him a good drink of alcohol and made him drunk. So they kept him there, and a dog team brought him to Little Forks. That was where his son was. And so the old woman come there. And he was like that for four years. Then he died.

So she was left as a widow. And a year after, she married a half-breed about thirty-five years old. She got baptized and was married in church. She threw all her Grand Medicine away and all the bad medicine the old man learned her, and she lived a very quiet Christian life. She used to say that God must've punished the old man—why he suffered his last days so much—when he did so much sin. He killed lots of people and made them crazy and twisted their mouth and, oh, did lots of bad things to all the people.

So she lived happily with her young husband. He was good and cared for her nice. She had no children with him 'cause she was too old. She lived to have great-grandchildren. Then she died. And all her children are dead. They died after her. Some of her grandchildren are Christians that took after her. But some aren't, that [took] after the old man. One of her grandchildren is living here at this reserve and some at Nett Lake. Oh yes, she died at Nett Lake and was buried in the graveyard.

So that was the end of her. She lived a very lonely life when she was married to this old man. This is the end of this story. Look for another soon.[1]

8

I'll Show That Man

That Stole My Daughter

Away from Me

This is a story of an Indian woman from the east. She married a man from Rainy Lake. When she was a girl, her mother didn't want her to get married and kept her pretty close. And when this man went there to this place and when he [went] home, she followed him without her mother knowing. And this man brought her home to his parents and married her. His parents welcomed this woman to their family. The young couple camped around the lake all summer getting a living for themselves. And when fall came, the old people had a talk with their son and said, "Does your wife have any parents? You must take her to her parents now. They must be lonesome for her now. And we will get youse ready if you want to go." So he said, "Yes. She has parents." And when he asked his wife to go, she was willing to go. And the old people made a canoe for them and gave them a gun and birch bark for a wigwam and also some food.

So they started off and paddled by canoe to Port Arthur [Thunder Bay]. They went by Dawson Road. And so they came to Port Arthur, after they camped five times crossing lakes and going through portages. And when they came to the places where the Indians were, her parents were not staying there. They were some other place camping. But her other relatives were there, and they all welcomed her husband. But they were told that her father was mad and [had] said that if he ever laid eyes on his son-in-law, that he would kill him. And she was told not to go where her parents were. And so they stayed right there, visiting with her brothers and uncles and aunts.

And after they were there for three days, someone went and told her parents that she was there with her husband. And, of course, the old woman was tickled to see her daughter and was getting ready. And her old man said to her, "No, you are not going over. All you will look at is friendship. I'm going over there and show that fool man that stole my daughter away from me that I'm brave enough to shoot him right down."

So away he came with two guns. And when the Indians saw him coming, they went in to tell the woman that her father was coming, but she did not come out, as she knew what her father was intending to do to her husband. And three men were in the wigwam visiting this man, and she was also in the wigwam with her aunts. So some of the old men tried to talk to this old man, but he would not stop to talk with them. He came right to the wigwam where his son-in-law was. And as he was coming in, he said, "Ha, Ha! I got you now. And I'm going to kill you right here." The man did not move at all but simply smiled at his father-in-law.

The woman was sitting near the door, like, and as her father was going to pull the trigger, she jerked the gun from his hands, and the shot went right through the roof of the wigwam. And one of the men jumped up and threw the old man down. And she jumped up and ran out with the gun and broke it in half. And she dragged her father out and gave him a good beating with a stick. And the old man jumped up and said, "That's not the only gun there is. I will get that man yet." So the other men all ran after him. As he was going down to the lake where his canoe was, he met his sister-in-law. She was younger than his wife, and she said, "What are you trying to do anyway?" And she grabbed him and threw him in the water and kept him underwater 'til he was nearly out of breath. So she let him go.

The husband didn't go out of the tent but stayed right there. And also the Indians hid all their guns so [her father] had nothing to use to kill his son-in-law. And some men came to town in Port Arthur and got some liquor and set the old man dead drunk. And then she and her husband went to see her mother. And after they told her what her father wanted to do, she said, "I do not want to stay with him anymore. If you want me, I will go along with youse." And so she got ready and came away with her daughter. She liked her son-in-law because her daughter was dressed good. And some of her other relatives came along with them. And as they were coming along, her husband told them not to say a word about what this old man tried to do, for his parents would not like it. And so they got there, and his parents were glad to see his in-laws all coming with him. And nobody ever said anything to his parents about what his father-in-law tried to do to him. So they stayed around there. And when the lakes froze up, the Indians went back home on foot camping along [the way]. And the old woman also went along.

So the Indians here moved back to their hunting grounds. And the woman and her husband moved [too]. And the man could not kill anything. And after for a long time, they did not have anything to eat. He use to go walking every day to try and kill a moose, but everything was scared of him. So one time again he went and slept. And that night he could not sleep. He was afraid. And so he got up and went home to his wife. But he was the same way. So the next day, they moved to his father's place. His father was killing lots of things and had lots to eat. So after they stayed there for quite a while, his father said to him one evening after he got back: "I went and killed a moose. Go there and make the hide and also the meat for yourselves." So the next day him and his wife started off. And when they got to where the moose was, there was nothing but bones there. Some kind of a wild animal had already eaten the meat all up.

So the man said to his wife: "I want you to go home to your people for your own good, as you will starve to death here. I'm going away someplace to die. Don't you know it's your own father that's doing this to us? He is making us suffer." But she said, "No. I will not go back to where I will see him. I will stay right here with you and try to keep you. And I want you to fight back too."

So they made their wigwam there. And she said, "In four days' time he will come to visit you again by spirit, and that's the time I want you to fight back." So sure enough! When four days was up, in the morning before daylight, the man awakened and felt his body some way as if he was getting big. So he spoke to his wife and said, "Get up. I'm afraid something awful is going to happen to us." She was also approaching motherhood, and he use to just see his child right through his wife's stomach, and [it] use to look like beavers to him. And his wife got up and said, "No, I do not want anything to happen to us."

So she took some dried blueberries and some Indian rice which she was keeping and cooked some for her husband and gave it to him to drink very hot. And then she start to dress up. And while the man was sitting there, something fell in front of him, and he grabbed it. It looked something like a little mouse. So he held it hard, and then he spoke to his wife and said, "Look what I have in my hand." And she said, "I told you I didn't want anything to happen. Hold it tight until I get through." She was warming his medicine rattler and start to *nahdahwiah* her husband. And also she destroyed the little wolf which the man had caught. This is what his father-in-law sent to him to become a *windigo* man-eater. Then he got all right. She asked her husband if he did not have any *pahwahgahn* to help him out in trouble like that. But he said, "No. I have nothing I can call upon to help me." So she did not say anything but went right on with her own *manitokaso*.

And then, next day, they moved back to his father's camp and stayed there then about ten or fifteen days after. This was about in March when the snow start to melt away when it's warm. A man came there and brought the news that her father was dead, that he froze to death while visiting some other people. And when he was coming home was the time he froze. A funny time for anyone to freeze. She did not appear to be shocked or did not care at all. She did not say anything, for it was her own self that destroyed her father. So the man went right back. Her mother and other relatives that came there with her that fall were not home yet over there.

And that spring, when the lakes broke up, all the Indians moved back and start to trap bears. So she and her husband also moved back. Now he was starting to kill moose, beavers, and all kinds of other things. So one time they went to see their bear traps across the lake, and she was left there on the shore to wait. So the man went. And he caught one bear in his trap and start to clean it. And all at once, he heard his wife yelling. But he did not pay any attention. He thought she was just yelling for nothing. So when he got through, he came down. His wife was sitting with her back towards him and something else was lying there. And when he came close, she looked up and smiled at him. He asked her what was wrong, but she said nothing. He went and uncovered this that was lying [there]. Here was a little baby boy. He got scared. He thought his wife would die, and he asked her how he would get her home. She said, "You don't have to carry me home. I'll get in the canoe." So she got up and went in the canoe. He tried to make her sit in the middle, but she would not. She said people would make fun of her sitting in the middle. So she sat in front with her baby, and he paddled home as fast as he could.

And when they came ashore, all the Indians came down, asking him if he brought a bear. And he said, "Yes." So she got up and got out of the canoe and took her baby along. She [had] made a basket of birch bark, and this was where the baby was sleeping. And one old woman took notice of her sitting there. And also she missed how she looked when carrying her baby. So she went up, and she seen the baby. And so she said, "Come and look here and see the little man." So they all went there. And then she went up, and all the old women start to make her bed and tried to make her comfortable and asked her if she was all right. And when she got better, her mother came and made a home with her then.

And when her boy was about three or four years old, she was

going to have another baby, and her mother and mother-in-law tried to keep a close watch on her. And that night, she went to set a net. And next morning, she got up early and went out. She knew she was going to be sick, so she took one of the birch barks and made a place there. [She] also made a fire. And that was where her second child was born. And her mother-in-law woke up and seen her daughter-in-law was gone. So she wakened the other old woman. All at once, they heard a child crying. So they ran out and seen what the woman did. So they took the child in. It was a girl. So she got all right again.

About four years later, as they were moving on foot in the fall, she was carrying again. She said to her husband, "Stop here and make a fire and throw some brush there." So the man did as his wife told him. Then she took some rabbit skins and sat down, and her baby was born. It was a little girl. And then he told her that they would camp right there. But she wanted to go where the trees were thick. So he went and made a wigwam and took his children over there. And his wife walked over there. So nothing happened again.

All their children grew up. One man and two women. Her husband was the first to die. He burned to death. He was out hunting alone. And when he was gone for three days, they went to look for him and found him burned to death. His moccasins, snowshoes, and gun were piled beside him, but his covering is what caught on fire. So she was left a widow then. She never married again.

The man's *dodem* was a loon, and her *dodem* was a lynx. She had a mare for a *pahwahgahn*, and that was why she had such easy times giving birth to her children. She used to *manitokaso* first when she would get sick [go into childbirth]. After she was alone, she start to *nahdahwiiah* the Indians, and that's how she made a living for herself. She named all her children when they were small, named them after the mare. This is the end of her story.[1]

9

A Very Young Man

Adopted Them for Parents

This is a story of an Indian woman. She stayed single for a long time. Also her parents lived long. The people use to all camp in one place to dance and *midewi* and do all kinds of things. There use to be many wigwams, and in the spring this was what they did. The men were playing moccasin game and also Indian dice game and lacrosse game, and the women were playing snake stick game and also squaw hockey game and dancing and *midewi*, and some were *manitokaso*. They did all their Indian beliefs there when they would all camp together.

So one day again, the women planned to play moccasin game again with the men. So at the end of this Indian village, they start to play moccasin—men on one side and women on the other side. And she was the one that was hiding the little balls they use in moccasin game, and her cousin was the one who was singing. And no one could not tell where she put this certain little ball. So they won that game. And every time she played, she always won. So she was a good moccasin player. She was into every kind of game that the Indians do such as dice game, bone game, and snake stick game. And she was also a fast runner and a good hunter because her parents had some kind of medicine for her to use when she was playing any kind of a game. She use to use that medicine for racing, and that's why she use to outrun the women in the squaw hockey. This was all what she use to do when she was young.

And when she got to be about forty years old, she use to never want any man. She thought they were not good enough for her. And then one time she wished for a young man about twenty years old. And she start to use love medicine on him. And sure enough! Not long after that, the man start[ed to come after her]. He was a nice-looking young man, and his parents thought a lot of him. He was respected by other people also. And when his parents knew he was after this woman, they tried to stop him. But he would not or could not [stop]. For such is love medicine. And the parents of this young man hated her very much, for she was too old for him. Also his sisters and brothers hated her. But he just turned against his own people, as he was so crazy for this woman. And she and her parents moved away from that place where the Indians use to camp for their Indian celebrations. And this young man followed her.

And so she married this young man. A day later, the parents of this young man went there to get him, and he would not leave his wife. So the two old women had a great old quarrel. His mother said, "Your daughter is old enough to be my son's mother, and it's a shame how she's going to ruin my poor boy." And the young man told his mother to get into the canoe. And he shoved his parents out into the water and told them to go away.

It was not her own will to use all this medicine, but it was her father that made her use it. She was always having lots of stuff by which she won. And a year later they had a little girl. When it was about two or three months old, the baby got sick and had convulsions for many days. They did everything to cure her, but nothing would help. They just sat and looked at it suffering. They made *jisukanun*, and they were told she had some bad dream, also the man, and they had to put the baby through the Grand Medicine. So they told the baby they would put her through the Grand Medicine. But the baby didn't live that long. So the man went through the *midewi* for his dead baby girl.

And a year later, again they had another girl. And they made more *jisukanun*, and she was told to *nahdahwiah* herself. And both of them were told to give the baby names. Also, they put her through the Grand Medicine. But in spite of all this, the baby got sick again and had convulsions for many days. And then some great *manitokaso* came there, and they asked him to *jisuki*, and he told the woman it was all her fault why her children were suffering. He also doctored the baby but could not do anything. He said that the baby was just covered with little bundles of bad medicine and that she would never raise her children but would always see them suffering. Unless she did something to stop it.

So her second baby died. And the man's parents were there and heard all this. They tried to make their son leave her, but he would not. He was so in love with her that he did not seem to care. But she was suffering. She never cried in front of people when her children died. But she use to go back in the bush and cry. And one time, an old woman heard her crying and talking, "Oh, *manito*. What could I do to undo all the bad things I did when I was young so my children would live?" And when she came down, she gave her father a slap and said, "Yes, it's all your fault why I'm in misery. You made me use all this medicine, you old devil." But her father did not speak to her. And later on he said, "Yes. It's true. You will always suffer for that. That's why I always told you never to marry. So I will give you some medicine never to have any children again." And she said, "No. I'm going to have another child soon."

So then they start to do everything in their power so the child would live. She even went through the Grand Medicine for her unborn child. And when her baby was born, it just lived a short time and died again. They put the baby through the Grand Medicine after it was born. She nearly died herself when she was giving birth to the child. And her parents gave her medicine so she would never have a child again. But she did not know.

So when her baby died, she said she didn't want any more medicine, and she wasn't going to do any of the Indian beliefs. And even her *nahdahwiiwe* she let go. Also her gambling. And about three years later, when she did not have a child again, she got mad, for she knew her father gave her some medicine to drink. And she gave her father a good scolding. And after, she let everything go.

She began to be a coward. She could never go anyplace in the dark. Or even in the daytime. Her husband always had to go with her, for she was that scared. And one night, when her husband was out walking, a woman came in and start to wrestle with her. She did not know who it was and was very scared. The woman would say, "You made a darn fool of me, and I'm here to square up with you." She could not get a hold of this woman, for it was a ghost. It was the ghost of a dead person. Her father scraped medicine off of this dead person's bones, and that was what she [had] use for love medicine. And when her husband came in, the ghost disappeared. And she was scared to stay alone. And sometime after that, again when her husband was out, a man came in again and start to do the same thing to her as the woman did to her. She would faint as soon as they would come in. Of course, she did not know it was a ghost.

So the man got worried over his wife, and he made a *jisukan* and asked some old man to go in. And they asked why she was always scared to stay home alone and why these people were coming then to fight her and who they were. So the *jisuki* man said it was because she robbed many people of their stuff by gambling and using bad medicine and also made many people lame by the race medicine. This was why she was scared. And the reason why these people came there was because she used that love medicine which was made from the rump bone of that dead person. And that's why they came there to scare her. And then she was told how to get rid of all this was to go through the Grand Medicine four times, one right after the other right away, and all these things would leave her. And she said she would not go through the Grand Medicine. Then she sent her husband away. For all the people said he would surely die on account of her. So the man left his wife. And her father died not long after. He was a bad old man, a great *manitokaso* but not much good. And he wanted his daughter to be like him. And she kept her mother, but she also died soon. And then she was all alone now.

Then she went to Kenora and stayed with her aunt. Nothing ever bothered her now. She wasn't over there very long when her aunt died. Her aunt was married to a white man. And she had another aunt there and got jealous of her and gave her a good beating. So she left Kenora and went in the bush without anything to eat. She had made up her mind to go and wander around and starve to death in the bush.

And for a few days she went without food. And as she was sitting around, she heard a shot and saw a duck falling. She did not know who was shooting this duck so she went and picked it up. It was killed only by one baby shot. And she said, "Yes, I use to dream of some little men in the bush. So thanks to you for this duck. And I will live now." So she cleaned this duck and cooked it. And she said, "People pass on the lake many times, so I will go down and watch for them to pass." So she walked down to the shore. And as she was going down, she seen some smoke, and she said, "Oh, they must be the owners of that duck which I ate." So she went down anyway. And as soon as the old women saw her, they jumped up and said, "Oh, here's the woman that's lost. You must be the one that fired that shot we heard as we were getting off here." But she said, "No." And they told her to eat and also asked her to go along with them. So she did.

And she lived a long time after. Her husband heard where she was, and he went back to her. She tried to tell him not to come back to her and for him to marry some other woman that could raise his children and one who was his own age. But he would not listen to her. So then she let him stay with her. They got very old. His *dodem* was lynx, *pishiw*, and her *dodem* is a duck.

And a very young man adopted them for parents, and that was their son. And he looked after them, 'til they both died. She died first, before her husband. She lost too much blood, and she also died of a broken heart. And her husband died soon after her. The end.[1]

10

They Moved On

to Different Places

This story is about an old man. When he was a young man, he was already married then, and his parents and grandparents were staying with them. There were the three families. And this man killed a bear, and they did not give any to the Indians which were living there close by. And later on, this man and his parents and grandparents moved away from there. And as they camped along [the way], his wife use to set snares. And in the morning before they moved on again, she use to come back and see her snares, but there would be no rabbits—only a stick or some other thing would be in her snare. And she use to wonder what it meant.

And when they got to their hunting ground, they killed lots of minks and furs and also moose. And they stayed on right there. And when they had just about eaten all their food up, he killed a bear. So they had food again. And they moved on to different places. And when they would camp in one place, at night his wife would fix up one of the furs, and that's what they would eat. And when they were just about starving, he start to *manitokaso*. And next morning he went along. As they were moving, he killed a moose. And when they came to their next camping place, his wife was busy cutting the wigwam poles for the three families. And the rest was cooking and eating moose meat. And it didn't take long for them to eat all the moose up. So they just kept right on eating the lynx skins, and all the other furs which they were going to sell. Even the moose hides. They ate that too. And after they had everything eaten up, they were just about starving. They could not kill anything. Everything was afraid of them. And for two months his wife never ate anything. She was just a living skeleton. They could just see right through her skin between her bones.

So they kept right on moving, camping along. They were weak from starving, and the man's grandfather was just about done for now. And they stopped and camped there. This old man wanted to kill himself. He said he was ashamed to die of starvation. And he talked to his grandfather [and told him not to kill himself]. When morning came, his grandfather said to him: "Get ready and go along. We have lived long already, and it's all right for us to perish here. But youse are young. Leave us here and go to where we left our food. And if youse do reach there before youse starve, come back and look for us."

And these old people were raising a young girl who was their granddaughter. She wasn't a bit thin, and the man told this young girl to stay with his grandparents and cut wood for them 'til they would get back. It was a four days' walk to this place where they left their corn, rice, and berries that fall. This was at Warroad before there was a town there. And his parents and also his wife went along with him. This young girl was crying because she wanted to go along. But he wouldn't let her go along with them.

And it took them a regular four days' walk to get to this place. And when they did get there, all their corn, rice, and berries were gone. Someone already took their food. His wife's parents were there. They wouldn't give them anything to eat. They would only come and ask their daughter to come over and eat. This was about in the springtime now, and the men were not able to go back and look for the old people which they left behind. And when the lakes were opened up, he start setting nets and killed some jackfish and ducks. He use to do all kinds of *manitokaso*, and he did kill something to eat.

It took him about a month before he was able to go back and look for his grandparents. And when he did go, he found his grandfather laying on the road with a gun in his hand. He was dead. And when they come to the wigwam, his grandmother was lying beside the fireplace dead. She died of starvation. And the young girl, they could not find her anyplace. They lost her for good. There was no bones or anything found that would be left of her. So they just left them there, and they went home. The end of this story.

THREE

SIBLINGS

Fig. 19. Drying fish at Lake of the Woods, ca. 1912. Photo by Carl Gustav Linde. Reprinted by permission of Minnesota Historical Society.

Fig. 20. Spreading rice to dry, ca. 1920. Photo by Frances Densmore. Reprinted by permission of Minnesota Historical Society.

11

Oh, Can't You Find a
Place in Your Heart for Me?

This is a story of a boy. He had one brother and three sisters. He was the youngest of them all. His parents were living also at that time.

And one day, his brother asked him to go out paddling with him. But the boy refused to go. And this made the older brother mad, and he took him by the shoulder and beat him and threw him into the canoe and paddled away. He did not get up to sit but lay face down in the canoe, thinking his brother would punch him on the back once in a while. But he did not move or do anything. And so his brother kept paddling along, and they came ashore. And his brother got out and killed a moose. He stayed right in the canoe.

And all at once, he made up his mind that he would go away. So he got up and got out of the canoe. He took some matches from his brother's coat pocket and also some other things. He was very sad because his brother was mean to him. He took his old coat and cap off and threw it on the water. And away he ran. He ran towards the north side. He did not care where he was going—only so he could get away from his brother.

And so when the man [his brother] came back to where he left his brother, he was gone. He looked out on the water and seen something floating around. And so he jumped into his canoe and paddled to it. And just as he was getting near it, it sank. And he thought that might be his brother. He start to cry. He left his moose and everything there and started for home. As soon as he got close, he started yelling to his parents and sisters saying his brother drowneded. And his parents did not believe him. They all accused him of drowning his brother. They went to the spot where he seen something floating around, but they could never find anything.

And so they all moved to where the moose was and camped there, drying the meat. Sometimes the mother missed one piece of her dried meat. Another time, she lost a pail and an ax. She never said anything, but she used to wonder who it could be. And she also thought it was some of the other people who were living close there. The old man was very sad. He missed his son, and he also took it very hard because his son's body was never found. For he always thought his son was dead. And that same fall, the old man died on account of all this.

People always thought him dead. But he was not—for he was seen many times. But nobody ever knew it was him. One time he was seen by his sister-in-law—the wife of the brother who beat him—as they were coming back from Kenora. One time her husband was drunk, and they stopped to make tea, and he fell asleep. And she went across to where there were some blueberries, and she was picking them. When she looked where her husband was sleeping, she seen a man walking around, and she wondered who it was. She got in the canoe and went back. When she got there, all their groceries were gone. Also her husband's moccasins. They did not know who stole them. They thought it was somebody else. And then another time a gun was lost. Another time an ax. And many other things. And one time again, some other old women seen him, but they did not know who he was.

And about three years later, when his mother and little sister were in the bush someplace smoking a moose hide, he made up his mind to let his mother see him. So he went up closer to her, and he spoke to her, saying, "Mother, do you want to see me?" And she turned around, and she said, "My son! Is it you? Are you alive?"

And he said, "Yes, I'm alive just as you are. I'm not crazy either. I didn't die. But I'm still mad, mad at my brother because he made me ashamed when he beat me up. I was very proud of myself that time, and when he did that, that was the time the bird that was in my body flew away. And that's why I'm wandering around. Because I'm no good anymore, and I don't want anybody to see me. And so do not tell anybody that you seen me. If you do, you will never see me again."

The old woman was very scared of her son because he was an awful sight with his old ragged pants. And [he was] dirty and filthy, and his hair was very long, and it was just all tangled up. But she soon calmed down, as she was very glad to know he was still alive. So she said, "Now, my son, wait for me here, and I will go and get something for you to eat." So she ran home and got all she could get and also a pair of moccasins. And she gave these things to him. And he told her, "If you want to see me again, come to the bay over there, and that's where you will see me." And away he went.

She told her little girl not to tell. The girl was about eleven years old at that time. And then she start to keep [things] and make moccasins for her son. Also other things. And several times she went and paddled around the bay. But she didn't see him again soon. But she use to see where he had been sitting, and she use to put moccasins and some food there. And when she would go, they would be taken already.

And about three years later, again she went to pick berries someplace alone with only her daughter. And soon her son came close again and asked her if they were finding any berries. She said, "No." And he told her where to go the next day. And when they went there, there was lots of blueberries. She did not see her son again, but when they were coming home, they found a birch basket full of blueberries. She knew it was her son who left them there. And pretty soon they had enough blueberries to last them all winter. And that night, while walking around outside, she told her daughter they would go home the next day. Her son must of heard her. He said, "Are youse going home tomorrow?" And she said, "Yes." She asked him to go along with them, but he refused to go along with them. So they left him there.

She never told of seeing her son. But she use to worry an awful lot to know that her son was going around the bush like a wild animal. He even told her once that he wasn't scared. Only at first he use to be afraid. There were so many wolves around sometimes he used to be afraid. But he had a gun, ax, knife, and also other things. She also gave him some traps.

Then he disappeared. Though she went many times to this place where he was, she never seen any sign of him. She use to go and put moccasins and food someplace, and then she would go [and] it would still be there. Then she gave up trying to find him, as she thought that at last he must have been killed by the wolves. She often walked around there and found caves where he use to sleep. But she never found any trace of him being killed. And for about five years, he disappeared like that.

And while she was camping one time with some Indians, she overheard some Indian men telling one another that they seen a man working in a logging camp there someplace, and when they spoke to him, he never lifted up his head to speak, so they could not make out who he was. She then thought to herself that it might be her son. So she got ready and went to all the logging camps she knew, and she did find her son. She wouldn't've known him only he asked her what she was looking for and she knew his voice. He was changed a lot by being shaved and his hair cut. Also he dressed like a man so different from the way she seen him last. She asked him to go home with her. She also told him that his brother was sick and might not live long and that it was time for him to forgive his brother. But he refused again. He said that he was all right wandering around and that he did not want anybody to know he was alive. He also gave her five dollars and told her to go. So she went home and she never seen him again. Her oldest son died. He was so worried and also disappointed that it was his fault his brother was lost. Soon the mother died too and also the other two sisters.

And then just the young sister was living. And she use to go from place to place. Finally one time, she went back to the bay where they use to see her brother. And just as she was going around the bay, she seen someone coming down the bank for water. She knew that was her brother. And then, after he was gone, she came closer, and she could see places where he had been sitting. Then she went ashore, got out of her canoe, and yelled to him. No answer came. So she said, "My brother! Answer me! I'm coming here to stay with you. Don't you know, my brother, that only us two are living? Our sisters and brother and also our mother are gone. Oh, can't you find a place in your heart for me? You're the only one I have now, and that's why I came here to find you."

Then she saw her brother coming towards her. He was different now. His hair was short. [He] also had on clothes. But he was living in some kind of a cave. He was very sorry to hear his mother was dead. He took it very hard and cried, saying, "I was cruel to my poor mother. Why didn't I listen to her when she pleaded with me many times to go home with her. For her sake, why didn't I go home? Only now I realize the heartache I caused my poor mother. Maybe it was on account [of] worry of me that she died." And then he said to his sister, "We will live right here. I will make a shack for you here. We will hunt wolves here this winter, for there is a lot of them here."

So they lived there all summer in a wigwam. He made two shacks, one for his sister and one for himself. And that winter they lived in their shacks. He was hunting, bringing home moose and deer meat. He also killed lots of wolves. He was very good to his sister. He use to go with her too when they would take their fur into town. And only then people knew he was alive and [had] lived in the wilderness for nearly twenty years.

And they lived there for a couple of years. Then one time he got sick, and he wasn't sick for very long. And as he was about dying, he told his sister that the time he disappeared for five years he went to Eagle River, and he had a wife over there and also a child. And he told his sister to go and see his child [and to] tell the woman that he was dead. And then he died.

There was no one there at all. She was just alone there. So when she got through crying, she set to work and made a hole, and she also dressed her brother and fixed him up nice. Then she buried him. And after she stayed there many days, she went to Eagle River and seen his child [and told] the woman that her brother was dead. The woman was very sorry to hear it. And she stayed with them for a long time. Then she came back there to her own shack and start to hunt. And she killed lots of wolves.

Then in the spring she took her fur to town in Kenora, and she got lots of money. Then she got in with a nigger man, and she came home with him and married him. He was very good to her. Also he was a good worker. She learned him how to hunt, and soon he knew just how to do things just like any other Indian man. And then they had a little girl that looked like her. And about two years later they had another little girl, which took after the nigger. And they always lived there. And then, one time when they went to Kenora, she seen a woman coming toward her with a little boy, and the women spoke to her, saying, "This boy is your relative. He is your brother's son. His mother is dead." And she did recognize the boy she seen as a little baby boy. The woman was the sister of the mother. The boy was nice looking like her brother when he was dressed up. Then they came home. And a couple of years later, the woman died that had this little boy. And her last words were for her [the boy's father's sister] to take this boy, as there was no one else to care for him. So she took this boy and raised him with her own little girls.

She lived in this bay for many years after. And her husband died while working on the railroad when they were dynamiting. She had a little nigger boy too with him. She died many years after. All her children, though, growed up. But this other boy, I don't know what become of him. If he's living, he must be very old. The children were all in school. The end.[1]

12

They Made Up Their
Mind Not to Let Their
Son-in-Law Go

This is a story of an old man who had two daughters. This happened at Lake Saulobishigokang. In the fall, they use to go back in the bush to hunt. And his oldest daughter married. And so that fall, they went back to the bush again and went with their son-in-law. And they moved from place to place until they came to the old man's hunting ground.

And the [son-in-law] start to hunt there, killing moose and caribou and also all kinds of fur. He was very good to his wife. Also to his father- and mother-in-law. He was a hustler and very good hearted, and his in-laws cared for him a lot. And so they stayed right there hunting. There were two other families there. And about Christmas or after that, his wife got sick and died. And then they asked the old woman what they would do with the body of her daughter, and she said that she did not want it to be buried there. She wanted them to hang it up on a tree, and when spring came they would bring it down to their place and bury it there. So they did hang the body in the tree, wrapped up in birch barks and blankets.

So then the old people knew that their son-in-law would not stay with them anymore, and then they would be hard up, for the old man was very old and could not hardly do anything. So they made up their mind not to let their son-in-law go. They still wanted him to remain there with them. And the young man was so sad over the loss of his wife. And when his father-in-law asked him to remain there and marry his sister-in-law, he did not think it quite right. He did not say anything. Not that he hated her. But he thought it too soon, when his wife died only lately. And also the young girl thought the same way. But young people long ago use to obey their parents. So when her father told her to marry the man, she did—although they did not use one another as married folks. The man was proud of the girl and felt kind of shy towards her. And also the girl [felt the same]. So the man remained there and got things for them just the same as before.

So when spring came, they were to move and take the body back to the lake where they called home. And so they took the body and put [it] on a toboggan and tied it on. And the old man was the one that was pulling it. And when evening came and they would stop and camp, the old man would take the body ahead and go and leave it there for the night. Next morning, he would go ahead and take it again. And the young man and young woman and the old woman use to come walking behind carrying all their things.

And one time when they were close to getting where they were going, the young woman was away behind. She worked at something that morning, and that's what kept her behind. So the old woman went along again and made a wigwam where they were going to stay for the night. And she also made a big fire, and the old man got back too. Also their son-in-law. But the girl was coming away behind, and it was now nearly night.

And as she was walking along, she heard someone saying, "Isht! Do you love the man you're married to?" And she would say, "No." But it kept on saying, "Yes. You do." But she tried to deny it. She was so scared now. The one was right behind her talking to her, saying the same thing, "Do you love him?" And when she would say, "No. I don't." Then it would say, "Yes. You do." She tried to walk a little faster.

She could see the wigwam now and a big fire. Still, the one kept on talking to her. She knew it was the ghost of her sister, and she was awfully scared. When she got to the door of the wigwam, as she lifted the blanket to go in, it pushed her and she fell right into the fire. The old woman was cooking some fat, and the grease was boiling. She fell and upset the grease. And all she could say was "Oh! It's my sister that's doing this to me. She's been following me all the way asking me if I loved the man." Then that was all she could say, and she died.

And the man got so mad, for he had learned to love his new wife very much. And he jumped up and ran outside to where the body of his first wife was. He kicked it and hit it and [said], "So! So you are alive, eh? For all the trouble we went through carrying your old body along and now you've destroyed your sister too."

And with that, he let it go and went back to the wigwam. He was very sad to see the burnt body of his wife. And next day, he put the body on his toboggan and carried it. They never stopped again anyplace but kept right on until they came to the lake. And there they dug two graves and buried the bodies of his two wives side by side. And then he told the old people he would stay with them and care for them all their lives.

And true to his promise, he did. And the old people were also very thankful for that. He also gave a lot of things away to his wives' *dodem*. That was when he *keewainige*. And the *dodems* fixed him up, and he was told he was free now to marry if he wished. But he did not marry soon. He lived with the old people and cared [for] and loved them as his own. And when both the old people died, he felt very lonely and lost without them, for they were good to him.

And when he got to be quite an old man, only then he married a woman who was much younger than him. Then they just lived as most people do. He was good to his wife, for he was always a good-hearted man. But he never forgot the trouble he went through when he was a young man. His wife was also a good woman. He never had any children. The end.[1]

13

If You Stop Along, I

Will Give Youse a Lunch

This is a story of a half-breed woman. Her father was part white and Cree, and her mother was a Cree. And her mother's brother had a son, which was her cross-cousin. And when they were kids, they played together, as they were nearly the same age. And also their parents always lived together at Ishtawahyang, near Winnipeg River—somewheres around there. And they grew up together to man and woman. Then they began to flirt with one another. But their parents never realized that they were doing this for quite a while. Then their parents found out. Her father did not like it. Also her uncle [didn't like it]. But anyway they got married just the same. Her mother did not seem to care. Also the man's mother [didn't care]. But the men disowned their children. Also they would not give them anything to use. But the man had a canoe, and she [her mother] gave them two strips of birch bark for a wigwam.

Then they went away and camped around. They did not have anything to use, but they did not mind, as they cared for one another. And there were three young men. They often went to see this young married couple. And one time these three men asked them to come to Rat Portage to where there was work. And so the woman and her husband came to where their parents were. And their mothers gave them grub and also other things to use. But their fathers would not see them at all. In fact, their fathers hated each other for that. So away they came with these three young men.

The woman's brother was married to a girl from Couchiching, and her brother never went back to where his parents were, and she knew that maybe she would see her brother there [at Couchiching] sometime. The three young men also had a canoe. So that was two canoes they came along with. And they come around Obishigokan. And then they traveled for many days. Then, at last, they came to Rat Portage. There were only about seven log houses there, the Hudson's Bay store and also other log houses for the men that [were] working. This was when the big tunnel was first started in Kenora—where the train now goes these days. There was a lot of blasting and other dangerous things. So the men started to work there for a week. Then they quit, as it was too dangerous. So they bought some things to eat and started off again.

They came on the Lake [of the Woods]. Only one man knew the way to come. And also some man in Rat Portage made out a map [to show] which way they would come. She did not know to speak Indian [Ojibwe]. She always talked English. And for many days they camped again. They met a few Indians on the way, but nobody ever offered to give them anything to eat. And as they were coming along, they had to stop on an island, for the wind was blowing hard and they could not travel out on the Lake.

And for ten or fifteen days, they had to stay on this island, for it was awfully windy. They got short of their food, and soon they were hungry. And one of the young men walked along the shore. He had no shoes on. And he looked out on the Lake. He seen a fish floating towards the shore. He knew it was alive. He stood and watched it for a long time, and as it was coming closer, he jumped into the water and grabbed it and then threw it on the shore. He took it back to their camps, and she cooked it and had something to eat.

Then one day the wind calmed down, and they started off again. They crossed the big lake. They did not have anything to eat, but they came to where there was some blueberries, and they stopped and ate some. But that did not seem to help them out. So they come away again and came to the mouth of the Rainy River. Of course, there were no white people there yet, nor any Indians either. But they came there anyway. And they killed some ducks, and she cooked them again and they had a good meal.

Then they started up the river and came to Matitinosibing, Sleeman, and seen some Indians there drying meat, and then they stopped. And the Indians gave them some meat, and then they came away again. They camped once. Then they came to the foot of the Long Sault Rapids. There were two tepees and one bark wigwam. There was an old man walking around with long hair and a pipe with a long stem on it. And when the old man saw them, he start yelling at them to come ashore, so they did. He was very friendly with them. He had three wives and also had a lot of chickens. He told them to stop and have something to eat, as he just killed a large sturgeon. The women were three sisters. And they began setting a place there for them to eat sturgeon, rice, maple sugar, potatoes, and tea and bread. They had a big meal. The old man was asking them all kinds of questions and also where they come from. And one of the young men told him how they nearly starved on this island. And then they were given some flour and eggs and also other things and what was left over when they got through eating. She took it all, as that was the style of the Indians long ago. And also one of the women gave her a dish full of maple sugar.

So when they were through visiting, they got up and went along again. And before they came to the big rapids, they seen another man walking along the shore. And when he seen them, he spoke to them again. They told him that they did not know which side to go over the rapids. So the man offered to come along with them. She got out of the canoe with her husband, and the man got in and showed them how to come up the rapids. And when they were safely on this side, one of the young men took a shirt and gave it to this man and thanked him and said that they had nothing and hardly enough to eat. So the man said, "I live up the river, and if you stop along, I will give youse a lunch." So they did stop along and had some more sturgeon. Then he said, "You will come to another big rapids called Manitobawitik [Manitou Rapids]. Youse will have to portage there, as it is very hard to get over that by canoe. And when you get through that, then there will be no more. Just the place where you're going." So they came away again. They had plenty to eat now.

They camped once. And it was about noon when they came to the Manito[u] Rapids. There was one bark tepee there and an old woman walking around. So they came ashore. And the old woman came down and asked them who they were and also where they were going and where they came from. And they told her. And she asked them to have lunch with her first, as she had a big kettle of sturgeon heads she cooked. So they went to her tepee, and she set a place there for them to eat. She told them that there was a lot of Indians up on the hill camping. This was where her old man was visiting. So they start to eat again, and before they got through eating, many of the Indians came down, and they were asked to stay there that night. So they did. The old woman gave her a big dish full of dried mashed sturgeon and some maple sugar, and also the other women gave her dried sturgeon skin, also sturgeon oil and other things to eat.

So the next day they started off. And when they came to where Emo is now, there was nothing but bush there. And at the island, someone was living there, but they did not go close. Then they came to Little Forks. There was some Indians camping there. So they were asked to stop and stay there again overnight, as it was getting very hard for them to paddle up the river as the river was running very fast. And the Indians asked them if they did not have a rope so someone could pull the canoe along. They did not have a rope. So one of the old women came up to her and showed her a *wikab* and said, "This is what we use for a rope."

So they went again, and as soon as they went around the point, they got off on the shore and start making a rope out of a *wikab*. They made two ropes, and the two men start walking along the shore and pulled the canoes and then they went faster. Then they came to Fort Frances. There were a lot of Indians camping around there. And they camped near the shore, as they were ashamed. The men start to work there, as the tunnel in Fort France was being started at that time and they were busy blasting. And one day, her brother heard that she was there, and he came there and asked them to go and stay at his place. So they did. But the three young men did not live with them anymore.

And they stayed there all the time. And a year later, she had a little boy, but the baby boy did not look right. On one foot he had a hoof of a pony, and he never walked. And a couple of years later, another boy was born to them. This baby boy did not look right either. He had no arms. But on his shoulders, he had hands. And a few years later, again she had another little boy with small feet. He had to use a cane to walk. The oldest boy never walked. He died when he was eight years old. And also the boy with small feet died when he was about six years old.

But the boy with no arms lived. He could do almost anything with his feet. He ate with his feet and also fished with his feet. He would put the fishhook between his toes, and when he knew a fish was biting, he would throw himself over and the fish would fall on the dry ground. When he was eating, he put the spoon between his toes and ate just like that. In fact, he could do almost anything. And when he was thirteen years old, some wealthy white man seen him and asked the woman and also the man if they would let him take their boy away and he would send them money all the time—all the money this boy would make. So his parents let him go. And for quite a while, money was sent to them. And all at once, they heard no word from this man. So their boy disappeared for good. They never knew where he was taken to nor what was done to him.

She had five more children after these three boys: two boys and three girls. The girls were born the right way and also looked the right way and also one boy was all right. But the other boy had a humpy back and a long face. So that was five children that lived. And people use to say that the reason why her first four boys looked like this was because she married her cross-cousin. They were related too close. So their five children grew up and married.

She never again seen her parents or her husband's parents. But they heard when they were all dead. And when her old man got to the age of seventy, he got blind. He couldn't see anything. He was in darkness, and he got very useless. So she had to care for him like a baby for ten years. Then the old man died and was buried. And also her son with the humpy back died, though he got to be a man. And also her other son, though he was married, he got crazy. He was a coward. He never went outside alone, and at last, he died too. But her daughters were all right and had children.

She got to be a very old woman. She died about twelve years ago. She was 102 years old when she died at the Couchiching Reserve. Her daughters are now very old. So that was the end of her.

14

She Liked Him as a Brother

This is a story of an Indian woman. When she was a young girl, her father died. And as he lay dying, he told his daughter that she had to marry this man. She did not like this man, but she lived with him because she promised her father she would. The old man gave all his things—his canoe, his blanket and shotgun and everything else—to him. He liked this young man very much.

So the young girl married him against her will. She was not acquainted with him, though she slept with him and sat with him. But she never spoke to him, although he was trying hard to make her like him. She never offered to go out with him either when he went out paddling. She never said anything when he went out gambling or dancing. She was entirely separated from him. They stayed with her in-laws. Her mother-in-law and father-in-law never spoke to her.

And in the mornings, she use to get up early and go back in the bush and cut wood. She would bring about three or four loads of wood. Then she would go and see her net. She would do lots of work in the morning. Still her mother-in-law would not even look at her. At last she quit trying to be friends with her.

So one morning, early, she went out to see her net. And she seen a moose walking along the shore. So she went back to the tent. And her husband was sleeping. His feet was sticking out. So she pinched his toe and said, "Get up! There's a moose out on the shore." So he jumped up, took his gun, and ran down to the lake and killed the moose. And he said to his wife, "This is your moose, and you can do as you like with it."

So the old people got up, and her mother-in-law got jealous of her and start to quarrel with her. But she never spoke back to her. And the man said, "I will take her away from here so she will not bother youse." So she got ready and went away. They did not go far, just around the bay, and they made their camp there. And she dried all her moose meat. She gave some to her father-in-law. She was a good worker, but her husband was useless. She did all the work herself alone and got along fine.

They stayed there all summer. The old woman used to come there and find fault with her and also [with] her work. She never spoke back to her because long ago it was a shame for a woman to speak back to a mother-in-law. Though she sometimes was mad. She never said anything to her husband either. He was so useless he never did anything right.

One day they were fishing for whitefish, and when they put their net out, it broke and they lost their net. And at the same time, they seen a beaver. And as he was going to shoot it, the shell blocked so they could not kill the beaver. Then, when they got home, he put his gun near the fire, so the shell would blow, and he forgot to watch it, so that his gun burned also. So they had lots of trouble that one day.

So when fall came, they moved back to where the man was going to hunt. And he was so lazy he never would go out hunting. She use to wade out in the deep snow carrying bundles of wood on her back, while her husband was in the wigwam laying on his back with no moccasins on. She use to go out killing rabbits and bring them home and feed her husband.

At last the man got sick. She never paid no attention to him to try and give him medicine. He got worse and start to bring up blood. They were very poor, as he never got anything for her. So when his parents heard he was sick, they came for him and took him to their camp. He was sick all spring. They put him through the Grand Medicine and *jisuki* and *nahdahwiah* sweat tent and everything else. They also gave him lots of medicine. She never bothered to help with anything.

So at last he died, and she was left a widow. She did not care. She only stayed there for a little while after her husband died. Then she went away and looked for her widowed mother. And a few months after, she had a miscarriage. So she was over with everything now and was single again. Her and her mother got along fine, as they were both good workers and good hunters. Only after that, her mother-in-law [and] also the old man wanted her there just to be mean with her. But she did not want to stay there.

Then her mother got married, and she did not like her stepfather very much. Her mother wanted her to get married to a certain man. This was a couple of years after. She said she did not want to marry anyone to please somebody else. She said she would marry the man she liked herself, and if she could not find anyone she liked, she would stay single all the time.

And all the people from all over use to come and camp in one place where they would have their sun dances and Grand Medicine and other *manitokaso*. And she also went with her mother and stepfather. And as she was sitting in the tent one day, an old couple came to the door with a blanket and some dress goods, also a shawl and other things. And they asked her if she would do as they asked her. And she did not say anything.

So they told her that their daughter died, and when they seen her, she reminded them of their dead daughter. And they adopted her for a daughter. So she was glad to make a home with them. The old people were good to her, and she was also good to them. And when the Indians moved back to their own camping places, she went back with her new adopted parents and stayed with them all the time.

And after she was with them for about nine or ten years, a man came there and wished to marry her very much. She liked this man herself. But she hated to leave her parents, as they loved her very much and she loved them. And she also loved this man too. So she made this man promise her that if he would never take her away from there but would always stay there with her parents, she would marry him. So he promised to stay there all the time.

So she at last married this man. And only then, she knew what love is. He was a nice man, and he was a good hunter. He was also a great *jisuki* and was also full of jokes. So when they were married for about two years, the man asked his wife if they would never have any kids. So she said she did not know. Then he asked her if she would take some medicine so as to have some children. So she took this medicine, and a year after, a little boy was born to them. Her parents were so glad and happy to see their daughter so happily married.

And when the little boy was four years old, her adopted mother died. And so the old man stayed there with her. The old woman was very good to her while she was living. At the same time, she use to go and see her real mother. And when her adopted mother died, she was very lonely, as she only had her boy and husband and her adopted father to cook for. And a little while after, she heard that her stepfather died. Then her mother came and stayed with her and made a home with her. And after a year or two passed, her mother turned around and married her adopted father. Then her own mother start to be mean with her, and she did not like that. So she went away from there and left her mother and the old man there and made another home for her own little family. She wouldn't of minded it so much, but her mother also wanted to be mean to her husband too.

And pretty soon, they had another nice place to stay. And when they were there for quite a while, the old man came there with his canoe and said that he thought more of staying with his daughter than any other woman. And so he stayed there. And the old woman came there also. But the old man told her to go away, that he did not want to live with her anymore because she was too mean and bold to her daughter. And he did not like that because he loved his daughter more than life itself and because she was so good to him. But she would not go away and start to be very mean with this old man and often sent him away. But he would not go away. And then they would all move away and leave the old woman there, but she would always follow them. And one time when they were moving away, her mother start to fight her and cut her across the eye, a big, long cut. Her eyelid fell and closed her eye. So then she took her mother along this time and kept her because she was getting old and was lame. And she also got to be good and was not mean to them anymore. And so they got along fine.

And white people long ago use to travel back and forth in canoes on the lake. They always had lots of liquor with them. So one time she heard these white men quarreling and fighting all night. So early the next morning, she got up and watched these men getting ready to go. And after they were gone, she went around over there to see if they forgot anything. And as she was walking around, she heard someone moaning, and she went [to him]. Here was a young man lying. His face was all bruised and cut. So she waked him up and helped him to get up, and she made signs for him to get [up]. And she brought him home and washed his face and put some Indian medicine on his face. Also [she] gave him hot water to make him vomit. He was sick for a long time, but she took good care of him, and he got better and stayed right there with them. She liked him as a brother and learned him to say "sister" in Indian: *duhwaim*.

Her mother got worse and died. Also her father died shortly after that. She was very lonely. She never had any more children—just the one boy, which was now very big. This white man taught the boy how to read and write and talk good English. And he stayed there all the time. He never wished to go anyplace to his own people. He stayed and worked for this woman which saved and took good care of him. And [he] also was looked upon as one of the family. The man was very good to him and called him *nita* [brother-in-law]. She also called him *duhwaim*. And he use to clear land and plow it and put out a garden of all kinds.

And then they start to live among Indians. And this white man use to be out nights, and in the morning she would ask him, saying, "Where you been, *duhwaim*?" And he would answer, saying,

"Oh, *duhwaim*, I was out with a girl." He would sound funny, and they use to laugh at him. And so it was like that for a while, and one time, he asked her what the Indians did when a man wanted to get married. Then she said, "Oh, nothing. If you want to get married, just go there and sleep with the girl and in the morning don't get up until you're told to get up. And if they don't want you, they will take a stick and send you out." And he said, "No. They won't do that to me."

So one morning when they got up, her *duhwaim* wasn't there. Then she knew he must be married, and they wondered who he was married to. So before noon, a man came to the door and said, "I do not object to this white man marrying our daughter." She was related to this man. It was her mother's brother's son, and his daughter was the one that was marrying this white man, and [he] said they liked him very much. And so her *duhwaim* was married now and stayed over there for a little while. He made a good son-in-law. When his mother-in-law said anything and he happened to understand, he would get up right away to do it himself.

Then he brought his wife to his *duhwaim*'s, and then they all moved to an island [Basil's Island, on Lake of the Woods]. And this is where he start to farm and made a living for himself and also his in-laws and his *duhwaim*. He had lots of children—all half-breeds with blond heads.

So when his *duhwaim* died, he buried her on this island. Also his brother-in-law and all the other ones died, and he buried them on this island and put crosses on their graves. He kept this Indian boy [his *duhwaim*'s son]. He was the first to have a gasoline boat. He use to go to Kenora, and this boy would be the one steering. And then he died, and his children and grandchildren stayed there farming on the island. None of his children are living, but his great-grandchildren are. The end.[1]

FOUR

WOMEN ALONE

Fig. 21. Woman paddling, ca. 1910. Photo by Frances Densmore. Reprinted by permission of Minnesota Historical Society.

Fig. 22. Women and children in Kenora, ca. 1912. Photo by Carl Gustav Linde. Reprinted by permission of Minnesota Historical Society.

15

Cloud Woman,

the Fast Runner

This is a story of an Indian woman. When she was a little girl, she was the oldest of two girls, and they were never in want of anything while their parents were living. And she was always the one who went out with her father when he use to go out hunting. Her father thought a lot of her. She was his favorite. She use to help him when he would go out setting traps for bears [and] also when he would go out setting snares for fox and wolf and other things. And he was also good to her. When he was fishing, she would always go along with him. And so she learned how to do everything by watching him.

Then, one spring, her father got sickly. But, still, she use to go around with him. Then, when it got hotter, he got worser, and just before blueberry picking time, he died and they were left all alone. She took it so hard. She was very lonely because she was never far from her father. And she also missed all the good things her father use to bring for her. Also she missed his loving care. She use to go out early in the morning and go someplace and cry herself to sleep. Her sisters and mother always tried to comfort her, but she would not be comforted. She never ate.

Then, when the Indians start picking blueberries, she use to go. And when she would sit and pick, she would start to cry and could not pick, as she would be blinded by her tears. Then she would also fall asleep there.

So one time when she was crying, she heard someone speaking to her, saying, "Do not cry anymore, as your days are long upon this land, and I will give you something here with which you will have fun. See this." And she looked to see the shadow of a large cloud pass before her. "This I will give you. Your body will be just like this cloud, and sickness will not kill you." She did not see anyone near her, but the voice she heard sounded from above her. So she stopped crying and wondered what it was all about. It was the shadow of this cloud which had pity on her. And that was her dream.

So then she made up her mind that she would not cry so much. She was now a young girl. She was able to care for herself. She use to go out fishing, doing just as she use to see her father doing. And when it was rice-making time, they went and made rice. She was a good worker, for she had no one to depend on now. She was the man of the family now. All the hard and heavy work, she would do it. And she use to always go out hunting and snaring fox.

That winter they were at Rainy Lake, someplace around the shore. They had their tepee, and in the summertime, the people would move to Fort Frances when the Hudson's Bay Company was there and this is where the Indians use to camp. And the man of the Hudson's Bay use to have two holidays in the summertime, and the women use to play squaw hockey and race. And she came there and played squaw hockey. She could run fast, as she knew before [already]. She was never tired, was never sick. And the Hudson's Bay man would hang up a flag and yards of dress goods and two kinds of wide ribbon, red and blue—three yards each—and a shawl and shoes and white cotton and a hat. This would be the prize of the women's race. So she was one of the many who were lined up for the race. They had to run a half mile and back again, and she won the race and was given the prize.

And every summer she use to win twice. And on New Year's Day, they use to race also, and she would always win. And for nine years, she was the one woman always taking the prize. And also when they were playing squaw hockey, the side she was playing on would always win. She beat all the best and fastest squaw hockey players. And the women use to quarrel over her—on which side they wanted her to play. And she always went on the young girls' side even though the women use to come to her with bundles of stuff, coming to ask her what kind of medicine she uses for running. And she use to tell them that she did not use any medicine at all. Some of the girls and women never looked at her. They were all jealous of her and hated her. But the Hudson's Bay people thought an awful lot of her.

So after nine years, she took three prizes a year on racing, and that summer she could not come to the first Hudson's Bay celebration. The Hudson's Bay man waited for her. Then the race had to go on without her, and an Ojibwe woman from the States won the race. That's when she was not there.

And the next celebration, she came there two days before—with her mother and sisters. Her sister next to her was already married. The Indians did not care for her to come, as they knew she would be the one taking the prize again. As soon as the Hudson's Bay man heard she came, he came over and got her and asked her why she wasn't there the first time, and she said she could not come. So he took her in the store and made her pick out the dress goods she wished to win. So she picked out a black silk which was very dear.

So when the day came, there were four women: the one[s] that came first and second [in the last race] and one new runner and herself. She use to fix her moccasins with medicine and smoke them so that no bad medicine would affect her legs while she was running. So they started off. The woman which won [the last race] was right at her heels all the time, and after they turned back, the woman was even with her and she could hear that she was out of breath. And the woman said, "I guess you will beat me." And she answered, "I don't know. I do not care to win this race." And after the woman was ahead of her, she said, "Now is the time to help me out, you that told me I would have fun. It would be a shame if I get beat." She was speaking to the shadow of the clouds. And right away, she felt her body light as a feather! And as if she was running on air, she passed the woman and was way ahead of her. So she won the race again and also took the prize of the outfit. And there was also a second prize but not as good as the first prize. The other two girls were way behind.

So then they got ready for the squaw hockey game. Many girls and women wanted to play against her, and only a few were on her side. And many people put their things for the ones to win. So they start playing, and one of the girls—the one that came second on the race when she wasn't there—was a good player. She was the best player where she came from and claimed to be a good runner too. But she could not do anything. When the fast runner got the balls, she ran. And this girl was right behind her. But she made a goal anyway. So they won that game anyway and divided up the stuff with the girls. They were talking and laughing, and this same girl come up to her and asked her what she was laughing at and she said, "Nothing." And the girl said, "Oh no! You're laughing at me because you beat me." And then hit her on the face with a crooked knife. She did not move or do anything. Then the girl walked away. The blood was streaming down her face. She was cut on her cheek. Then the girls took her to their tent and washed her cut and put some medicine on her. Many of the women had it in for her and tried to do her wrong all the time. But she did not care. And her face healed right away.

And while they were staying there, the Hudson's Bay man came there and asked her if she would go to Kenora and race a woman which was the champion runner. And she said she was willing to go. There was a celebration in Kenora, so she went with the Hudson's Bay man and his wife and her sister. It was night when they came to Kenora by boat. She was scared because there were so many lights. She was taken to a restaurant. And they slept there. And next morning, they had breakfast in the restaurant. At two o'clock she was to race. Her boss bet on her so many dollars. The prize was fifteen dollars. So when two o'clock came, they were on the road. They were to run half a mile, then back again. She had on two long skirts and her beaded moccasins on. The white woman had on shorts with no stockings on. She was not a bit scared though there were many people watching them. A [gun] was fired, and then they were shoved to go.

The white woman was a fast runner and was ahead of her from the first. She did not mind her. She ran steadily along, and when they turned back, she ran ahead of her. And just when this white woman wanted to pass her, she spoke to the shadow of the cloud again. And right away, she thought she was running on air again! And as she was coming close to the line where they were to stop, she could see the Hudson's Bay man waving his hat and yelling for her, saying, "Come on!" Then she ran with all her might and beat this woman by far and broke her record as champion runner. So fifteen dollars was given to her.

And the next race was men and women—just a little ways—and only one prize of five dollars. Her boss told her to run again. And she won again. So that was twenty dollars she had now. And she was to get another five on the bets. So the Hudson's Bay people told her that was enough and told her to wait for them 'til the next day.

So her and her sister walked around town listening to all the music. All at once her boss came running to her and asked her if she would race a man which was betting fifty dollars he could beat her. And she said she would. And her boss said, "If he beats you, I lose fifty dollars, and if you win, you have twenty five and I have twenty five dollars too."

So she stood on the road again ready to race a man. Everybody said she could not beat this man, but she was not a bit scared. The man was also dressed in shorts. So off they went again! The man was very slow, but she did not mind him. She ran as fast as she could, for they had to run a longer ways anyway. And then she beat him! And so that was fifty dollars now she won by three races. The Hudson's Bay man was very proud of her and brought her home again.

While she was in Kenora, there was a nice-looking half-breed that fancied her, and she walked around with him and talked to him. And that fall, this man came to Rainy Lake right to where she was staying and stayed there. So she married this man. He brought a lot of stuff for her. He was a good man and was good to her. And the next summer again, when the Hudson's Bay man gave a prize for the winner, she was not able to run, as she was carrying a baby. Then someone else won. Someone else took her place. But the Hudson's Bay man was never satisfied.

She had two girls, and [with] the third one, she got sick on her face. Some old Indian man did this to her by Grand Medicine. She got *nahdahwiah* men to doctor her. Then her baby died. And she got strong again. Worms were eating her flesh sent by the Grand Medicine Men, but the Indian doctors doctored her. And when her little girl was four years old, she got strong again. And she was mad. She made up her mind that she would start racing the women again. Also start playing squaw hockey. She talked through her nose, as this was where she was sick. And when she would run, she always beat the women and girls. And when she would play squaw hockey, she would always win. And she would always say— to make the women mad: "It's all right if I have to talk through my nose [because of] what the old Indians did to me. Only if they break my legs, I will not be able to run anymore." And she always tried hard to beat anybody. And at last, the women got scared of her, and they never raced her again. And her daughters grew up to be big women and got married and had children. Her husband died and her daughters and mother and sisters [died]. When she got older, she was never tired. Though she would walk and work all day, she was never tired.

And about eleven years ago, she was killed by a train right in Rainy Lake Reserve. She was crossing with a dog team, and her toboggan got stuck in the track. And as she was trying to pull it out, the train struck her and killed her right there. So that was the end of her. She did not die of sickness. Both her grandchildren died. So none of her family are living. The end.

16

Her Dead Grandmother
Told Her to Straighten Up

This is a real story. This happened at Asinkamisquawbikinind, [which] means Stone Painted Red. And at this place lived a little girl. Her father was a good hunter. He killed everything, and he use to win a lot of nice things when he would gamble. The little girl use to say that he use to fight her mother, and she use to run away, far in the bush. And one time, when she was about nine years old, her father start to fight her mother again, and her mother ran away. And she ran after her, and she got lost. She went further than her mother, and she never knew that she stayed away for four days. And she slept all that time. She dreamed that she was in a place where there were a lot of people and she was very happy and had nice things to eat. And when she woke, the sun was up. She slept near a stump on some muskake [muskeg] where the moss was soft. She could see some low-bush cranberries, and she started to eat them. She never had anything to eat since she left home. And this is also where she was blessed so that she could *nahnahdahwiiway*, to doctor people.

So after she got through eating these cranberries, she went around there playing. She was just as contented there as if she had her home there. And as she was playing, she seen that the trees were kind of thin and clear on one side. So she went that way, and she walked a little ways. Then she come to a lake. So she went along on the shore to get a drink and played around there again. And she thought she would go back to where she [had] slept. And she went further along the shore. She come to a point, and she went over this point. She could see a canoe out on the lake, and she could see that there was somebody in this canoe. And she could hear them saying when they seen her, "This must be the little girl who got lost. She's been gone now for four days." Only then she knew that she's been gone for four days. And she was scared to go home. And she stood there looking at these people coming, and she thought to herself that she would hide. So she ran back into the bush, and she hid in some thick brush. And when the people came there and looked for her, they couldn't find her. So they went back and told the people. And she laid there. She could hear the people talking. They were looking for her. And the men went back in the bush and went through the bush. And when they passed her, she lifted up her head to see where the men were now, [and that was] when someone grabbed her. She got so scared she start to cry.

It was an old woman walking behind that had seen her lift her head up and went up to her as quiet as she could and grabbed her. And, of course, all the other ones come running back, and the old woman told her, "I'm not going to let you go. I'm going to keep you as my own little girl. I'll take you home to my place, and you will have nice things to wear." So the little girl stopped crying. And she also wouldn't go to see her father. She hated him. And the same with her mother. And the old woman took her home to her wigwam, and she stayed with her there.

And her mother use to come there, but [the girl] never spoke to her to be friendly with her. She just had no use for her own relatives. And her grandmother on her father's side use to come there and quarrel with this old woman she stayed with and use to even fight her. And the little girl grabbed the old woman [her grandmother] one time and gave her a beating, and she never came again. And even her parents use to bring her nice things to wear, but she never made up with them again. And they use to say to this old woman,

"It's on account of you why she won't come to us. You talked her into it." But the old woman spoke to them, saying, "I never told her anything to do. Only if you did care for her, youse wouldn't of carried on like the way youse did. You scared her. [That's] why she ran away, and I ain't going to let her go unless she wants to." But the girl told her [adopted] grandmother that she didn't want to go back.

So they lived together just the two of them. Her grandmother was very good to her, and she was a good girl. Also she was a smart girl. And when she got her first monthlies [menstruation], she stayed right in with her grandmother. Only after she was well, they moved away from there. They use to go around camping in the fall. Her grandmother learned her to do everything that the Indian woman makes. She could beadwork on a frame and also [do] the other kind of beadwork and tan hides and make mats and cedar bags and yarn bags and make nets and birch barks for wigwams and baskets. And she learned how to trap, set snares, and set nets. She also made snowshoes. So they always had lots of things. Also lots of nice things to eat. They were both good hunters.

And she stayed single for about twelve years. And she was also a good, quiet girl. She never went or spoke to any young man. Her grandmother told her one time that she should now get a husband. But she said, "I don't care about having a man to bother us." The reason why she said this was because [of] how her mother and father use to fight, and [she] thought all men were alike and she never wished for anyone. Her grandmother made a bed for her on the other side of the fireplace. But she never slept there. She slept with her grandmother.

And when she was about twenty-five years old—that's after she stayed with this old woman for fourteen years—they went away to a place called Mushkiginicomisibing. That was where they use to camp in the fall. And they went there to hunt and fish, and they stayed there 'til the lakes freeze up. They gathered up an awful lot of meat, fish, muskrats, and rabbits, and they killed a bear and made lots of bear grease. And while they were there, her grandmother got sick. She was so sick that she thought she wouldn't live. And she sent word to someone who was passing by to tell the people that her grandmother was sick and that she might not live—so that people would know how they were. She never slept, watching over her grandmother.

And one time, she fell asleep, and she dreamed of the time she was lost. She dreamed that someone gave her a rattler and other things they use when they doctor and spoke to her, saying, "Try this on your grandmother. She might get better." And so when she woke up, she start to make a little rattler and start to *nahnahdahwia* her grandmother. And the old woman seem[ed] to be brighter when she got through. And so that night, she started again on *manitokaso* and *nahdawiiwa*. And before she was through, she heard somebody outside. It was her father and mother and some people coming to see how they were. She didn't stop with her *manitokaso* but kept right on 'til she got through. And her father and mother made their wigwam close [to] there. And about four days after, her grandmother got better and was up and around.

So then, from that, people knew that she was a *nahdawiiwa*. And she was wanted from one place to another to doctor the sick. And about two years after, her and the grandmother moved to Ahnibikawinigahming to make rice in the fall. [Her grandmother] got sick again. She tried to *nahdahwia* again, but she couldn't do anything. And when she knew that her grandmother was going to die, she got ready to take her to a place where other people were. But before she started, some people got there. So she kept her grandmother there. She lived only two days. When her grandmother died, she let her *nahdawiiwa* go. She threw her rattler away. And she buried her grandmother right there, and she was very lonely.

After she lost her grandmother, she wouldn't go back to her parents. She wouldn't stay with anyone either. She just wanted to be alone. There was no one who could be in her grandmother's place. And men wished to marry her, but she never cared for them. So she just lived alone there. People told her that she better move away from there. And she told them that she couldn't move away from where her grandmother was buried. She moved just a little way from where her grandmother died. And she lived there for about two years.

And her sister younger than her lived there. She had three children. But she never lived with them. Her brother-in-law wished for her. He use to bother her an awful lot. And one time at night when she was alone, he come there and wanted to sleep with her. But she took a stick that was still on fire, and she hit him with that and sent him out. And she didn't like that. So she made up her mind that she would go away from there 'cause she didn't want her brother-in-law to bother her. And she went along with some people to Rat Portage to pick berries that summer. And she left that place for good.

And there was a man there that wished for her. He was a half-breed. And so, at last, he did marry her, and [they] stayed over at Rat Portage. She made him a good wife, and also he was good to her. And first she had one boy and then a little girl and three boys and then a little girl. So that's six children she had.

And then she use to say that, after all her children grew up, then she start to worry an awful lot. Her sons use to drink an awful lot, and she use to get up through the night to go and see what they were doing. And her daughter was not one bit like her. She was one of the fast girls. And she use to have to get up and look for her daughter. And then her daughter was only fifteen years old when she had a baby, and they didn't know who the father was. And then her husband got sick. He was so ashamed of what his daughter did. The girl use to drink and fight the same as the boys.

[The woman] worried so much that her hair got gray, and [she] got old right away. And she worried over her old man too. And then her older son went away near Winnipeg to work. And all at once, he came home through the night, and he packed up all his things and gave her sixty dollars, and he went away to someplace else. And after he was gone for a while, one time early in the morning, two policemen came into their house and searched the house asking for her son. And she didn't know why they were looking for him. She thought it was only a fight. Her son was accused of murder, and he was arrested and taken to Winnipeg. And he was kept there for three years. And at last he was found guilty. He [had] murdered a man, a bartender. So a telegram was sent to them that their son was to be hanged that day. And as they were sitting around crying and mourning over their son, [her husband] sat on his chair smoking, and she was laying on the floor crying. And when she got up and spoke to her husband, he was dead.

So after her husband was buried, she was out of her mind. She was crazy for ten days. She sat and never ate or [went] to sleep either. She was always seeing things. Sometimes she would see a bear passing in front of her or a train, and she would tell the people to get out of the way of the train. And sometimes she would see her dead son killing somebody right there in front of her. For ten days she was like that. At last, she thought her dead grandmother came to her and told her to straighten up, that she had many years more ahead of her, that it wouldn't be nice for her to die crazy.

So she thought. She wakened about noon, and she felt like a different woman. She was very weak, and her mind was very tender. And she wondered if she [had] slept that long and if she dreamed all this. And she was so glad that, once more, she had heard or dreamed of her grandmother speaking to her. And she thought, "I will live some more, as my grandmother wants me to live."

And she got up and went out. She looked around, but she did not know where she was. She knew that there were men and women watching her, but she didn't ask any questions. This was in a hospital where she was. And when she knew that she was in a hospital, she asked them what was the reason why she was there 'cause she didn't feel sick. And they told her that she would of been very sick if they didn't bring her there—that it was over ten days ago since she had anything to eat. And she told them she was going to get better. And they told her they knew. And she asked about her children. They told her that they were well. And so they gave her something to eat.

So she got all right. And she came back to her own home. And she hated the white people then 'cause she thought they all killed her son. And then she come back to the lake.

Her youngest girl was put in [residential] school. Also the two younger boys. And the girl which had the baby stayed right in town. And her other boy was married to a girl from Port Arthur.

And she come back to the same little shack where she and her grandmother use to live before. She lived there all alone by herself. She was pretty old then. Her youngest daughter got out of school and got married. And they came there and lived with her mother.

Before her daughter came there, she caught a little baby bear and raised it. And when it was small, wherever she went, the little bear had to go too. And when she went out paddling, the bear had to go [with her]. And when it got to be very big, she didn't know how to get rid of him. She got scared of him too. But the bear never did her any harm and never scared her. It was as gentle as it could be. And after her daughter came to live there, her son-in-law killed the bear. And she never could eat the bear meat 'cause she was so good to the bear and the bear was so fond of her. So after that, she couldn't ever eat a bear again.

And her son-in-law made her a little house where she could live as she liked, 'cause she never cared about living with anyone. And he also made their home and stables. They kept a stopping place there for the people that were going back and forth to Kenora and Fort Frances.

So she got to be very old [so] that she had to walk around with a cane. And her other two sons got married and had children. And their children had children. Also they had children. So that was three times she had great-grandchildren. She had a nice home in Kenora, but she rented it. The [Indian] agent took care of the rent for her. She use to get the money, like every three months. And so at last she died, and after they got through dressing her and put her in a coffin, she turned to stone. And the white people in Kenora wanted to buy her body for so many thousand dollars, but the daughter wouldn't sell her mother's body for any money. So all the children are dead now. Just the great-grandchildren are alive.

[The woman] use to say that, after her being such a quiet girl, she raised such a boy and girl to worry her so much.

Well, that's all. Of course, this is not all of her life. There's some parts which I do not know.

17

She Was Left There
to Starve, but She Was
Too Smart for That

This is a story of a good woman, honest and brave, a good, strong working woman. She did everything for her husband. Kept him clean and worked for him. But he was still mean to her 'cause she didn't have any children, And that was why he was always beating her. He wanted her to have children. But she could not help it. She wanted children just as bad as he did. She use to cry an awful lot, wishing she could do something to have children. He did everything to her. He use to leave her and go and marry someone else. Then he would come back again whenever he was pleased, and she would be just the same. She was never mad or jealous.

And they use to go out on the lake moose hunting. This was at the lake in Tower, Minn[esota], where they were. And one time, again, they went out moose hunting in the spring in about June, and they traveled for two days. And the third night, they stopped on the shore. And the next day, they killed two big moose, and she cleaned them and dried the meat. So they went up into the woods to get some birch to make [a] birch-bark wigwam and also birch bark for a canoe. And she come down with her load of birch bark, and she seen their gun there. So she took it along and went back for another load. And when she came back again, their canoe was gone. And also her husband.

So she was left there alone with no canoe. But everything else was there: her kettles, tea pail, ax, knives, and all her clothing and blankets were there. And she also had the gun. So she walked along the shore thinking that her husband was out paddling. But it got so dark that she went back to her wigwam and went to bed. So the next day she waited and still he didn't come. So she knew that her husband left her there for good. So she made up her mind to stay there until death would come to her.

So she made birch barks and tanned the moose hides and pounded meat. And then she got some cedar and made the frame of a canoe. Of course, this was about ten days after she was left there. So she stayed there and did all her work, making mats and all kinds of things. She had her sewing along with her.

And then, later on one evening, she went around the point to the bay and sat there. She seen a moose in the water. So she waited 'til it came closer. Then she shot it and killed it. So she start pulling it out, but she couldn't. So she left it there. And early the next morning, she got her knife and cleaned it. And as she was pulling all [the] inside[s] out, she dropped her knife in the water. So then she had no other knife. So she took all her clothes off and dived for it. But she nearly drowned. And as she was coming out, she kicked something under the water. Here was her knife. So she got through cleaning the moose. And she moved around the point into the bay so it would be closer to where the moose was. And she cut it up and dried it. But she left her canoe frame over at her first camp. So she stayed there again.

You see, she would've got home all right if she wanted to, but it would of been hard for her. She was on the same side of the lake as where her people were. She had no parents, but she had aunts, uncles, brothers, and sisters. But she didn't care to try and get home. She was just as well contented there. She had two fireplaces a-going. She would cover the other one with the ashes so it wouldn't go out. She had matches. But she was saving them unless she really had to use them.

She was there about twenty days now. The only thing she didn't have was a comb, and her hair was a sight! She had her two hides tanned and smoked all ready for use. And she had the hides of the moose she killed on the frame and was scraping it.

And there was a young man out for moose hunting near. And he come to this point and heard someone pounding. He didn't know what it was, so he went near. And the pounding went on again and like someone scraping. So he went nearer, and he saw a woman scraping a hide. Here was the woman he always wished for! And still he was more in love with her then. So he got out of his canoe. She did not see him. She was busy cooking and scraping a hide.

So he went up to where she was, and he spoke to her and said, "So this is where you are making leather." And he gave her an awful start! But she calmed down. Then he told her that her husband went home and told her people that he lost her and [that] he had hunted and waited for her for three days. And [he] said it was at a different place, and all the people went to where she was supposed to be lost and searched for her. But they finally gave up and thought her dead by that time. And the man told her that [her husband] was married again to another woman which was no good at all.

So she gave him something to eat, and they sat down and had a nice meal. So the young man stayed there and married her. So the next day they put birch bark on the canoe and finished the hide she was scraping. They stayed there for five days, and they finished everything. And the young man was so happy that he at last got the woman he always wished for.

So one morning, he told her they would go away that morning. So she got ready, put her things in her own new canoe, and the man went around the point to where she lived first. And he came back walking kind of fast and said to her to hurry up. So they did. And he made sails on their canoes and away they sailed out into the lake. And as they were going, she took notice of him always looking back. So she looked back, and she seen a man walking around where they camped. He had on a white shirt and red on his hat. She knew it was her husband, the one that left her there, but she didn't care 'cause she had a nicer man now. And this man yelled to them to come back. But they wouldn't. They kept right on. They were crossing the Lake [of the Woods] to her husband's people. He had brothers and sisters, and only his father was living.

And so they come to this place, and his father said to him, "My son, I hope you are not taking another man's wife." And he answered him and said, "No. I found her scraping a moose hide as I was coming along the shore of the Lake. She was left there to starve, but she was too smart for that." And so they stayed over there at her in-laws. And one of the man's aunts said to him, "You were a lucky man when you found this woman. She's so smart and keeps you clean."

And then, about two or three years later—the Indians use to move to one place—and she and her husband moved to this place too. And she made new mats and birch barks. Everything was new and so nice. And they happen to make their wigwam near her first husband's old wigwam. His wife was filthy and dirty looking. And they already had three children. And their bedding was old and dirty, for his wife was lazy. But the other woman was always smart and kept everything nice and clean. So often the women would say to this man that he made an awful mistake when he was mean and at last left her in the wilderness to die, and now, although he had another wife, he had to live among dirt. And many a time when she was home alone, he would come there and bother her or to try and make [her young husband] jealous. But he never was jealous or [said] anything to his wife 'cause he trusted his wife. He knew she was true and honest to him. And he liked her too much to hurt her feelings.

And so one morning, all the people were going away to a different place. And early in the morning, she got up and went to see her net and caught some fish. And she come back and cooked her man's breakfast. And after they were through eating, they got ready. And some of the Indians were gone already. Anyway, this man and his wife and children [were gone]. And so they took all their things down to their canoe. But when they got there, the canoe was cut twice, and so they were left with no canoe. But some of the old women got to work and sewed up the canoe and put tar on it. And so they went, them too. And they traveled in the night 'til they came to where the Indians were camping, and so they stopped there.

And the next morning, this man [the first husband] was already again getting ready to go. And as he was taking their things down, he made fun of the canoe that was cut up. And as he was getting in the canoe, her young husband said, "You are always running away from me." And the man said, "Yes, and I was the one that cut your canoe." And, of course, the [young] man got up, ran into the water, and grabbed the canoe and pulled him out of the canoe and dipped him in the water three or four times and knocked him on the face. And then he let him go, and he said to him that he did not want him to do anything to him or to tease him anymore. And so he let him go.

Then he and his wife got ready and went again. And they camped in a different place, and the [first husband] camped alone someplace near where the Indians were. The Indians were all going to rice making.

And so they got there. And the men use to have all kinds of games such as lacrosse and moccasin and the hand game. Every time they would have this lacrosse game, the man [her first husband] would hit the young man on purpose. But he would say he didn't. Of course, the young man never said anything to him 'cause he didn't want to have another row with him again 'cause his people were always talking to [telling] him to behave. And so he never paid no attention to him although the man was always teasing him. So she lived happily with her young husband. He was good to her.

18

Let Them Stay Single

All They Want To

This is a story of a woman. When she was a girl about ten or twelve years old, her father died, and her and her mother use to stay all alone in the bush. Her mother was a great old woman to make things such as mats, rabbit-skin robes, and birch bark. And the girl learned how to do all these things. In the summer they set nets. They use to make a lot of rice and dry berries. They also use to put away loads of maple sugar and syrup. In the fall they would kill lots of fish and rabbits and dry meat for the winter. And they lived in a wigwam *mitikogiwam* all winter. Her and her mother use to work together. They never lived among people. They always lived among islands near the Lake [of the Woods], where they could get to kill rabbits and fish.

So then she was a young girl now. They also killed weasels. In the spring they would kill muskrats. And one spring, her mother found five little baby fox. They took these foxes and kept them on an island. They fed them on fish, and when fall came, they killed these foxes and sold them. They were black fox and silver fox and a cross fox. So they got good money for them. And the woman got some men to make a little shack for them. So that winter they lived in a shack.

She was then about nineteen years old. She never went with any man yet. She was some kind of a quiet girl. When she was among people, she was always out of sight or in the tent. She never went with any girls either. She only went around with her mother.

And her mother use to talk [to] her often to try [to persuade her] to get married. But she [the girl] would not speak to her [discuss marriage] at all. And one time when they were camping among Indians, a young man came to the tent to try and go with her. But she jumped out of her bed and ran to where her mother was sleeping. And her mother said to her, "You mustn't do that when anyone [someone] wants you. You have to get married anyway. And people are making fun of you." But she would not listen to her at all. She said she was awfully scared of men. So the old woman said to her daughter, "If you had a man, we would not work so hard to try and get food for ourselves. The man would always support us."

So one time, she [her mother] made up with the parents of a young man which she wished her daughter would marry. And they said that they also wished for her daughter, for she was a good worker. So she told her daughter: "You must not say anything. Marry this young man, for he is a good hunter and he will be good to us." She never spoke to her mother at all. So the next day the old man took over his son's belongings to this girl's tent. And the young man also went. He stayed there about ten days. And all that time, she never spoke to him at all. So at last, he picked up and went home to his parents. He never bothered her again. The old woman was very sorry for the young man. So she told her daughter not to do that again if anyone wants to marry her.

So she was single for a while. Then a man from Leech Lake asked to marry her. And she did. They stayed there for a while. Then he wanted to take her away to Leech Lake. But she wouldn't, until her mother told her to go.

So away they went. And when they were there for about ten days, she only knew then that he was a lazy man. She use to set her net, and in the morning she would go and see it and cook some fish. Then she would tell him to get up, but he would not. He never did any work, and she was very poor, for she only took [had brought] a little [few] of her clothes with her. And she did not have anything [like beadwork] to work at. So she was very lonesome. All she use to do was make grass mats and cedar-bark mats. She had a nice canoe of her own. She use to ask her husband to bring her home to her mother to get her clothes, for she had nothing to wear. But he use to say, "No, you stay right here." When his parents would tell him to do anything, he wouldn't. He had lots of brothers and sisters, and they lived in a *shabodahwan*.

So one morning, she went to see her net. And when she came back, she cooked the fish and tried to make him get up. But he wouldn't. So she went out and start to work on her grass mat. All at once, towards noon, she could hear them crying. So she came running to the tent, and she was told her husband was dead. He slept for good. His brothers and sisters could not wake him up. So they dressed his body up, and [he] was buried. She did not care at all.

Next morning, she finished her grass mat, and one old woman there made out a map [to show] how she could come home. So when the Indians moved to some other place, she came home. And when she got to her mother, her mother said to her: "My daughter! Why are you coming alone? Where is your husband?" But she said, "Oh, they buried my husband up." And her mother said, "Does your in-laws know that you came away?" And she said, "I don't know. They seen me coming this way." So then the old woman did not say anything else to her daughter. Only she was sorry to see her daughter so poor.

So she stayed with her mother again for a long time. She was like a man. She could kill a deer anytime she wanted to. And a long time after, she married another man from Nett Lake. He was a good hunter and was very good to her. Gave her all the things she could use. And she made nice things for him and kept him good. And the man never asked her to go anyplace with him. He stayed right there.

And about two months after they were married, one morning

the man did not get up soon. And after she got through cooking, she tried to make him get up. But she couldn't, for he was dead. He died while he was sleeping. So then that's two husbands that died that way.

So after that she stayed single for nearly eight years. She use to snare cross fox and silver and black fox. Like, rabbits and foxes meant good money those days. So she lived very good. So then the old woman never said anything to her daughter again, for she thought her daughter had some bad dream and [that was] why her husbands died that way. But the girl said that she did not have any dreams.

So after she was a widow for many years, she married a man from near the Ocean Shore [Lake Superior]. He stayed right there with her and her mother. He was a hustler. But he was awfully mean to her. He use to lick her an awful lot. Then one time, about three or four months later, they went out hunting on the lake—just the two of them. He got mad with her and start to give her a beating. He kicked her and clubbed her 'til she did not breathe at all. So when he thought her dead, he took her and throwed her over on a rock and covered her up. So away he came home and brought the news that he lost her. So the old woman got in her canoe and came along the shore. He did not tell just where he lost her, either.

And the woman, here, she pretend she was dead. So after he was gone, she crawled out and washed her face. She was aching all over. She was on an island. No way of getting to the mainland. She had nothing to eat and nothing to cover with. No ax or anything. She could hardly see. Both her eyes were swollen and bruised.

She was there about three days, and she was about starving now. So she start to yell and shout. And while this old woman was going along the shore, she heard someone yelling on this island, and she went [there]. She was with a young girl, and when they got to the island, here was her daughter sitting on a rock all bruised and swollen up. And the old woman got out of her canoe and ran to where her daughter was sitting, saying, "Oh my poor girl! Such an awful life you're in to be treated like this by your man!" And she said, "Yes, Mother, and you always told me I would live good if I married any man. Here I am bruised and half killed and nearly starved."

So she took her daughter home. And when they got there, the man already was gone. He never showed up, for he really thought he killed her. So she got better again, and the old woman never said anything to her again, for she knew it was all her fault her daughter had to go through all this trouble. Only she use to say to women: "Mothers, never tell your daughters to get married when they don't want to. Let them stay single all they want to."

That was four men she married. And yet she married another man about four or five years later. She never had any children with these four men. Only [with] the fifth one. She had a little girl with him. He was good to her. He thought a lot of her. He was a French half-breed and was also a Catholic. She was never well again. The man [had] nearly killed her, and she never got over it. But her husband took good care of her, and they always lived very good.

And their daughter grew up to be a young woman, and she used to be a great girl to walk around town there in Fort Frances before there were so many houses there. The Indian agent and Hudson's Bay Company were there. And some boys use to tease the Indian agent about this girl. And he use to say, "I wouldn't be seen with her." And, of course, her grandmother heard that the agent said this to her granddaughter, and she made her granddaughter wear some love medicine. She also got in with the agent and got some of his things. And then pretty soon the agent got in love with this girl. He was so crazy after her. And then, at last, he married her. And he use to take her to places to be fixed up like a lady, and he made her wear white gloves. So one time they were asked to dine at [the minister's] house. And she ate with her white gloves on. And, of course, he couldn't tell her in front of the people to take her gloves off!

They were married for quite a while. She kept their house as clean as any white woman. She died soon after that. She was buried right in Fort Frances Cemetery. Her husband put a nice gravestone on her grave. The old woman [grandmother] died also. And the woman died too.

So that's how the woman turned out to have the Indian agent for a son-in-law. The end.[1]

19

Why Do I Have to Die Now
When I Have a Man and
Children to Live For?

This is the story of a woman and of her great adventure when she was lost, of how she wandered around. She went out picking berries, and she went out so far into the bush picking eye berries. And when she filled her pail, she knew she was lost. She did not know which way to go. It was kind of a cloudy day, and she walked and walked and sometimes she would run. Of course, she had her pail of eye berries. At last, several days after, she come to a lake. And she creeped down. She heard voices, and she went down. She seen people eating, and as she was going towards them, they seen her and were scared of her. So they jumped into their canoes and left all their food there 'cause they thought she was some kind of *windigo*.

And at her home village, there were people looking for her all over. [They] didn't know what happened to her and where she was. She was about thirty or forty miles away from her home.

[The people] were scared of her when they seen her coming with her hair hanging, hardly any clothes on. She was running around the bush wild, and even she got so's that she was afraid to see anyone, in fear someone would find her.

And at last she got used to being in the bush. She took all the things that these people left. She took an ax, knife, and tea pail and some food. So she got settled in one place. And she use to tell that the mosquitoes were awful and of the little beasts she seen and funny-looking snakes, birds, and all kinds of beasts. She wasn't scared of these at all. Only to see a human person she was scared. She use to cry an awful lot.

She use to snare rabbits with twine. Then she was all right after she got this food. And when it was nearly all gone, she started off again. That was after twenty-five days she was lost. She come to where there was no water. For four days she traveled with no water. Only at the swamps she would suck the damp moss. At last she threw her blanket and tea pail and everything away. Only the ax and knife she had.

And as she was walking along, she come to a road. She did not know what it was. Only in pictures she use to see railroad tracks. And this is what the road was. Then she come to a little house. The door was open, so she went in. She was awfully thirsty and hungry, so she took a drink of water. And before she had time to have a bite of anything to eat, she fainted. And the man that was living there came in and seen this woman laying there. He thought her dead then. He yelled to his partner, and he came in. Then she come to again, and they fed her.

Then they took her to the station and sent her to Kenora. They thought she was crazy. She nearly got out of her mind on account of being lost for forty days, and she was scared all the time. They took her to the doctor in Kenora. The doctor said there was nothing wrong, only she was frightened and went so long without water or food. She wandered around too long. If she went for two or three days longer, she would have wandered to death.

So they got her clothes—she was all in rags—and they kept her there in Kenora and sent word to locate who owned her. And the two men that found her in their shack—the oldest was the youngest man's uncle—and the young man fell in love with her and wanted to marry her.

And one time she got in one of the boats which were going back and forth from Kenora to Fort Frances, and she come home to Fort Frances, where she got lost from. The railroad track where she went to was the C.P.R. [Canadian Pacific Railroad] track. So when she got home, all her people were glad to see her 'cause they thought she was dead. She was in the wilderness for forty days and the time she was kept in Kenora.

And after she was home, this white man come after her. He was a Frenchman. So he made a home for her on the lake near her people, and she lived with him happy and had four children with him. Then she died, and she said before she died: "Why didn't I die the time I was in misery tearing through the woods than at this time when I want to live? I have a man and children to live for, and then I have to die when I was living happily with my family." Then she died and was buried.

And about a year after, one of her own brother's oldest daughter married her husband, and she started to housekeep for her aunt's husband. And the old man is still living today. He is so old and gray, and he has to walk with a cane.

At the time she was lost, her parents got all the *jisuki* men to find out where she was. And some said she was dead, and some of them said she was living and was to be found and brought back home alive. This was a great habit of the Indians, when anyone was lost, to put up a *jisukan*.

And when she got home, all the people brought her something nice to eat. And some brought her nice clothes and print for her to wear. They were all so glad. [There was] a great rejoicing over her when she came home from Kenora. And people from different places said that she was seen three times during the time she was lost. The end of this story.

20

Leave Me Here

to Starve Alone

This is a story of an Indian man. He already had two wives. His wife which was the oldest one, he had two daughters with her. They were grown-up girls when he use to move around. He always had two wigwams, as he had children with also the other wife.

They went to pick blueberries where a lot of Indians were camping. And while they were there, one young girl got sick there. Many Indian doctors tried to doctor her, but they could not do anything with her. She was very sick. So one time this old man was called to go and doctor her, as he was a regular *manitokaso*. The parents of this girl told him that if he could doctor her to live, he could take her for his wife if she got better by him. So he did *nahdahwiah* her. Gave her medicine to drink. For a long time this young girl was sick. But at last she got better, and then he took her to his wigwam. That was now three wives he had.

He lived in the same wigwam with his young wife. His other wives never said anything to him or anyone because this girl was given to him and, only by him, she got better. His daughters were very fond of his young wife because she use to go with them, and she was just as young as these girls, her stepdaughters.

And there was one young man there which had his mind on this girl. He was going to marry her. He hated this old man for taking this young girl for his wife, and he said he would get even with him some way. This young wife was very unhappy, but anyway she stayed there, as she was afraid this old man would do something awful to her.

He was very good to her. Also the other wives and especially the two young girls [were also good to her]. And when fall came, they moved to this old man's hunting grounds. He was a good hunter. He brought home all kinds of meat and things to eat. His family had three wigwams: one wife and her children in each wigwam, and in one wigwam the young wife stayed and he stayed there with her. And all that winter they lived very good.

And after Christmas, about in February, he would go out hunting, but he could never kill anything. At last, all their meat and things were gone, and they had nothing to eat. He would go out all day and come home in the evening with nothing at all. Everything was scared of him. Even when he would shoot anything, it would not even hurt it. He could not even snare a rabbit. He got weaker every day. And after for so many days of walking around and nothing to eat, he was so weak that one morning he could not get up. He spoke to his wives and children and said, "Now, my children, I can't do anything for youse anymore. So get ready now while you are strong enough to walk and go someplace to try and make a living for yourselves. Leave me here to starve here alone. But if youse do not go, you will also starve here. It's someone that I made mad—why we are starving like this. Or maybe I will become a *windigo* if you stay right here with me." Before he said this, he use to go into his sweat tent and also in a *jisuki*. But even the spirits would not come, and that's why he was so sure that it was someone that was doing this to them. And that's why he told his wives and children to leave him.

No one did not intend to go away. They tried to snare rabbits, but they could not kill anything, them too [either]. One of the old women use to go around picking old bones and boil them over and over until there were nothing left of them. So the oldest woman of the three wives told her two daughters and five children that they would go away. And they did. She had seven children. They were all able to walk. The other wife had five children. They were all small, and she could not very well carry them, as she was too weak.

So this older woman went along. She slept once on her way. And in the morning, she went and cut a bark off a tree—balsam—and boiled it for a long time, and she gave this to her children to drink. So they started off again, and towards evening, they came to a place where some Indians camped that fall. They found some old fish there, and they cooked this fish, drank the soup, and ate the fish and made their camp right there. One of the girls went out cutting wood and came running back to her mother and told her that she found a bear while cutting wood. They all ran to where the bear was, and the girls killed the bear. They took it home. It was so fat when they skinned it and cooked it. They start killing rabbits too. And they were not afraid anymore. And after the young girls were good and strong again, the oldest girl said, "I am going back to where we left our father and the other ones." And her sister said, "I will go with you." Their mother gave them meat and fat and told them just to give their brothers and sisters something to eat and the two other women. But they were not suppose to give anything to their father.

So the two young girls started off. And after they walked a little ways, they seen someone coming staggering along. When they got closer, here it was this young woman [the youngest wife]. She was so weak she could not walk straight. When they met her, she said, "Oh it's awful! The two children have starved. Now they're dead. And the woman is just about starving. The baby is just biting her tits off. He's always nursing. And also the two little girls are just about starving." They told her to sit down there. Then they made a fire and made a little soup for her and told her where she could find their mother. So they left her there and went right on.

So when they came to the wigwam, they did not see any sign of life. No fire or anything. No one was strong enough to cut wood. The oldest girl went right in, but the youngest girl was afraid. When she went in, she seen them all lying down as if they were sleeping. They made a big fire and made a big kettle of soup and pulled their stepmother up and gave her some soup. The two little boys were already dead, and the little girls were dying. They spilled soup in their mouths, but they were dead. And the baby that was nursing was just crazy. He was eating his fingers up and biting off the heads of his mother's breasts. They knew he was to become a little *windigo*. His eyes were blazing, and his teeth rattling. So the old woman killed the baby boy.

The girls tried to arouse their father, but when they pulled the covering off his face, he was dead already. They took his body, and something flashed like lightning. That was his power leaving him. The girls wrapped up the five little bodies and put them together. Also their father's body. Then they took their stepmother and wrapped her up in a rabbit robe and put her on a toboggan and took her along. She was the only one alive there. Six died of starvation.

And when they came to the place where they had met this woman [the youngest wife], they found her lying there. She was also dead because the fatted soup she drank killed her. So they brought their stepmother to their own camp and nursed her back to health again. Seven died and nine lived. There was sixteen in the family,

So they stayed right there, and the old women use to set nets under the ice and snare rabbits and also kill some other things. They lived good. And when spring came, after there was no snow on the ice, the two girls again said that they would go again and try to find some Indians. They knew that some Indians must of moved down to the lake again.

So they went. And sure enough, they could see that there was Indians camping. The oldest girl went along and yelled, "Oh, people! There's only nine of us alive. Seven of us died." And the Indians that were camping there knew who they were. The parents of this young woman that died were also there and also the relatives of these other women were there. So the Indian men went back with these girls. They went back for these bodies and brought them down to the lake and buried the seven bodies there. So that was seven graves there. Then, after everything was over, they moved to where the Indians were camping and stayed around there.

This woman use to say that she was sorry that she did not let her oldest little girl come when she cried after them when they came away. She would have lived if she let her come along with them. Now none of her children were alive.

This old man which was the father of the young woman who died knew that it was the young man that did this to these seven people that died. He was very mad. And [he was] sorry for his daughter. He made up his mind to do something to this young man too. So one time he seen the young man talking and laughing, he got so mad that he took his ax and went up to him and [said], "You are the one that killed seven Indians and were the cause of my daughter's death. I hate you for that, and also you are not fit to live. So I'm going to kill you right here." Then he hit him on his forehead and killed him right there. So that was the end of him also.

The Indians made a big meeting, and they said for no one to say anything about this old man killing this man—that he destroyed seven lives and it was enough for him to be killed too. So they left it that way. But the father of this young man was also mad, and he killed the old man by his bad medicine. And it went on like that between them all the time.

But then the white people were among them now, and that was the only reason why they came to be good friends. And this woman and her children all lived along and were able to make a living for themselves. But the other woman died that same summer. She had blood poison. It started from her breasts when her dead baby bit them off. She also died of a broken heart.

These two young girls both got married and had children of their own.

From that time, then, the Indians asked the Hudson's Bay man if he would not send some men out during the winter time to go from camp to camp of the Indians [to] get all their furs, and from them, people would know how they were getting along. So that was why the traders then traveled all over to the Indians. Because many a time, Indians starved because of some bad medicine and power by someone sent to them. And these traders use to find people like that and save them.

The brother of these two girls, when he got to be a man, he was very brave and strong, although he had nearly starved when he was a boy. He went to the Soo [Sioux] Indian country to battle with the Soos and came back safely with some men he went with. Also he was a great *manitokaso nahdahwiiwe*. That was the time when they were starving. They dreamed of these things, and that's why they didn't die also. His sister, younger than him, she could do her *manitokaso* such as *nahdahwiah*, and she was good at it too. Everybody called on her to *nahdahwiah* somebody. The boy though never did as his father did. Although many times he was told to doctor a girl and if she lived he could take her for his wife. But he never did it, as he was afraid the same thing might happen to him as his father.

They were the only two there out of that family that did some *manitokaso*. They did live a long time, but they're all dead now. His *dodem* was a duck, and that's her *dodem* also—a duck. That's all I know of this story.[1]

21

The Old Woman Doctor

This is a story of an Indian woman. She was a doctor woman—in Indian, *nanadawiiwe*. She went through a rough life. She got married to an Indian. He was married already, so she had a co-wife. He was a great hunter, and he went out with her to hunt ducks. And then they upset the canoe, and he swam ashore. But she hung on to the boat, and she was blown away by the wind for about four hours. And she come to a grassy point, but still she couldn't reach the shore. It was awfully slow getting to the shore. At last she swam ashore and dragged the boat along 'til finally she landed. And she was soaking wet and cold. She had no matches to light a fire and no paddle to use. And there was a little wind. So she took her clothes off and hung them up to dry. Then she raced around the bush to keep herself warm. She use to say that was the hardest part of it, as she was cold and had nothing to eat.

She was about nine or ten miles away from home. There were no people close. The first house was about eight miles away, and the wind was blowing against her. So she went along the beach in the canoe with a stick for a paddle. She kept along the shore until it got so dark that she couldn't see at all. So she put ashore and got off and got some grass. She put the grass in her canoe, and then she lay down in the canoe. Finally, she slept.

It was daylight when she woke. The wind was still against her, and it was blowing harder than the day before. She kept right on again going the same way, and she had about six miles to go yet before she would reach the nearest house. So at last the next evening she finally come to the house. So the people gave her a good drink of whiskey and put her to bed. And for four days she was unconscious. And at last she come to and got better. And her husband come as soon as he heard she got there. Then he took her home.

So they kept on living that way, hunting and fishing. And she had three children. And every time the child would come to the same age, they would die. And her husband would be fighting her, kicking her, and was awfully mean to her. Then his two wives would get after him, and they would lick him.

Then she parted with him, and then she started with her *nan-adawiiwe*. She was getting nice things for it. She got along so fine with all kinds of nice things. And she was a great woman to tan hides. She wasn't in the same place she was when she was married. She went away to the Lake of the Woods. And that was where she was living fine when she got in with a young man and married him. And they had a little boy, and she had to support him herself. [Her husband] was good for nothing. But he was good to her, so she had him rigged up in beadwork at last. So he would trade. The boy was about three years old when a man gave him a pony for his beadwork. And in the wintertime they come to Hungry Hall with the pony. And the man she was first married to was there 'cause that was where he lived.

So about a week after they came there, this other man wanted to take her back from her young husband. The old man scared them so much that the young man run away, and she had to go back to the old man. But she never did like him. Her little boy got sick and died. He was lonesome for his father. And after the boy died, she use to fight this old man. And he use to say all kinds of wishes so the young husband would die. He use to dream and talk to his *powagunuh*. At last, they heard that the young man froze to death. And soon after that, the old man got blind and was sick. Then he died, and she was left a widow again and was free from her husbands. But her mother-in-law and father-in-law and the two brothers and sister of this old man wanted her to stay with them.

And then, that fall, they went back to their hunting grounds, and they nearly starved. They couldn't even kill a rabbit. It was this other young man's parents that were doing all their bad dreams to make them unlucky so they would starve to death. They were mad 'cause it was this old man's work, the reason why he [their son] died. So they moved away and left her there alone 'cause she cut her foot. She didn't have anything to eat. She hardly cut wood for herself. They told her they would come back for her. And she waited five days, but nobody showed up.

So she started off, and it took her four days to get to where they were camping. And then they only thought of her work. She did everything: cutting wood and tanning hides for them. She knew they were going to make a slave of her. So she did not stay there at all but went to another place. And then, from there, she went home to where she belonged. And the young man's parents were glad to see her back and were good to her. She made a home with her own parents and sisters.

And the next summer, she went around with her own sister—that was two years after her husband died—and she met her brothers-in-law and sisters-in-law. They started fighting her. They tore all her clothes and cut her hair and cut up her canoe and tent and beat her. They were mad just because she had on good clothes and was making a good living for herself. That was the style of the Indians long ago. When the husband or wife dies, the in-laws take everything the widow has if he or she doesn't give something (*keewainige*) in place of the one she married.

So after all her bedding and things were taken away from her, she sat there and didn't know what to do. So she left word there and said that she was going to get married the first chance she had and wasn't going to give them the pile of stuff they wanted her to give them. Some kind people then lent them a canoe to go back with, and she and her sister went home. The time they tore her clothes and canoe, she was coming there to make a visit at her old man's grave. But she never came again after that.

Then, a year after, she got married to an older man at Whitefish Bay. He was a widow like herself. He was all kinds of *manitokaso*, *jisuki* and Grand Medicine king and kind of an Indian fortune-teller. He knew what was going to happen ahead of time, and nearly all the time his dreams came true. He had lots of bad medicine, and people use to say that he wished to keep other people's luck. And they claimed that he use to make people crazy. Everybody was scared of making him mad. And he use to be the only one to kill game or fish. And the other people wouldn't kill anything. And that was the reason why people thought him bad. So they kept on like that for many years, and he cured lots of people. And he was a great old gambler.

So she lived there with him all this time as his wife 'til all her in-laws with the first husband were dead. Some got blind and crazy and crippled. Some just got sick and died. And he put her through the Grand Medicine dance several times. Then he got sick with smallpox and died, so she was left a widow again. And she started *nanadawiiwe*. And she was a hunter. She killed furs and fish and made rice and made a good living.

She is a real Indian woman. She dresses like an Indian. She dreams of all kinds of games such as the Indian dice game and snake game and the caribou bone game. She gives these out to her namesakes. And she gives out songs she dreams of and all kinds of games and songs. She did not have any children—just the four that died. None are living.

She's still living yet today. She is very old, but she's still on her *manitokaso* and naming lots of children and giving out dance songs and these games of all kinds. She use to make a nice, big cooking and pretend she was having a feast with the dead people. And she would make a speech over it. Then she would pretend she was sending it to the dead people, and she would pick out people who are living and they would eat it. And she would say that these dead people would send the dishes back filled with life for them. And she had lots of other kinds of feasts. And she would make the people believe she had visitors from heaven. And when she would doctor anyone, she would tell them to go through the Grand Medicine, and she would dress them up herself putting red paint and everything on their faces. And sometimes they would live, but sometimes they wouldn't get better. She was just trying to keep up the same way as her old man.

And lots of other rough life that is not fit to tell. She's living alone—hardly any relatives—at Whitefish Bay. She's old and help-less as a baby now. This is all I know of her. The end.

22

She Used to Make All Kinds
of Little Things for Her Boy

This is the story of an old Indian woman that lived for ninety-six years. When she was a young girl, about twenty-six years old [ca. 1865], she married an Indian man from Leech Lake. They used to have an Indian war dance long ago, and at one of these dances she fell in love with this man. And her mother didn't want her to marry this man. One night later she got ready through the night. She got all her things and canoe, birch bark, and some things to eat. She even took her father's gun. And then she run away with this man. And then they went away to Leech Lake by canoe, and it took them about ten days to get there. They killed moose and dried meat. They had lots to eat as they traveled along.

Then they got to Leech Lake, and her mother-in-law didn't like her when she got there. And about fifteen days after she got there, her husband was awfully jealous, and he gave her an awful beating just for nothing. She didn't deserve it. You know what it is when a stranger gets to a place. All the people wanted to see her. Even all the men passed close [by] her tent just to see her because she was a nice-looking girl. She had long hair. When she was sitting on the ground, her hair used to lie right on the ground. And she was whiter than any of the other girls.

And after her beating, she only then thought of what her mother said to her. She used to go in the bush and cry. He used to fight her and kick her, and she had such lovely hair that he used to just pull her by the hair and drag her around and fight. And about a year after, she become a mother of a little boy. And about two years later, she had a little girl. Her little girl was two years old when she died, and about a month after the little girl died, he gave her another good beating, and she went back in the bush crying. Some woman come to her and said, "Why don't you try and go home?" And she answered her and told her that she didn't know which way to go, that she didn't know the place.

So she stayed around there. And some old people lost their daughter, and then they adopted her as their daughter. So she stayed with these old people and kind of left her husband, but still he was hanging around her all the time. And one time he went to her and said to her that if she would get ready he would take her to see her mother. He said that they would come through Big Forks through Rainy River and out to Lake of the Woods right through to Nâyawangashink if she promised to come back with him again. So she promised to come back with him, but in her heart she knew that she wasn't coming back with him again.

So they started off. This was in the spring in May after they got through making sugar. And they came by this way that the man said they would come. And when they reached Nâyawangashink, her mother was glad to see her and her father was the same way. They all welcomed her with joy. And lots of the people missed her hair, but she never told who pulled all her hair off.

So he got kind of mean with her again. He never fighted her there, but he was sulky and mean with her. And in the fall, he begged her to go back with him, but she wouldn't go. She told him that she wasn't going to go back with him. So he said to her, "All right, if you don't want to go, I will take another woman with me." And she told him, "All right! You can do it!" She got so's that she just hated him. She didn't care whether he came or got married. So he came away with one of her cousins, her father's brother's oldest daughter. Before that she used to tell them what her husband used to do to her, and I suppose her cousin didn't believe that he was that mean.

So she didn't care what her husband was doing. And they were gone all day and all night and all day the next day. And that night, when she was sleeping, this man come to her tent and snatched her little boy. And just then she wakened, and she knew right away that this man was taking her boy. She jumped out of bed and ran out, but he was already in the canoe with the little boy. So they followed—this girl's parents and herself—but they couldn't find them, as it was pitch dark. So they went back.

And that was the only reason why she was downheart[ed]—was when her little boy was taken away from her. He was four years old then—going on five. And she worried so much about her boy because there was no way of hearing how he was.

So all that winter she stayed there. And she used to go to Kenora—well, it was Rat Portage at that time. She went and traded some fur, and she bought her boy pants and shirts. She used to make all kinds of little things for her boy. She used to say that she was very lonesome for her boy. She even used to go in the bush and cry.

So she got ready that fall, and about in March she started off from Nâyawangashink. She walked to Leech Lake. She passed through the Manitou [Rapids]. It took her about sixteen days to walk to Leech Lake. She didn't have anything to eat, as she couldn't very well carry anything. She used to get up early in the morning and start off, and when the snow was thawed, she would stop and kill rabbits and then eat. She had a rabbit robe coat and all her little boy's things she made and all her moccasins.

And she got to Big Forks, and this is where she seen some people. They were going home to Cass Lake. So she went along with these people. She waited four days for them, and it took seven days to get there. She knew the way they came, and she asked these people along which way a person goes. So she got to Leech and stayed at the old people's place that adopted her. They were busy making sugar when she got there. She didn't see her little boy, as they were four miles away, and she didn't like to just go over there.

So her adopted father went over there and said to this man that he should bring the little boy back so's he would see his mother— she come far enough to see her little boy. And the man was quite surprised to hear that she had arrived in Leech Lake. So he did bring the little boy to see his mother. He was six years old then. And the man said to his son, "This is your mother." And the little boy said, "Yes, I know this is my mother. I've been lonesome to see her long ago. And I suppose you're not lonesome to see her because you used to fight her often." So she give the things she made for her little boy: moccasins and beaded leggings and this rabbit robe coat and pants and shirt. So he took the little boy home. And he used to bring the boy often to see his mother. She stayed over there and helped make sugar, and he got so's that he wasn't afraid to leave the little boy there.

And she seen her cousin. She was abused just the same as she was.

She got tired waiting for the lakes to open. So this man and his wife [her cousin] went away to hunt muskrats, and the little boy was left with her. Then she had a good chance to come away. Then she got ready. Her adopted parents gave her a canoe and got her ready. So she started off, and she paddled all day. Then she got off and was sitting around on the rocks when she seen a canoe coming. It was this man's brother and his wife going after them. So she hid there, and they passed by. So she stayed there all day. And in the evening, they passed going back.

So then she started off. And she come to this place where there was a camp. This was at night. She got out of the canoe and went to this shack. There was two old people there. The old woman was very glad to see them. And the old woman told her that these people came there and told them not to let her go by, that she was kidnapping this boy. But she made them understand that it was her own boy and told them how she was abused. She showed them her head and all the scars on her head. So they told her to go and gave her lots of grub to eat. So she started off again. She paddled all night and all day. Her little boy was happy to be with her.

And as it was coming noon, she come to where white men were working. So she stayed at the point, and then she paddled across where they wouldn't see her. Then she got out, and she made a portage. She carried her two box[es] of sugar and all her things. Then she went back for her canoe. And she passed them, and she paddled on. She paddled day and night. She never camped. And then she come to Big Falls, where there was lots of sturgeons, and she got one sturgeon. And she had to portage there again. And she come to a dam, and she seen another white man there. He helped her with the canoe.

Then, finally, she got to the Rainy River, and then she camped on the Canadian side. She cleaned her sturgeon, and she got birch bark there. So she started off again, and she come to the Manitou Rapids. All the Indians were busy killing sturgeon, and she stayed there for three days helping the people. She then had lots of sturgeon and maple sugar, so she started again. And she passed through Long Sault Rapids. They were killing sturgeon, but she didn't stop there. She went through Rainy River and out to the Lake of the Woods. And she got to Nâyawangashink. Then she went to Rat Portage to see the Indian agent, as that was the first place where the agent was. And the Indian agent told her to put her boy in [residential] school, but she didn't put her boy in school just then. But later she did.

She stayed around close to Kenora 'cause she was afraid that this man would come and take her boy again. And about four years later she put him in school. And she stayed around there. Her little boy was about twelve years old then. Then she heard that this man brought his wife home, as she was very sick. But she wasn't scared now, as she knew that her boy was in a safe place. And one time, when she was going around getting birch bark, she was going over a hill. She met this man and he asked her where the boy was, and she got right mad. She had a little ax in her hand, and she made a sham she was going to hit him. "I nearly killed you!" And never told him where the boy was.

But he heard from someone else where he was. And while the

boys were playing football, the boy seen his father, and he ran into the school. But the man was permitted to see his son for twenty minutes, and he gave his boy twenty dollars, and the boy gave this money to the agent to keep. And then one time the woman was washing her things on the shore. The man came there and said to her that he was suffering because she wasn't good to him. And she answered him and told him that she didn't want to have nothing to do with him 'cause he made her suffer enough when she stayed with him. She told him that he pulled all her hair off, and it was enough for her. And her cousin was just about dying at that time. So he cried and left her alone.

So she married a white man. He was a cook for loggers, and she stayed right there helping him. And then her little boy was born, and her cousin died, and the man went home. And a little while after, she got lame. It was this man who did it to her. But her husband took her to Winnipeg and [she] got cured, but she did limp a little. And then her boy got out of school and helped his stepfather.

So her husband died, and she married again to another cook and they lived the same way. He was a white man, and a little girl was born to her again. And she lived with this one for quite a while. They moved from [logging] camp to [logging] camp in the winter times. And in the summer they worked on the [log] drive, cooking. She lived with this one for sixteen years. Then he died, and she never married again.

FIVE

FRIENDS AND FOES

Fig. 23. Moccasin game, Lake of the Woods, 1922. Photo by Carl Gustav Linde. Reprinted by permission of Minnesota Historical Society.

Fig. 24. Boats traveling between Kenora and Fort Frances, ca. 1912. Photo by Carl Gustav Linde. Reprinted by permission of Minnesota Historical Society.

23

I Have a *Pawahgun*

That Gives Me the Power

This is a story of a man who lived with his parents at a place called White Horse. When he was a boy, his mother died, and then it was only his father that took care of him, as he was quite small—about eight years old. And for quite a while, his father was single. Then one time he took notice of his father dressing up. That's when his father gave things to his in-laws [*keewainige*]. And pretty soon his father brought home a woman and married her. He was very sorry to know that his father already was forgetting about his mother. And he was also very lonely. For it wasn't long that his stepmother start to be very mean to him, and she was also always asking him to do this and that. And she never spoke to him the right way. And also she never gave him anything to eat that was nice. She always gave him what was the very poorest.

His father use to be away all day, and his father always said to him to listen to his stepmother and do as she says. And also for him not to go anyplace all day. But he use to get tired, for his stepmother was always scolding him. And he also never got anything to eat while his father was away. And when fall came, they moved to their camping place and stayed all winter. His stepmother was even worse. She never spoke to him right, and he felt very bad. He was quite a big boy now.

And then one night when he was sleeping, he dreamed that his dead mother came to him and said, "My poor son. That's why I felt very bad when I had to leave you alone in this world. I knew that no one would care for you as I did. But I want to tell you this: when your stepmother says for you to take what she left in the kettle, go and take it and sit right where she will see you eating." This was all his mother said to him.

So next morning, his stepmother told him to get up, and he did. His father was eating already. They were eating a porcupine. And his stepmother said to him, "Go and take some porcupine. I left some in the kettle." So he got up and took his old birch-bark dish and looked in the kettle. Here was a small piece of porcupine cut from the poorest part on the stomach with the tits right on. He took it out of the kettle and put it in his dish. And as he sat down, there was a large chunk of bear meat with the fat right on! His stepmother looked at it surprised, and she said, "Oh! What is that? I must of made a mistake and left you the wrong piece." And she said, "Bring it here." And as he was going to hand it back to her, his father said, "Don't take it back from him. Let him eat it." So he ate every bit of it himself and had a good meal. And after that, his stepmother use to look at him for a long time. And when he would look at her, she would look away.

And then again one time, as they were having their supper, they were eating a big jackfish, and his stepmother said to him, "Go and take some fish from the kettle. I left some for you." So he got up again and took his old birch dish and looked in the kettle. There was a very small piece cut from the very tail part. He took it from the kettle and sat down. There was a half of a whitefish in his birch dish! Again his stepmother looked at it and said, "Where did this whitefish come from?" He did not say anything but kept right on eating the fish. His stepmother looked at him. All he seen was hatred in her eyes. But he did not care. Also his father did not question him. And many times that happened. When his stepmother gave him the very poorest to eat, as soon as it was in his old birch dish, it turned to something very nice.

And then one day as he was laying in their wigwam, his stepmother came in with a little ax. And when she seen him lying down, she went right close to him. But he did not move. He knew she was going to do something. So she said to him, "When I give you something to eat, why does it turn to something very nice? Do you have any kind of dreams? Why [do] you have the power to such? Tell me right away. If you don't, I will kill you with this ax." Then he said, "Yes. I have a *pahwahgun* that gives me the power to turn anything the way I want to, and if anybody gives me the worst to eat, it will turn to something very nice every time." Then his stepmother turned around and sat down and stared in one place for a long time. And after that she never gave him anything to eat that wasn't no good.

So when spring came, as the snow was beginning to melt away, the sugar trees were ready now for sugar water. And one night as he was sleeping, his mother came to him again in a dream and spoke to him, "My son, you must leave this place, as your stepmother is going to do something to you. She is going to fix up a dish of something very nice to eat, and she's going to put [in] some bad medicine and give it to you to eat. If you eat it, it will destroy you right away. So take my word and don't take anything from her but go away. I will be on your side all the time and guide you."

So next morning, his stepmother woke him up very gently, and she said, "It's time for you to get up now. I have something for you nice to eat. The people had a big feast this morning, as it is the first time we ate sugar this year. And I left some for you." Then he got up. He remembered his dead mother's warnings that night. And when he got through washing his face, his stepmother handed him a dish of maple sugar, and it was fixed very nice with all kinds of other things mixed with it. He took the dish of sugar and looked at it. Then he pushed it into the middle of the fireplace and said, "I do not want to eat. I will give it to my grandfathers and grandmothers to eat." Of course, the birch dish and sugar were on fire right away. His stepmother looked at him very hard, but he did not care. He got up and went outside. His father never said one word to him. So he walked away.

It was very warm now in the spring. And then he came to a

smooth rock, and he stopped there. He put a rock there and lay down on his back. He lay there looking up in the skies and then he fell asleep. He never moved once but lay there as if he was dead. He would waken sometime in the night, but he never moved. He went right back to sleep again. And after he lay there four nights, and in the morning he wakened and looked up in the skies, he seen a buffalo jumping around among the clouds. And as he was laying there, someone spoke to him. It was his father, and he said, "Oh, my son! So this is where you're fasting." But he never spoke. His father gave him some fire coal and told him to mark his hand how many days he was there now. And then the old man walked away.

But the young man he never moved. He was always sleeping and dreaming. He now had many *pawahgun*. But there was something else he wanted to find out. He wanted to be the headman of a battle with the Soos [Sioux]. [There were] also other things he wanted to learn first. And next morning, his father came again and said to his son, "How many days more do you think you can go?" And he lifted up his other hand, which was not marked. His father was very heavy-hearted because other men fasted for five days only. So his father gave him more coal and told him to mark his other hand. Then his father told him to try and be brave. And his father left him.

He was numb now all over. But he did not give up. And on his eighth day, he wakened again. His lips, mouth, and tongue was so dry. And he looked up towards the sky. He seen a little stream of water pouring down. It poured into his mouth just enough to wet his dry mouth. Then his father came to see him again. He had a piece of lead, and he put the lead into his son's mouth. This lead was supposed to moisten his mouth. And it did. So his father left him again. Then, when the tenth day came, he wakened. And he was just numb all over. He did not know how to move his legs or his body. But, anyway, he turned on his stomach and bent his knees. His father came just as he turned around, and he said, "Well, my son, it looks as if you are ready to get up now." Then he handed him another chunk of fire coal and told his son to eat this fire coal and also to mark himself across his eyes with this fire coal. Also he marked his other hand. That meant now that he fasted for ten days.

Then he got up and looked around. And his father showed him the way. There was green cedar brush on the path all the way from where he lay for ten days. Then he walked on these cedar brush. His father was walking behind him. And when they got to their place, there wasn't a soul to be seen because all the women and men were in their wigwams because they were not supposed to look at this man that fasted for ten days when he was coming home. His father called to him and said, "Son, this is your wigwam here. I wouldn't let you go into the old one, as it is too dirty." Then he went in. It was just a new wigwam, and there was fresh cedar brush spread inside. Also a new mat. Everything was clean.

He sat down, and awhile after, men start coming in covered with blankets. They were bringing all kinds of goods, blankets and guns and also other things. All the men were marked across the eyes with coal. Also, all the women were marked like that because that was the old Indian style. When they were to look at the one that fasted, they had to be marked across the eyes with coal. If they didn't, they would scare his *pawahgun* away.

And right away, there was a young girl brought to him that was sick and dying. He got a *nahdahwiah* drum and rattler and start to doctor this girl. After he doctor and *manitokaso* over this girl for two days, she got a little better. And when she was there for four days, she fully recovered and walked out of the wigwam. Then there was another little baby brought into his wigwam. The baby was very sick, so he start to doctor him again right away. And when the baby got a little better, he was asked to name the child and he did so. The baby got better again. He was praised from all over, and sick people were brought to him all over. And he doctored them all. Also children were given for him to name all the time. Also there were always dishes of the best food brought to him to make a speech. This he always did.

And then again one time, there was some tobacco brought to

him. It was from another place where there was Indians. There were four sick [people] at this place, and he was wanted to come over there. So he got ready and went. And every night he went to these four different people and doctored these people. It was not long then they got better again. And then he came back.

He was a great man. People thought an awful lot of him, and he was also given many nice things all the time. And there was a girl that was very sick, and then he doctored her again and she got better. And this girl was given to him to marry. And he said to the parents of this girl that he would wait 'til he came back—that he was going to go out traveling first. "And when I come back, I will come for her." He also told the parents of this girl that he would take care of this girl. They understood what he meant. He was going to the Soo Indian country first for a battle. He was not intending to marry yet. He had a cross-cousin there, a man. And he went to see his cousin and told him, "That girl I doctored was given to me to marry, and I do not intend to get married yet and I want you to marry her, if she will have you. But don't tell her because I do not want to do anything to disappoint them. So just go to her, and if she likes you, just marry her."

So he came back to his own place, where he had a home. And all winter he hunted and trapped. And when spring came, he told the people there to make him a large wigwam, which they call *moshabewicomig*—and everything. He also gathered the men which he knew was fit to go with him to the Soo country. He told them to fast and *manitokaso*, and only those who had the birds of the air for *pawahguns* would go. And if anyone had some kind of a beast for *pawahgun*, such a one could not go.

He knew just how many days it would take him to go there and just what time they would overtake the Soo Indians, and he also knew that he would bring all the men safely back. So when forty days was up, they went away and traveled day and night, only stopping for a little time to *manitokaso*. And when they came to the place where it would only take half a day to get to the Soo

Indian country, they stopped there. And he said to the men that there was one in the bunch of men that had a beast as a *pawah-gun* and that it would be this man which would cause them some trouble. And he also told them that there was blood on their path, and whoever this man was, it would be best for him to go back from there and wait for them along their way. But no one seem to want to go back.

So they started off again. And when evening came, they came very close to the village of the Soos. They could just see the smoke from the fireplace of the Soos. And when night came—just at the time when people went to bed—then they crawled to the end of the village where they seen a wigwam and heard some women talking. They crawled closer, and there was two girls sitting near the fireplace talking and laughing and braiding their hair. They were nice-looking girls. And there was one old woman and another one already in bed. They did not know whether it was a man or [a] woman that was already in bed. So this man and another man crawled closer and watched these girls.

And after the girls went to bed, they crept into the wigwam and laid down beside these girls. And when the girls knew they were there, they took and covered them up. And when the girls spoke to them, they could not understand them and then the girls knew that they were Indians [Ojibwes], but they did not move. So he signaled to the girls to get up and come with them. Then he took one girl by the hand and pulled her up. She got up and smiled. Then she put her moccasins on. Also she took another pair of moccasins. Then she spoke to her sister. And she got up too and put her moccasins on, and she took her grandmother's moccasins. The men took them by the hand and led them out of the wigwam and took the girls to where the other men were. And then some of the men stayed there with the girls, and the rest went to the other end of the village and start to fight with the Soos.

This was at night. And they start shooting one another, and one of his men got shot. And they killed three men and pulled the skulls [scalps] off them and away they ran. And as they were running, they heard one man shouting. He knew right away it was one of his men. So he and this other man ran back and found him, wounded. And they picked him up and ran away. They came to where they left the girls and the other men and away they went.

It was coming daylight now, and they hid in a little bush. They could hear the galloping of many horses around them, and when the noise was dying away, they start walking. And as they were going along, he knew that the Soos was coming behind them. And he told his men they would have to stop. So they did stop. And he *manitokaso* and asked for a heavy rain. And right away, there was a heavy rain, thundering and lightening, and there was a heavy fog. Sure enough! They heard again the galloping of the Soo ponies going by. The Soos did not know that they were hiding near there.

And while they were there, he doctored this man that was wounded on the leg. He knew this was the one that he had dreamed would be shot. But none of the other men was wounded because they all had some kind of birds for *pahwagun*. And this man was the only one that had an animal for *pahwagun*. And that's why he was so clumsy. And while they were there, they heard the Soos coming back. They were all crying, every one of them. The girls were not a bit moved. They were glad to be taken away because they liked these two men that were bringing them home with them.

So they started off. And when they came to where the men left their canoes, one girl got in [the man's] canoe and the other girl got in [the other man's] canoe. These were the ones they liked.

And then, one morning early, they came along singing the war songs. And the people back there heard the men coming along singing. So they all got in their canoes and met the men. They were singing a war song with the words that they were bringing home three Soo Indian skulls and two Soo young girls. This was their war songs. The two young girls were lying flat in the canoes so that the Indians which were coming to meet them would not see them right away. And the women also met them. And also three canoes each had these three skulls hanging on a stick. They were tied in little frames, and the hair was just hanging down.

So when they came ashore, the Indians gave them a nice feast. And the women all got busy and start cutting poles. And in a short time, they made a dancing place with poles and brush. Then they took these Soo Indian skulls in this dancing place and start to have their war dance. And also the Soo young girls went in to watch the dance. All the people got some nice food ready and also some nice print and took it into this dancing place. This meant that they wanted to hold this Soo Indian skull, that they wanted to dance with it, them too. Old women too were just as anxious to lay hands on it. Even little babies that would be able to take [hold of] anything, they were given the Soo Indian skulls to hold. This was their style, but I do not know what it means.

And for four days, they danced. And they quit just before sunset. And they would start early in the morning. And there was one old man there. He was very bold. And when he would dance around, he would go very close to where these Soo Indian girls were sitting. And he would lift up his ax and want to hit the girls. But then he would dance away again. He did that many times. And the man did not like that, and he got up and talked: "I do not want anybody to do anything to these girls. I want them to live. That's why I brought them here. If I wanted them to die, I would've killed them myself. But I want to marry the girl I brought home. And also the other girl, well, she can marry the one that brought her here. So we will quit dancing right now. We will not have any trouble because I love this girl, me too [I do], and I don't want any[one] to kill her after I've brought her here."

So the dancing stopped, and he took these two Soo girls out. And the other man came, and they went home. The girls liked these men very much. Then they got ready and moved away. They camped from place to place making a living for themselves. The two Soo women use to sit together, talking and laughing, and their husbands could not understand. Only sometimes. And the men too use to sit and talk to one another, and also their wives hardly understood what they were talking about. So all summer they lived around.

And when fall came, the man had an *ogima* dance for the first time. There were many people there again that came to his dance. He sang eight *ogima* dances. They were long dances. Then, after he sang those eight songs, he got up and said that was enough. And he also told the Indians that there were some strange Indians near—just like they were watching from close [by] there. And he went out and explained to his wife that there was Soo Indians near. She made signs to him to get ready and get in their canoe.

So he told the Indians to do this too. And they did. Only one old woman and her old man stayed. The old man said that he was going to eat first before he went. He also said that this man was such a *manito* as to know everything. The people kept on calling to these old people to hurry, but they were awfully stubborn. They denied what this man said. They thought they knew more than him. So the other people all moved to the mouth of Pasgandibâwisibing, and they all camped there preparing for their enemies, the Soos, to overtake them. And in a short time, they could hear shouts from where they moved. They knew that these old people were getting killed.

And when they went to see, the old people were killed, and their skulls pulled off. So the man got mad. And he told the men that he was going to follow these men—that he knew exactly where they were stopping, and he could overtake them if he hurried. So some of the other men went along with him. Also his wife went along with him.

And early the next morning, they came to the place where they were hiding, and him and his wife crawled closer. There was some man there mending one of his moccasins. He had his back towards them, and they could tell that he was a young man. And there was another one sleeping. Also other ones. And all at once, one of the Soo men seen them watching them, and he jumped up and ran off. And also the other ones ran away. And this young man that was sewing his moccasins jumped up with only one moccasin on and ran. The man took his gun, and as he was aiming to shoot, his wife grabbed him and made signs for him not to shoot. So he lowered his gun, and then the young man kept on running. All at once, he fell to the ground. He gave up because his bare foot hurt when he was running. His wife ran and dropped to her knees beside this young man. It was her brother. The other Soo Indians got away. But they came home with this young man, his wife's brother. And when they got there, the Indians [Ojibwes] nearly killed him. But the man pleaded for him to live.

So after that, they went away and went to a hunting place where they stayed all winter long. Sometimes he use to be afraid of his wife and brother-in-law. He use to imagine when they were talking that they were saying, "Let's kill him and leave him here." But then they would laugh. He learned his wife and her brother to talk a little Indian [Ojibwe]. Also they learned him to talk Soo. So when spring came, they moved back to the summer camping ground again.

And then his wife had twins, a boy and girl. And the twins grew up and three more children came: two girls and one boy. So they all lived.

And he was a great *manitokaso*, *ogima* dance[r], *wahbahno* dance[r], *jisuki*, *nahdahwiah* and also other kinds of *manitokaso*.

And then the twin girl grew up to be a woman and received her first sickness [menstruation]. She had a wigwam of her own back in the bush for ten days. And when she came back, she went with her mother and went to pick berries. And when they came back, she made a feast to eat these blueberries for the first time. Then her mother told her to cook. She had her monthlies again, so she cooked and set a place for her father to eat. And when they got through eating, her father said to her, "Did anyone come here today?" And she said, "No." And he said, "I've eaten something that's dirty." Then he start vomiting for a long time, and all at once, a little bird fell from his mouth. He took his medicine rattler and tried to doctor it, but it died. So then he had nothing now. He lost all his *manitokaso*. Everything. And he was very weak. It was [caused by] his own daughter, when she had her sickness and when getting up and walking back and forth. [That was] why he was like that.

But he never said anything to his daughter because she could not help it. He got to be very old. All his children grew up. Also his brother-in-law got married to an Indian [Ojibwe] woman and had children. So there were quite a few Soo Indians in Pasgandibâwisibing. The end.[1]

24

It Won't Be Her

That Will Know

This is just another short story of some people who were all living in one place doing all kinds of things such as dancing and *midewi*. And there was one young man there that was sick, and all kinds of *nahdahwiah* men were doctoring him. Some were *jisukis* and other kinds of *manitokaso*. And there was one young girl there who was a queer person. She hardly ever spoke and never paid any attention to what was going on. Also she never went anyplace where there was amusement. And one morning she said to her father—he was an old man, and he was one of those that were doctoring this young man—"Father," she said, "You *jisuki* last night. Did you not have some kind of feeling that there are strange people watching us here?" And her father said, "No." And she said, "I'm afraid that there is some strange person watching us every day."

So her father went around telling the Indians. But no one would listen to her. They said, "It won't be her that will know if anything is going to happen to us. There are men here every night that *manitokaso*. Surely they would know if there was anyone around."

So again that night she went to bed and slept. She wakened all at once and knew someone was fussing around her. She sat up and felt the hair of this person. It was a man with long hair. His hair was like horsetail hair. The man shook her and told her not to tell.

So he went out. She did not say anything until that morning. She told her father they would move that night to a big island. She also went to her sister and told her to get things ready. Also her grandmother. She told her father how this man came there that night. She knew it was not one of the young men there. It was a Soo. She could tell by the feeling of his hair. The old man told the Indians to move. Also to take this sick man to this island. But no one would listen to him or his daughter.

So that evening they got ready. Her parents, sister, grandmother, and some other relatives all got in their canoes and went to this big island. On the other side of this island, they camped. They never made a light, as they were afraid that the Soos would see the light. Some other old women too got in their canoes and went to the island. But all the men stayed there, as they did not want to get the name of a coward. Her people never knew or seen her to *manitokaso*. But she use to do it secretly.

And after they were over [on the island] for one night, she said again, "The Soos are watching the Indians [Ojibwes] all day long and are watching for a good chance to overtake them. They are going to try and take a girl along alive." Then she thought of the girl that was staying alone in the bush for receiving her first sickness [menstruation]. She then again *manitokaso*, and she said, "I wish those two older girls would have sense enough to go and get their sister and bring her here." And sure enough! The three girls came there that night. And some more old women and also women with their children came. The Indians over there would not come. And there were about ten wigwams of Indians there now. She was always scared. She was always looking towards the place where the Indians were on the mainland.

And when they were there three nights, she could not sleep that night. She knew for sure the Soo Indians would overtake the Indians [Ojibwes] in the morning. And sure enough! Early that morning, all at once, they could hear men shouting and yelling, and they also could hear shots. Some of the Indians anyway had time to jump into their canoes and came to the island. Eight of the Indians were killed right away. The sick man was killed.

And there was a girl, she was the very first person which one of the Soo men went into her wigwam and tried to do something to her. She jumped up and yelled. And all the men jumped up. But some of the men could not find their guns, as already early that night someone went around and stole their guns that had power enough—so as not to waken the men. So eight of them were killed. There was ten of the Soo Indians. Only then those that hardly got away thought, "Why didn't we do as this girl told us to do?" If they had listened to this girl, they would have prepared for it and have their guns ready. Also [they would] dig holes and send their children away, as that is what they use to do when anyone would know that the Soo Indians were near. But they would not listen to this girl because she was never anybody and was always alone. But they found out for themselves.

This young girl, she jumped into a canoe—and also another woman and her two children—and they pushed all the canoes out on the lake so the Soos could not go after them. And they went to the island. The fog was so thick no one could see them. But the shots were passing by them.

Also there was another girl there. She was so scared she could not even move. So at last, she ran down to the river and hid among the tall grass. And she seen everything that was going on.

The Indian [Ojibwe] men killed three of the Soos, and after, the Soos ran away with the three bodies. As soon as they were out of sight, she could hear them crying along [the way]. And as she was standing there, she seen one of the men move and then fall down again. She was afraid to go and help him. At last he got up and came walking slow down to the river. And there was two canoes floating around. He got into one of these canoes and shoved his canoe along. He was bloody all over. His arm was broke. She watched him go around the bay out onto the lake. Just as he went around that bay, two Soo men came running down and took all their guns, blankets, and other things and away they went.

She sat there for a long time, for she was so scared. And this man whose arm was broken, he went along yelling, and the people at the island heard him and they said, "I guess that's an Indian [Ojibwe]."

And the woman that came away from there with her two kids knew it was her husband's voice. Then she got into her canoe and brought him back to the island. He was just covered with blood. Also his skull [scalp] was taken off. But he lived again. Came back to life. And the girl, she was still standing in the water. A paddle floated to her, and she grabbed it. A little while after, another paddle floated to her. She also took that. This was now in the afternoon. And then a canoe floated around there, and the little waves dashed it near to where she was standing. She took this paddle and hooked and brought it closer. Then she grabbed this canoe. She waited 'til it got dark, for she was afraid the Soos must be there someplace watching for someone to come back. She got in the canoe and went slowly along without making any noise. She came out on the lake and paddled to the island. She was more scared when she was coming close to the island that the Indians might shoot her. She went along slowly. She heard someone say, "Who are you?" Like it was a little bird. And right away she answered and called herself by name. And the woman said to her, "You are alive, eh? And we thought you were dead." Then she said, "Oh yes. It was just by a miracle why I'm alive." So she got to the island.

There were some men that were out hunting at the time when the Soos came. And the next day, they came home and found no one over there but just the bodies of these people which were killed. And they said, "Surely they must've gone to that island." So they went to the island and found their wives and children unharmed. So the next day, they came back to the mainland and dug holes to bury those that were killed. They heard the Soo Indians going along crying, and they came around them. And that was why they knew the Soos were there. And then they came right home and found the bodies lying around.

This man whose arm was broken lived anyway—and his skull was cut off! So never again did the Indians not do what anyone said. They always were prepared. And the men were so angry that the next summer they went and killed some of the Soos, them too. So then they came home safely. Everyone of them. This is the end of this.[1]

25

I Knew I Could Go There and

Bring Home a Man for Myself

This is the story of a young girl. Her *dodem* was a caribou. When she was about seventeen years old, she fell in love with a married man. Of course, he was young. But he had a wife and two children. Still, she flirted with him. And then, this man got ready and said he wanted to go [to] the Soo Indian country for a battle with the Soos. And for four nights, the men got ready. They also danced for four nights. And all that time, she was in the bush alone making many pairs of moccasins. Her mother wondered why she was doing this. She never told anybody what she intended to do.

Then, that morning when the Indians were ready to go, the women use to paddle along a little ways with the men and tease them, splashing water on them. This was the style of the Indians long ago. Then the women missed the girl. She was not there any-place. Then, when after they came back she was not there either, her mother looked for her all over. She missed her daughter's canoe and blanket. So she did not say anything, for she knew then her daughter was going along with the men to *nuhdoobuhni*. She also thought she must know for sure that she can come back safely again by some kind of *manitokaso*. Why she is going, of course, she did not know—that her daughter was in love with one of the married men that were gone.

And as the men were going, this man got off. For he knew this girl was waiting for him there, as they had planned to go with one another long ago. And he got into her canoe. And when they came to Warroad, they got off there and start to walk from there as that's why it's called Kuhbaikuhnong when the Indians use to stop there with canoes and then walk from there to go and battle with the Soos.

And as they were going, when they would stop at dinnertime, the headman would tell all the men to *manitokaso*. He would also ask her if she knew of anything to help her through—why she came along. She never said anything, but she started to *manitokaso*. And she made a speech of a little wren and that was the best thing to have a dream of—especially on going to war with the Soos. The headman said that it was all right for her to go.

She was always walking behind with this man whom she ran after. And then they came to a place where the headman said that they were all suppose to *manitokaso*. And everyone did. And she said, "We are in danger. I think I see blood on our path ahead." And one of the men use to never *manitokaso*. And the headman told him, if he did not know of anything to help him through, it was best for him to come home, as it would be all his fault if they would get beat. So the man came back home. As he was not fit to go along, he would surely be killed. Then, when she start to *manitokaso*, she did not see any blood on their path again. So the headman said, "Tomorrow morning we will overtake the Soo Indians." But she said, "No. We will not have time to wait that long, as there is a river here a little ways. It goes into a lake. And just before noon, some of the Soo Indians will pass here. They are moving, and that will be the best time. We will see them."

So they did go to the river and waited for the Soos to pass by. And sure enough! The Soos were paddling by, and they overtook them. Her husband, or lover, killed one first, and she ran and cut the skull [scalp] off. He also killed another. And the other men killed one. So that was three they killed. And away they came home.

And the women here also used to watch for the men day after

day. So one morning just about near noon, they could see the men coming a way far. They were coming along singing. They sounded so nice, as the new *nuhdoobuhnis* were saying, "So that's how the Soo heads look." That was their songs. And the older men were singing, "She is bringing home one Soo Indian head." And also she came along singing, "Yes. It wasn't just for nothing why I did go after the men. I knew I could go there and bring home a head. Also a man for myself." All the men joined in singing with her right away. Also over there where the people were waiting, they were singing and rejoicing with the ones which were all coming home safely. For they all knew that everyone was alive. For if there was one dead, they would also come crying. And that was why they knew everyone was alive.

So they came ashore, for everything was prepared for them. The wife of this man did not say anything when she seen her husband coming home with this girl also coming right to her wigwam. She was just as happy and proud as the rest of them. She was dancing away with this Soo Indian skull which her husband killed and brought home.

So then he had two wives and also got so many feathers for his bravery. Then everybody lived happily hereafter. He had children with his new wife, and his wives never quarreled either. His *dodem* was a *wasisee*, a bullhead. Well, this is the end of this story.

26

He Gave Her a Folded
Birch-Bark Map

This is a story of a Cree woman. They were living someplace near the prairie. She was just a young girl living with her parents and another sister younger than her. Her sister was lame. And there were also some other people living there. This was on the river in Winnipeg—somewhere around there. She was a very lively girl. Smart. And she use to work around doing things. They also had shacks and wigwams outside these shacks.

And one evening, she was doing something, going back and forth from the river to their shack, and as she was going down again, she seen a man lying on the side of the road. She ran back and told her mother, but her mother would not believe it. So she did not go again. And later on, the old woman told her husband. And he said, "Why do you think so strange of it? We have two young girls here. It is not strange for a man to come around here—unless no one wishes for our daughters at all."

So no one mentioned it again. And after everyone was gone to bed, the lame girl could not sleep. She was sleeping with her sister. She thought she heard someone walking around outside just like as if trying to get in. Then she would speak to her father. And at last, her father told her to shut up and to go to sleep. So she did not say anything again, and she fell asleep.

And early the next day, the other girl got up and went right out to see her net. There was a heavy fog that morning. And as she was busy taking the fish out of her net, all at once three men in a canoe were right beside her holding her canoe. And as she was just going to holler, one man grabbed her by the mouth, and she hardly made any noise. And she pulled his hand away and made another noise. And this time she was gagged with an old rag. They threw her in their canoe and tied her up.

And this lame girl, she got up as soon as her sister went out. And she heard her making this noise. She told her father to hurry up. She was afraid her sister was drowning. The old man ran over there and yelled to his daughter. There was no answer back. Of course, they could not see, for the fog was too heavy. And only when it cleared away, they seen her canoe floating around. And the other canoe, which was along the shore, that was missing. And then they knew that she was taken away by somebody.

These men took her along. She was all tied up in the canoe. She wiggled hard and would nearly upset the canoe. She did not understand what they were saying, but she knew they were Soo Indian men. And each time she would move, one of the men would lift up his little ax and want to hit her. So she did not move again, as she knew he was ready to kill her at any time. And when they came to the road at White Horse Plain, they all got out. They lifted her out, and they put a big stone in this canoe and shoved it out on the river. They also threw the paddles in this canoe. And she remembered which way the wind was takin' it and also just where it would come ashore.

There was one older man there and two young men. One of these young men was quiet and nice looking. But the older man was homely, and she was awfully scared of him. She did not mind the other two. And he made her walk all the time. She use to be so tired! And when they would stop to eat something, this man would dance around her, lift up his ax, and make signs that he would cut her skull [scalp] off while the other young man would be singing. And the nice-looking one would never say a word but go right on cooking. Or he never smiled when this man was dancing. He acted as if he pitied her. And she too depended on him.

She use to walk along tied onto one of the men. And she would look around trying to remember which way they were going. Also how the place looked. She never cried. These two men would try to make her laugh. They would tickle her. Also do many things, but she never smiled but always sat with her head down. She use to go along too and break little sticks with her feet. Of course, they never let her do anything. And they walked all day and all night, and towards morning, the men slept and the other one went some other place. He came back just at noon bringing some spuds and corn. And they cooked the spuds and also the corn. And the men slept again, and she couldn't sleep at all. She could not untie herself, and she said, "Oh. I use to dream long ago that I could get out [even] if I was tied in iron." But before she could do anything, they all wakened, and they started off again. She was so tired.

Towards morning, they stopped again and they ate. They gave her some hard grease to eat, and she took this grease and rub[bed] some on the ropes on her wrists [and] also other places where she was tied. And after they got through, the man start to sing, and the other one danced around her and would always lift up his ax to hit her. And then he would laugh. And after that, they all lay down. They tied her onto their legs, and they all went to sleep. They also covered her up with an old blanket.

She lay down, and she thought, "I use to dream of a big ant. I wish it would come here and chew up this rope. And I wish these men would sleep soundly." And she also fell asleep.

And when she awakened, the sun was up high, and it was very hot. She got up very quiet. She knew this big ant was chewing away at this rope on her wrist because it was greasy. And just as the rope was to fall apart, this young man whom she liked lifted up his head and seen her sitting there. There were tears in her eyes, for she knew if she could not get away from them, she would be killed or be abused by the Soo Indians. The young man got up

He Gave Her a Folded Birch-Bark Map 169

very quietly, and he came closer to her, and he took her face in his hands and looked at her for a while. She could not keep her tears back. Then he took and kissed her. Then he took his knife and cut the ropes from these men's feet and also cut her loose and made signs for her to jump. And he gave her a folded birch bark and also made signs for her to take both these other two men's moccasins and throw them away along the road. And she did jump and ran away as fast as she could run. She opened this birch bark. Here it was—a map of the road!

She ran all day. She knew this young man must of planned for her to escape—why he made this map for her also. Before she left him, he made signs to her that, if she did not come away, she would be killed as soon as she was brought to the Soo Indian country. And when she seen the places where she broke the sticks, she knew she was on the right road. And when night came, she was so scared that she did not [know] when she went off the road. And she dropped down and fell asleep, as she was so tired.

And when she wakened again, the sun was up high. She got up and looked around. She looked at her map but could not understand it. So she started off anyway. She did not know where to go, but anyway she went. Night came again, and she slept. Next morning, she start walking again. She could not get anywhere. And the third night she heard some kind of noise. It sounded like a bull, and she got scared again, for she thought maybe it was a buffalo. For she did not know whether she was coming closer to the prairie or leaving it further. And then morning came again.

She never had a thing to eat all that time nor anything to drink, but she did not feel hungry or thirsty. But she was afraid there— lost in the wild bush. Night came again, and she slept again. Next morning, she got up and start walking again. Soon she came to a narrow path, and she start walking on this narrow path. Soon she seen stumps where someone had been cutting trees. She walked along although she was afraid, for she thought maybe they were Soos. But she kept on anyway. Soon, she came to a wider road, and it led her to a big clearing where there were many little stacks of wild hay.

She kept right on. She seen a little shack in this clearing, and she went along outside the wooden fence. And as she was getting closer, she seen a woman walking around. There was a lot of cows around the field. And she said to herself, "This must be one of the cows I heard night before last." And when this woman seen her, she waved and came running to meet her. She was a white old lady. She took her by the hand, led her into the house, and asked her if she was hungry. She did not understand, but the old woman made her understand by signs and gave her something to eat. Only then she knew she was hungry! She was very thin, for that was four days she never ate a thing and she was always on the go. Her old clothes were ragged. Also her moccasins. And her hair was all strangled up, as she [had] never combed [it] since she was taken away from her parents.

And when she got through eating, this old lady's husband come and her two sons. She told them how this Cree girl come there. And then they asked her if she was the one that was lost. And she said, "Yes." They also asked her by signs how she come to be alive and got away from the Soos. She also made them understand that the Soos were sleeping, and [she] cut the ropes and got away. Also how many days she was in the bush without food. These white people were very good to her. They made a nice, soft place for her on the floor to sleep. And did she sleep good that night and rest! They told her that already some Indians came there and told these people she was lost and if she happened to be found, that she was to be kept there 'til the boat would pass there again sometime. The men got their guns ready in case the Soos came there to look for her. But they never came there.

The next day the old woman washed [clothes], and she offered to help her but the old lady would not let her go outside. Instead, she was told to do something inside or to sit down and rest. She use to wonder what the white people meant every night and morning: they would kneel down and talk. And when they would get up, the old lady would come over and pat her on the shoulder and point towards heaven. She use to think it very nice to hear them talking.

She stayed there for a few days. And one time, another white man and his wife came there, and they were talking for a long time. Of course, she could not understand what they were saying. And this man made signs for her to go along with them. She hated to leave this old lady, but she did not want to refuse. So she went along, got in this rowboat, and she was taken down the river. She did not know if this was the same river that went out on the lake where she was taken away from. This woman was talking to her very rough. She even made her lie down in the canoe so no one would see her. And she did. And they just went a little ways, and then they come to their own place. They were talking to each other very hard. She understood they were quarreling. And the woman told her to get out. And she did. Also the woman made her go into the house right away. And for two or three days, she stayed there. The woman was very mean to her, and she was always locked in an old shack where no one would see her. And the woman hardly ever gave her anything to eat.

Then, one time, another old man came there with a younger woman. This woman talked to them for a long time. She could not understand, but, anyway, she knew they were talking about her. Then the young man start to talk for a long time. Then the old man told her she could go along with them. And she did go along with them. And when they brought her to their own place, the young man went to the stable and hitched up his horses and told her to get on the wagon. And she did. He went back into the house and brought out a gun and away they came.

After they went a long ways, the place seemed to look familiar to her, and she knew she was close to her parents now. She felt like jumping off the wagon and walking the rest of the way! She could now see the bay where the Hudson's Bay store was. And the young man never said anything to her. At last they came up to the shacks. She did not know what to do. A woman came running out.

She was Cree, and she said, "Oh, you are alive! We all thought you dead. And your people are all so very lonely. Your dad is just brokenhearted." And the Hudson's Bay man was very glad. He gave her clothes to put on and took her home to her parents. Her father then got better and rejoiced [and] gave a big feast with a regular speech and told the people he was happy his daughter was found alive. He always thought the Soos were going along making fun of her. The end.[1]

27

The Moose Was
Wise Enough to
Bring the Boy Back

This story is of an Indian the white people called the old dog driver. He use to always drive dogs. He lived at Hungry Hall right at the mouth of the Rainy River. He use to wear deerskin pants and a moose-hide coat all trimmed with muskrat fur. And his cap was of otter skin. And his mitts were of muskrat fur. This was how he dressed in the winter times. And he would always drive some dogs. He used to go back and forth to Nikaseewiniguming and Hungry Hall. And one time he went to a place called Yellow Girl, Osakwiuese. He heard there was a girl over there who was very smart. She could do all kinds of beadwork. And when he saw her, he wished for her. So he went to that place, and he gave an otter skin and one beaver skin, a blanket, gun, and canoe to this old man and asked for his daughter. So the girl was given to him to marry, and he did marry this girl. And the old man gave him a blanket and a shotgun and a canoe.

And so he came away with his new wife, and he come to this place they call Nikaseewiniguming. And they lived there. And they use to put out a garden every spring. He had a little bear he raised and a little moose, and he also had four dogs. And they had a little boy. And one day they went out picking berries when their boy was about four years old. They made a swing for the boy, and the woman watched her boy from there. And once, when she looked to see where her boy was, she could not see the boy. So they ran all over looking for him. He was lost.

They were crying and running all over the woods. And after they couldn't find him there, they ran along the shore. And the woman was running along crying. And when she looked, she could see a moose coming and another baby moose and a little boy behind. Here was her little boy!

She did not hear her little boy when he said, "Oh, look at the little moose!" And he [had] chased after it. And the big moose was wise enough to bring the boy back. This was the same moose the man raised. When it got big, he had let it go. And it had a little moose, and this was the little moose the little boy ran after. They were so glad and thankful that the moose brought their boy back. The boy was gone for about two hours. And all that time they ran all over.

And when they got into their canoe, they could see the moose still standing looking at him. He was as tame as a horse. He use to go and pat him on the head. But the little moose he couldn't get a hold of him. The moose stayed on a big island there at the lake, and he made a mark on its ear when it was small. He never went there to hunt for moose. He use to go to a different place far away from there to kill a moose. He was so used to it he never felt right when he killed a moose. And one time, another man killed a moose on that island, and it had a mark on its ear. And when he went there again, he didn't see his tame moose. Then he knew it was killed.

He was a good hunter also, and one time he went out moose hunting. He was paddling back and forth there taking moose meat home. And one time he had a whole moose in his canoe going home. The lake was calm. No wind at all. And he seen some kind of a beast stick its head out of the water. It had long horns on its head. This was right up beside this island. And after it went back into the water, he seen a bunch of foam coming towards him. He got scared and started to paddle fast, but it was coming faster. He took some tobacco and put it in the water. But still it did not stop. And he said, "Well, I guess I will perish here. Whatever it is that is destroying me." He took the moose hindquarters and the arms and threw them into the water. He knew he was sinking now. But it didn't stop. Then he took the heart and threw that into the water. Only then it stopped—as if someone let him go. Then he paddled as hard as he could right away. It got dark, and it began to rain and thunder and lightening. He got ashore to this big island and stayed there 'til the storm was over.

And after the wind stopped blowing, he put his canoe into the water and was just about to start when he heard somebody talking. They were saying, "What a joke we did on that man when we scared him to give us that meat which was to be given to his twins!" And they would laugh. He wondered who they were, and then he heard another voice sound like an old man saying, "Sh! Don't say that. You should be thankful youse got the meat. You should not make fun of it." And he looked around, but he could not see who they were.

He was there all night. And in the morning, he went home. And when he got to their old log shack, it was so still. But he could see there was fire inside. And when he went in, he seen his wife sitting on something soft and there was something covered beside her. And the woman said, "Guess what I have." And he said, "I can't guess." And she uncovered a pair of twin girls, and only then he thought of what he heard them saying on the lake—whoever they were. He was so thankful he had put the meat into the water. And he asked his wife how she ever managed giving birth to the twins herself alone with all her pains. And she said she tried to do her best, and it wasn't very hard. And his little boy was sleeping. The woman said the boy cried because they were girls. He wanted a little boy so he could play with him. And they told him not to cry, that his little sisters would sew and wash his clothes for him. So he was pleased with that. And they stayed there. The woman got better, and the girls were growing.

And when they got to be about four years old, the man again was out hunting. He was gone for three days. And as he was coming home—just as he was quite a ways out on the lake—he seen a pack of wolves making for him. He had his toboggan full of meat. So he let go his toboggan, grabbed his gun, and ran back towards the shore and climbed up a tree. And the wolves just got there. There were twenty of them, and they started digging the tree and some tried to climb the tree. And he started shooting them, and he killed eight and wounded four so they couldn't walk. And all his shells were gone, and he started setting fire to rags. He tore up his shirt and the little dried branches and all the things he could set fire to and threw them down. And the eight wolves hated the smoke, and they ran away. And when they were far away, he went down from this tree and killed the four he wounded. He was so worried that his children would be out on the ice playing. His home was just around the point. So he started off running, and when the wolves seen him, they stopped and looked at him. And sure enough! When he got to the point his girls were playing on the ice. He yelled to them to run home. And they did. And then he went back for his twelve wolves.

And later on, his wife got sick and died, and one of his twin girls died. And his other daughter got to be a woman and got married. And his son was quite a man. So he stayed there in the same place for many years. He was awfully lonesome staying there alone. So he got married to a widow woman like himself. And he was married for another eighteen years. His daughter died. He didn't have any children with this widow woman. They were both too old to have children. She had sons at Hungry Hall, and in the wintertime they used to stay at Hungry Hall or they use to go back and forth.

And one time when he was going to his trapping place, as he was coming back, he seen someone crawling on his knees, and he went up to him. Here it was a white man nearly froze! So he put this old man on his sleighs, and his dog team brought him home. And then he brought him to Rainy River. He was froze all over on his feet, hands, and face. The old man paid him for saving him, and the old man thought an awful lot of him.

And after the old white man got better, he lived near the lake. And when the old dog driver use to go back and forth to his trapping place, he use to stop at this white man's place. And again one time, as he was passing there, the white man asked him to stop and have dinner with him. And the man went in. This white man had a fox hanging which he killed. When he went out and went for water, the old dog driver got up and started fingering at the fox skin. And when the white man come in, he prepared their dinner. The old man forgot to wash his hands. So they had their dinner. And after they got through, he started off. And he just went a little ways when he started to have convulsions on his hands. And he stopped and made a fire. And when he knew it wouldn't stop, he came back to this white man's shack. And the man put him in a sleigh and brought him home. You see the fox was poisoned, and the old man didn't know. And he got poisoned too. The white man hired a horse from there and brought him to town, but they couldn't do anything. He only lived ten days, and then he died.

So that was the end of the old dog driver. The white man was very sorry to see him die, for it was only because of him that he was still alive. So he was buried. And the old woman lived for ten years. Then she also died. This is the end of this story.[1]

28

She Knew the Bear Wanted
Her to Go Someplace

This is the story of a family. A man had two daughters and two sons and another baby tied in a cradle. He and his wife were living south of Red River near the prairie. And in the fall, people long ago use to move away to their camping grounds for the winter. And so when fall came, these people moved away to their own camping grounds where they use to go every winter. When they got there, they made a large wigwam big enough for all of them. [They were] also getting everything else for the winter. The two girls were grown up, for they were the oldest of them all. The two boys were also quite a size.

They all went to set lynx snares in different directions. The two girls use to go together. Also the boys. But the man use to go alone, and the woman always stayed home with her baby girl. The man brought home a lot of meat. They also had many hides on frames the woman was working at. And one morning, the man said to his children, "Never go anyplace alone. And always take a gun." Because he had seen the tracks of many wolves, and they were very large and he was afraid the wolves would overtake one of his children if they were alone. And he said that if they knew the wolves were near, to make a big fire and stay near the fire, as fire was the thing wolves were afraid of. So when the boys and girls were out hunting, they were always on the lookout for wolves, but they never seen any tracks where they went. And so every day they use to go hunting and bringing home fur and also other things. And soon they forgot about what their father said to them.

And one morning again, their father went early, and the girls also got ready to go and see the lynx snares. And the boys also went to see their traps. And the woman was just the one staying home. So after she put her baby to sleep, she start cutting wood. And she also start to carry in some snow to melt so she could cook some meat and corn for her children and husband. And as she was carrying in snow, she looked up and seen a pack of wolves coming very near her. She jumped up and ran toward the wigwam, but she just got halfway, and the wolves sprang upon her and tore her right up to pieces and ate her up.

And there was a big stage full of bear meat and moose meat, fish and rabbits, and the boys were the ones coming home soon. And the youngest was running ahead of the dog team. There was two dogs, and as they were coming around the bend of the road, he seen someone trying to spring onto the stage of meat. He knew right away it was wolves. He drew back and told his brother, and he looked too. He seen many wolves rushing around the wigwam and the hides, and he told his brother to climb up a tree there and gave him some birch. Then he untied his two dogs and let them go. The dogs ran home, and the wolves killed them right away. And the oldest boy said that he would go back and run across the bush to the road which his sisters would come from. He knew his sisters would come along talking and laughing, and the wolves would hear them and they would also be ate up.

So away he ran. And sure enough! When he got on the road, he seen his sisters coming. They were talking. He ran as fast as he could and made signs to them to be quiet. One of the girls said, "Look at that boy running to meet us. I wonder what's wrong with him." And when he came closer, he said, "Be quiet and don't talk. There's a pack of wolves where our wigwam is, and they are trying to get on the meat stage. I do not know whether our mother is alive or dead." So they did not know what to do. They were afraid to go home, and yet they wanted to know whether their mother was alive or dead. And also their baby sister.

So they started for home very quietly. They went along making big blazing fires on the road. And when they came closer, they made another big fire, and then they came in sight of their wigwam. It was very still. Of course, they had two guns and the other girl had an ax. So they went closer, and they could hear their baby sister crying. Then they knew that their mother was killed. They ran into the wigwam. Their youngest brother was already there trying to stop the baby from crying. He told them, when he seen the wolves going away, he came down from the tree and ran home and found his little baby sister alone. Then he started to cry, and the baby wakened also. And then he tried to stop it from crying. They went out, and all they could see was blood all over and the guts, bones, and head of their poor mother. So the girls right away picked up what was left of their mother, and they tied it up in a new tanned moose hide. They seen the tracks of the wolves coming from the way their father had went that morning. And the tracks had gone back the same way.

Then they tied the bones of their mother on a toboggan and got everything else ready which they needed. Their little baby sister was crying. They could not stop it because it wanted to nurse. The girls made some soup and gave it to the baby to drink. The baby would stop crying for a little while. So they started off, pulling the toboggan along. And as they were walking along, they were afraid of the wolves very much. As they were going along, they came to the place where their father had been ate up. All that was left of him too was the head, guts, and the bones with the flesh eaten off. He must of made a fire, and as the fire was going out, he was going for another stick of wood and this was when the wolves ate him up. After they finished him, then they followed the road to the wigwam and ate up the woman.

Then they gathered up the remains of their poor father and tied it up in another new tanned hide and put it alongside the remains of their mother.

They traveled four days, stopping to camp three nights. Then they came to a farm where there was a house and farmers. There was a woman there, and these farmers took pity on them and made them stay in a little storehouse where there was a little stove. Then this white woman got some cow's milk and put it in a bottle and tied a rag onto it like a nipple. The baby did nurse on it for a while. But the baby cried and cried. It could not be comforted. The girls were all tired out, and the farmers told them to stay there. They could not understand them talking, but by signs they could tell what happened by the signs they were making.

So they stayed and slept there that night. And the next day, they were too tired to start off again. The farmers were very good to them, also giving them some nice things to eat. And also the men asked them if they would not let the men bury the remains of their parents there someplace. But they refused as they wanted to take them to where Indians were and to make a real burial speech on them. And that same day, the wolves came following their trail right to where they were staying. But the farm men killed two of the wolves. They were black wolves from the north, the same ones that killed their mother and father. One of the wolves got away.

And the next day, they started off again. But still they were in fear of this other wolf, although it was wounded and there was houses here and there. And all day they walked, and they came to the place they call Saging [Fort Alexander]. This is where the Hudson's Bay post was, and there was also a [Roman] Catholic school there. And then they told the people how it all happened. And the next day, their parents were buried by the Indians. Then the people took pity on them. And the Hudson's Bay man was told about all that happened. So he took these two boys and put them in this Catholic school, and he also got work for the two girls. And at the same time too, they were learned how to read and write. And their baby sister? Well, it couldn't be stopped from crying, and it could not be fed either. So it died of starvation four days later, although many of the women done their best to try and feed it. And then this one was buried too. And also the youngest boy was very lonely. His grief was very deep over the loss of his parents and little sister. He could not stand it. Although he was put in this school, where there were many other boys playing, he got thinner every day. And late in the spring, he died of loneliness.

And then there were only three left. And the oldest girl, some people took her or else adopted her. The man was a French half-breed, and he was married to a Cree woman. They weren't what you call well off, but they wanted her there to help them with the work around their place. They had cows because they were farmers. And so for four years, she stayed with them. For two years she went to school, and the other two years she helped around. She knew how to milk and tend to the cows. Also she did the housework, washing, and cleaning up. She was a good worker, and she was not a very crazy girl either. In fact, she was very quiet—[different] from the type of girls these days. But she was ruined.

The woman was always sickly because she was having kids. And so the girl was left alone to do most of the work to help this man. At last, he did not even let his wife help him [with] anything. He only wanted the young girl to go with him to get hay, or when he would go out hunting ducks, he wanted her to go along. She never thought anything of this man until one time he tried to make love to her. She did not want him, but he forced her to. And she was scared of him because he threatened to destroy her. And he also gave her clothes and money without letting his wife know anything about it. And, at last, this girl knew she was to become a mother. She did not know what to do, or she did not know whom to go to with her trouble. But she stayed right on and worked as hard as ever. She could not hide, for she was beginning to be in the shape now when she couldn't hide anymore. And the woman also knew it was her husband's child.

So one day when her husband wasn't home, she start to scold this girl and fight her. Then she threw her out—and all her clothes.

[The girl] gathered up her clothes, and an old woman took her in. Her baby was born soon, and then, when the time came for the Indians to go out buffalo hunting, she got ready to go too. And as the people were going, she nursed her baby first, and then she took it to the father of the baby. He was cutting wood. She gave the baby to him and told him to keep it—that she didn't want it. So away she went—leaving her baby behind.

She went along helping the people, and she was paid good, for she was very smart. The men were bringing back pemmican and buffalo hides to the Hudson's Bay [post]. And one time, someone asked her who she left her baby with. She said that she gave it back to the father. And they said she was very brave to give her baby away. And she said, "Yes, I'm brave. If there were anybody going to the Soo Indian country I would soon go along." The men said she couldn't go because she was too much of a coward—why she was saying all these things. They were all against her. They even said to her to that she couldn't take this French half-breed away from this woman when she tried to do it. She did not care what was said to her.

And about four days later, they seen people coming. These were the men who were going to the Soo Indian country for a battle. And some of the men there yelled to her: "Here come the men that's going for a battle." They were just teasing her. She jumped up and said, "I'm going along. I don't care if I get killed either. I was going to die long ago anyway, but it was only [for] my brother and sister why I lived. And now I don't care if I die because I throwed my baby away, and I also disgraced myself by having a child with a married man." So she went.

The men did not want her to go, but one man said to let her go—that they would use her for bait. So they did let her go. And when they came near where the Soos were camping, they stayed there that night and was going to wait for morning. They all fell asleep. Because the Soo Indian chief knew that the Indians were near, the Soos came there and circled around them. The chief also knew there was one woman there that was going to be used for bait, and he told the men not to kill her.

And she wakened from her sleep. She knew the Soos circled around them, so she start crawling towards the bush. The Soo men were laying down. They made room for her so she could crawl out. She jumped up and ran, and as she was running along, she come to a hole and she crawled in. Soon she heard yelling. She knew the battle was on. She did not move. She knew she would be found anyway.

And as she was sitting in this dark place listening to the shouts of men, someone came to the door of the hole and crawled in. She was not scared. It came closer and lay down. It would push her in more. Once in a while, she felt it, and it had fur. And they stayed there. Then it went out. The noise was quieting down now. Then it came back again. She seen it was a big bear. Oh, she was scared! The bear came and pulled her out and looked at her. Then it would start walking. Then it would come back again and pull her. She knew the bear wanted her to go someplace. So she followed the bear.

The bear seemed to be in an awful hurry. He would look at her. Then he would start to run. So she ran, her too. And they came to a lake where there was canoes. The bear threw one in the water and gave her a paddle and pushed her into the canoe and pushed the canoe out onto the water. She start paddling as hard as she could. When she looked back, the bear was going along tearing up all the canoes. Also breaking the paddles in half. And as he was tearing up the last canoe, the Soo men came running down yelling away. The bear ran along the shore as hard as he could. He was coming the way she was going too. Of course, the Soos did not have any canoe to follow her. They just had to stand on the shore and watch them. And when she came to a rapids, the bear was already there waiting for her. She was very scared of it because she did not know what he meant by this. And then she remembered, when she was a little girl, she use to dream about a big bear going around with her protecting her from everything.

Then she went to where the bear was waiting and got out. The bear picked up the canoe and portaged. Then she got [in the canoe] again, and the bear [was] running along the shore around points and bays and everything. Then she come to another rapids. Already the bear was there again, and she did the same again. She got off, and the bear took the canoe over [the portage] again. This was in the night now. And then she slept in the canoe. And while she was sleeping, all at once the canoe jerked, and she woke up. Here it was the bear waking her up! It was broad daylight. Then she started paddling again. The bear swam across the river, and she knew he wanted her to go on the other side. When she came around the point again, it was a big lake. The bear stood in one place looking across the lake. It was getting sunset now, and she did not know where to go. At last, the bear got on his hind legs and looked again. She also got up and looked. She seen a smoke from a fire. Then the bear looked at her. He turned and walked into the bush.

She did not know what to do, and she knew not where she was either. But anyway she paddled towards the place where she seen the smoke. And when she came closer—it was now quite dark—she seen a woman sitting near the campfire and two other men. She did not know who they were, and she was also scared of them. They were laughing. She went closer. They were sitting down talking. Then the woman got up and came down to get some water. She was saying, "We might make it to Nigidawitiqueyang tomorrow." She was very surprised to hear where she was—far away from home. She did not speak, and then she went closer and she could hear them talking. The woman was saying, "I am very scared. Just like there is someone near looking at us." Only then she spoke up, saying, "Yes, I'm near here looking at youse. I wanted to find out first if I could understand your language." And they all ran down and asked her where she came from. She told them that she came from Saging.

Then she got out of this canoe and sat down near the fire, for she was cold as this was early in the fall. She had never ate anything since she went to the Soo country. And only then was she hungry.

The woman gave her some hot tea and also something to eat. Then they slept. She lay down near the fireplace and slept.

The next morning they started off. She had some of their things in her canoe. And then they camped again. The woman told her that the young man was her brother and that he was single. She said that she was not good enough for any man. And she also told the woman her story of going to the Soo country and how the bear led her away from danger and brought her to this place where she found these people. The woman said, "So! This woman here was saved by a bear!" They took four days more. Then they came to the place named Shebashkodeang, where there were a lot of Indians.

Then she married this young man, and they had a little girl. Her sister-in-law was very good to her. Also her husband was very good to her. Then, when her little girl was three years old, she went out picking berries one time. And all at once, she seen a big bear coming. She knew the bear was mad. He came and grabbed her little girl and, right in front of her, tore her little girl to pieces! And away the bear went again. She came home crying. And then her sister-in-law thought of the time when she told her about the bear. And she hated her.

She could not help it. She was very sorry to lose her little girl. And she knew well enough why the bear did it. Because every spring and fall she use to make a little birch pan and put some sugar and other things in it and go and put it someplace where the bear would come and eat. And she never did this since she got married. And this was why the bear tore her little girl to pieces. Because she did not do what the bear wanted her to do, and this was why the bear got mad. Her husband did not blame her, but her sister-in-law blamed her, and she was awfully brokenhearted.

So when the remains of her little girl were buried, she could not stand it anymore because she had went through too much: her parents ate up by wolves; her little sister starving to death; and, her little brother dying of a broken heart. And her shame of what she did and then throwing away her child. And now, when she was happily married forgetting the past, her little girl was torn up by a bear in front of her! All this passed in her mind. She wished the bear tore her up too. She couldn't go on living. So that night, after her baby was buried, she went out and hung herself. She was found dead the next morning, and she was buried. So that was the end of her.[1]

29

She Knew That This Woman

She Dreamed Was the Bear

This is a story of an old woman. She went through a rough life. When she first got married, her husband was a good hunter, and he was a man not what you call wicked. And they had children. They had three boys and one daughter. The boy and the girl were the oldest. The girl was the oldest of all. They lived in a bark wigwam at the mouth of Mosaysibing. This is somewheres on the Lake of the Woods side. And close there, there was a village of Indians where they use to camp in the summertime.

And the children, of course, long ago they use to go around in the canoe paddling, playing around that way. And the boy and the girl were going out paddling, and some other children were going out paddling. They were from this village. And they got into fighting, and the girl and boy came home crying. And it kept on like that all summer 'til rice making. And, of course, all the Indians went away to where there was rice.

So this woman and her family moved to where they were rice making. And then the children started to fight again. And just as they were getting through rice making, at last the woman and this other woman quarreled and [had a] fight. And this woman said to her that that winter they wouldn't kill enough game or food to live on that winter. So she didn't say anything like that to her. And, of course, when fall came, it was the habit of the Indians, when they got through rice making and killing fish, they moved back to their hunting ground. So this is what they did.

And about five months after the quarrel with this woman, it happened that they didn't have anything to eat. They nearly starved. Her husband couldn't kill anything. The children were crying and sleeping all day 'cause she didn't have anything to feed them. And they had a big dog. So she killed this dog and scraped it. And she cooked it and fed her children on this dog. And she ate it herself. Her husband wasn't home. He was away all day trying to kill something to eat.

Her man came home with nothing that night. So she gave him the dog to eat, and he ate the dog. And after he got through eating, he said he was going to walk all night. He was going to see his uncle, his father's brother. He said he would be gone two days and that they would eat the dog while he was gone those two days.

So he went away that night. And after he went, she went to sleep, her too. And that night she dreamed of a nice-looking woman, dressed in red. And this girl told her in her dream that if she would find her the next day before noon, it would stop them [being] so unlucky—that she was to look for her early the next day. So that night when she wakened, she did her *manitokaso* and talked of her dreams she had before.

And when morning came, she was anxious to get out of her sleep. And she combed her hair, and she painted her cheeks with red and got ready. And she took her mallet that she use to dream about. She went out, and she looked around. And she walked around the wigwam, and at once, she knew which way to go. So she went at once to this place. And she walked about half a mile from her wigwam. She come to a place where there were two cedar trees lying. They were blown down by the wind that took up the root and earth. And it seemed like that there was something there that she was going to see.

So she poked her mallet in this ground. And she seen a she-bear stick her head out. So she hit this bear on the head and killed it.

She couldn't drag it home 'cause it was so fat she couldn't lift it. So she went home and got her girl and boy. So they took a toboggan and took this bear to their wigwam.

So she skinned the bear. And she took the head and hands, feet and heart, grease and tongue, and she kept that. Her husband was gone one night, and he was to be away one night yet. So she had lots of grease now 'cause the bear's fat was five inches thick. And [she had] all kinds of meat for them to eat. She knew that this woman she dreamed was this bear 'cause she use to dream of her before she knew that it was a bear. So that means that she winned [won] her husband's luck back.

So her husband got back, and when he came to their wigwam, he could see blood all over outside. And he shouted, "Who came and destroyed my children?" And she answered him, saying, "Don't say that! I got your children something to eat." So when he came in, he could see meat and everything. So she cooked these things she kept and had a regular feast with their *pawaganuh*. There wasn't anyone else [camped] there close to them. They were there all alone. He brought some maple sugar and rice and dried blueberries that they stored away that fall for spring.

And then he was in luck and killed everything. They got seven bears that spring and a thousand muskrats. And that spring some Indians come there to camp, and these people they had trouble with were brought there too. They were nearly starved 'cause the man got the bad luck. And someone told her that this man said that whenever he sees her husband that he would shoot him. And then he soon heard what this man said.

And about in April when the lakes opened up, he was going to bring his fur to Fort Frances to the Hudson's Bay store. And on the way, they camped on their old camping ground. And the next morning, they were gonna go to Fort Frances to sell their fur. And it happened that this other man was going too, that same day. They lived right on the right hand side of the creek, and there was an island right opposite this creek and it was a point, like. And in the morning, when she was cooking, they seen men coming around this point in a canoe, and they knew it was this man.

So they came right to where they were sitting and yelled to her husband, saying, "You're the one I want to see." And he answered, "Yes, I'll be down." So he got up with his gun, him too. And as he was going down the bank, this man lifted one foot out of the canoe and fired at him. Then he put his foot out and fired again. And her husband shouted and said, "He's killing me!" Then he shot him too and killed him. And this man that was in the canoe started to cry. And he said, "Why do you cry?" And her husband died brave with a shout on his lips. So they both killed one another.

The woman and her children were sitting watching her husband getting killed. And as the sun was away up, the two bodies were lying together covered with brush. And men came and put clothes on them and buried them on the island side by side.

It was on account of these children fighting. And next, the two women fighting. Then the men finished it by killing one another. She used to say she never cried once to let anyone see her. But she had it in her heart that she would of just like[d] to kill this woman, her too. So after the two men were buried, she started off with her children and came to Fort Frances and brought the fur to the Hudson's Bay and sold it.

So she stayed around Fort Frances quite awhile—around the Indian villages. Then, after a while, she had a baby with some man. Then, in the fall, she went away back in the bush and camped alone with her children. Then her baby was born back there in the bush. And one of her children use to tell that her baby was born dead, and she buried it right where she had the open fireplace in the center of their wigwam. And when she moved back to where the Indians were, they asked her where her baby was. And she said, "Kiniboban." That means, "It died." And she said that so many times.

So she had another baby. And it was full of scabs, and it died with that. And then, again she had another baby, and it was just the same way. Their hands and face were all full of scabs. Just like it were burns. So that was three babies she had while she was a widow. And the last one she had, she got one of these *jisuki* men to find out for her what was the reason her children were full of scabs and died that way. And mind you, the *jisuki* man told her that it was on account of her burying her baby in the fireplace. Of course, she didn't bury her baby there alive. But the hot ashes burned the flesh of the dead baby. And that was the reason why her other two were full of scabs just like they were burns. So she didn't have any more children after the last one died while she was alone.

And then, later on again, she got in with one man from Hungry Hall. Well, she married him, and then he moved her down to Hungry Hall. And all her children went along with her.

She was a great old *manitokaso*. She was a *nanadawiiwe* and all kinds of *manitokaso*. And her husband was a great old *jisuki*. Oh, they went at it fine! They got along fine for about fifteen years. I would just like to have a picture of her right now! She dressed in red, blue, green, yellow, black, and all colors of beads and different kinds of ribbon on her hair. And a feather sticking on her head. Earrings. And beads on her moccasins. And her face was painted. She dressed like this every day.

And every time, people would call [her] to *nanadawiiwe*. She use to have a maid with her to drum for her when she was doctoring anyone. Twice she asked me to go along with [her], to go and drum with her. And she gave me a shawl and six yards of prints. She always got someone to go along with her. So she kept on like that for a long time.

And then her husband died. She didn't have any children with him. So she was a widow for two years. Then she married her brother-in-law again. He was a useless man. He was a drunkard. And then she start to drink too. And she just went to nothing. And when she got sober, the people use to get her to doctor them, but she wasn't so good as before. Then her oldest son got sick and died. And the younger one also died. And then her daughter got sick and died too. Her daughter was married eight times but never had children. She never had grandchildren. Then, when all her children died, she died too and left her useless old husband.

And when she used to *nanadawiiwe* someone, when they were getting better, she used to give them a name and give them a snake game and the Indian dice game and the medicine rattler that they use when they *nanadawiiwe* anyone. This is what she used to give to the ones she doctored when they were getting better.[1]

30

I Want to Be Your *Pawahgun*

This is a story of an old man. It starts from at the day he was born. He use to tell himself that he knew when he was an infant first before he was born. He knew that his mother had the inside of a moose and the head, nose, and tongue which she was going to use for his feast. And also other things. He use to think he was in a tight wigwam, and he never moved. Sometimes he use to be rocked hard. And then, one time, it got very tight for him there. Then he start wiggling himself and turned, and then he pushed himself out into the light. He seen a lot of old women. They were all excited and yelling. Then someone slapped him, and then he cried for the first time. Then he was wrapped up in warm clothes and put to bed. He slept for a long time, as he was very cozy.

And when he was two days old, he saw some old women cooking. Then, again, he heard an old man talking about something. He knew, then, this was his first feast. He listened very closely and took in every word this old man was saying. His mother was holding him. He seen all the things his mother kept for his feast. He was very pleased to know that his parents were doing everything for him. Then, from that time, he did not know. Only 'til he was a little older.

He remembered again: one time someone was singing, and he was rocked. He was tied onto a cradle, and he was crying. He stopped crying and looked. It was his mother rocking him, and she was singing. Then she put him down and untied him. He looked at his hands and wondered what they were. Then [he looked] at his feet. Again, he did not know what they were too. He was scared of [his hands] because sometimes they would scratch his face. Then his mother took him again and tied him up and put him up against the wall. Then he looked around. Soon, he got tired and fell asleep.

And when he got older, his mother use to make him sit up. And soon he was able to sit up alone. Then, later on again, he began to wish for things, and they were beyond his reach. Then he wondered how he could move around. Then he use to lay down on his stomach. Then he began to creep around a little. And then he began to wish he could walk around too. Then he tried. He got up and stood on his feet and took a step. Then he would fall. Oh! It use to hurt him to fall! But he tried again. Then, at last, he was running around. All this he knew. He remembered it all just like yesterday.

Then, when he got to be quite a big boy, he use to dream of a pigeon coming towards him. And the pigeon would say, "I want to be your *pawahgun*. I will take care of you. I will also bring you things. And you also see me: how I look. You will also look like that too." Often he use to dream this then. He never said anything about his dream but kept it to himself.

And many times after that, too, he use to dream that this pigeon would bring him something such as shoes and [a] cap and other things. And also, every fall, this pigeon would come to him and tell him just where to go so he would find a bear to kill. And sure enough! When he would get up in the morning, he would get ready and go. Then he would find this bear and kill it. The pigeon also one time brought him a house [in a dream]. And sure enough! He made a house. And after that, the pigeon brought him two ponies in a dream. And a pig. And soon again after that, he [got] two ponies and one pig. Also one cow.

He was now a young man and was living by himself alone. He was single for a long time. And he was a good worker. He was very white in complexion, as the pigeon gave him to be white. Then, again one time in his dream, he dreamed of this same pigeon bringing him a girl and saying, "I am bringing you this girl to live with. She will help you with everything. Be good to her." When he wakened next morning, he wondered what the pigeon meant by bringing him a girl.

But soon he forgot all about his dream until about ten days after. As he was sitting around alone, he seen some people coming in a canoe. He did not know who they were. They came closer and came ashore, got out of their canoe, and came up to where he was sitting. There was an oldish man and woman and their young daughter. He asked them in[to] his house, and they came in. His house was fixed nice inside. He had nice things. And then they told him that they were bringing this girl for him to marry. Well, then, he could not refuse! He then thought of the pigeon bringing a girl for him.

He took this girl and married her. He was good to her. They were never in need of anything. Then, again one time in his dream, the pigeon came and brought him a little boy and said, "I am bringing you this boy for your son, and I warn you to be very careful, for he might be the cause of some trouble later on." And when the boy was born, nothing happened, but he use to often wonder what the pigeon meant by saying this. And three more little girls were born—all two years apart. Each time it was the pigeon who brought them to him in his dreams.

And when the boy was grown up, he use to often talk to his son never to kill a pigeon if he seen one anyplace, no matter if the pigeon was very close. He told his son never to do it, and the boy told his father that he would try to remember what his father told him.

The pigeon use to come to him in the night, always had something for him, and he would always get what the pigeon brought him—although it was only in dream that the pigeon came. Well, it was his *pawahgun*.

Then, again one night he dreamed about this pigeon getting

I Want to Be Your *Pawahgun* 199

killed by his own son. He did not think anything. But later on, when he never dreamed of this pigeon again, he wondered what was wrong. Then he asked his son if he ever killed this pigeon, but the boy denied it. But it was him who killed this pigeon that same day when his father dreamed of it being killed. But he did not want to tell his father. He killed the pigeon with a bow and arrow

Then their trouble began. The pigeon never came to him again. And then, when another child came to them, the baby [died]. And three more children came, but they all died at birth. He never knew anything again or where to get anything again. The pigeon never came to him again in his dreams. Then they had another little baby boy. It lived, but his wife died instead at this little boy's birth.

Then, when his wife died, he then made a *jisukan* and got a *jisuki* man. And while they were *jisuki*, the boy was asked to tell if he ever killed a pigeon. And only then, he told that he killed this pigeon one day when it was following him all around. And after he killed the pigeon, he took and hid it and never told his father. And the *jisuki* man told them that it was all on account of him killing this pigeon why there were many deaths in their family. And also he told them to get ready so that this boy could go through the Grand Medicine dance as he wasn't well. He was kind of crazy. And then the boy did go through the Grand Medicine dance, and he got better.

And later on, as all his children grew up, they all stayed in the same house. There were three grown-up girls and his son, a young man. And his other son was small. And as they were living there, they use to be afraid of someone around there dressed in white. They use to see it walking around, and they were very scared. And then, again one night in his dreams, this pigeon came to him and said, "This coming summer, someone will come here. And when he gets here, you are to listen to him very carefully and do as he says. I will show you right now what he will do, and you are to do it [and] your three daughters and little boy [as well]. But your other son that went through the Grand Medicine, he cannot do this that youse will do. He will have to leave youse and go some-place else."

Then he dreamed that the pigeon took him by the hands and led him away to a big house and took him inside. The inside was varnished, and there was many seats and a platform. And the pigeon took him up to the platform and made him kneel down. And he also saw his three daughters coming in and his youngest boy. And they all got baptized except his oldest son. Then he wakened. He never said anything but kept all this to himself.

And next summer, a man came there. He was a minister. He camped beside his house. And then he remembered what this pi-geon said. And he made up his mind to do as he was told to do by his *pawahgun*. Then he asked [told] the minister that he wanted his four children to be baptized. Also himself. And, of course, the minister was glad to baptize them all. And he did.

And his oldest son? Well, he could not get his son to be baptized because this white bird told him not to. Then his daughters all grew up. His daughters married all white men. And this was where a lot of half-breeds came from. And even the youngest son married a half-breed woman. But the oldest boy married an Indian woman and was always an Indian.

So when after all his children got married, he lived alone in his home and lived on his cattle and pigs, selling them one by one. And after he sold all his cattle, he got sick. He was all alone for several years, and when he got sick, his youngest son and his wife came there and took care of him. And then, when he got very sick, they brought him to town to a doctor, but the doctor could not do anything for him as he was too far gone. And he was only there several weeks. Then he died, and they covered his body up with a quilt. And when they got ready to dress his body up and were pulling the covers off, the first thing they seen was a small, wee pigeon sitting on his chest. And when they wanted to take this little pigeon, it flew away.

So the pigeon was always with him right to the end. But it was only on account of his son killing a pigeon why they had so much trouble. They were told that none of his family was ever suppose to kill a pigeon.

So he was buried, and that was the end of him. I do not know what became of his children, but he left all his land and home to his youngest son because they were the ones that took good care of him when he died.[1]

ACKNOWLEDGMENTS

A grant from the Social Sciences and Humanities Research Council of Canada funded the research. Archivists at the National Anthropological Archives in Washington DC and at the Minnesota State Historical Archives in St. Paul provided invaluable assistance. Visionary philanthropist Peter Barnes offered a truly remarkable retreat to think and write at Mesa Refuge. Graduate students Jordan Davidson and Jennifer Lys Grenier provided research assistance. Friends Marika Ainley, Lori Beaman, Ellen Bielawski, Julie Cruikshank, Susan Drysdale, Virginia Kerns, and Lynne Phillips believed in the importance of this work. Family Michael, Sam, and Bella were trusty companions. Above all, friend and editor Krisha Starker discussed almost every word with me along the way and knows how much this work means to me. Finally, I hope this book acknowledges my deep respect for Maggie Wilson and Ruth Landes as pioneers in writing women's lives.

Thank you all.

The original stories are in the Ruth Landes Papers at the National Anthropological Archives at the Smithsonian Institution in Washington DC. They are archived in order according to handwritten numbers that appear at the top of the first page of each story. Stories 1–60 are in box 37; stories 61–119 are in box 38. The original numbers of the stories published in this book are listed in brackets below.

1. She Got In with Him Again After They Were Widows [111]
2. Why Didn't You Take Good Care of Her While I Was Away? [12]
3. You Can Have Him All to Yourself [16]
4. He Made Up His Mind to Look After Her [109]
5. The Wind Took the Canoe Right Across the Lake [83]
6. We Will Take You and Love You as Our Very Own Daughter [99]

1. Landes described this arrangement in the preface to the second edition of *The Ojibwa Woman* published in 1971. In the 1930s it was standard practice for the anthropology students trained by Franz Boas and Ruth Benedict at Columbia University to record oral narratives by working with a few individuals—then known as "key informants"—who were locally recognized as repositories of cultural knowledge (Black-Rogers 1989; Cannizzo 1983; Darnell 1992). Typically these were senior males (most anthropologists were also male) who told tales of tribal origins and exploits in war (Kehoe 1996) or who elaborated complex ethical beliefs to explain social practices and patterns (Radin 1927). Ruth Landes alone had paid attention to the stories of individual women's everyday lives and dilemmas. Frances Densmore (1928, 1929) had recorded women's cultural knowledge as it related to her own ethnological interests in games, songs, crafts, and subsistence skills, but she did not record storytelling as art or as autobiographical/biographical narrative as Landes and Wilson did. Landes was atypical among anthropologists of the time not only because she was principally interested in women's lives but also because she was more interested in individual agency and expression than in the prescribed rules and standardized norms that her peers and professors were codifying. Landes described Maggie Wilson's storytelling practice: "She would explain the traditional rules impeccably, only to top this with accounts of big violations by individuals. . . . Her discussions always followed this sequence: specific social rules were taught and heavily sanctioned by gens, family and supernatural powers, but these could be and were universally set aside" (1966, 5). There is no doubt that the archive of Maggie Wilson's stories reflects themes that were of mutual interest to Wilson and Landes just as the archives based on Franz Boas's research with George

Hunt (Cannizzo 1983) and A. Irving Hallowell's research with William Berens (Brown 1989; Hallowell 1992) reflect the mutual interests of those anthropologists and their Native collaborators. For further discussion of the research collaboration between Wilson and Landes and the critical reception of the work of Ruth Landes, see Cole 2003.

2. The masculinist bias of the period was noted by Hallowell in his 1938 review of *The Ojibwa Woman*: "Since male ethnographers have given us most of our accounts of the life of native peoples, it is well to have a culture systematically studied and presented from a feminine point of view. Landes has been successful in carrying this out, as I can testify from my own investigation of a western branch of the Ojibwa. . . . Since, in Ojibwa society the role of women, as culturally phrased, is very much more circumscribed than that of men, one might gain a totally false impression of the actual life of women without such data as Landes gives. She is able to show, and rightly I believe, that women not only have an immense amount of freedom in this very individualistic society, but that they are often successful in flaunting customs and vetoing traditional standards" (1938, 892–93).

3. Ruth Landes Papers (RLP), box 38, National Anthropological Archives, Smithsonian Institution, Washington DC.

INTRODUCTION

1. "The Story of My Mother," RLP, story 119. My account of Maggie Wilson's early life draws on this story, on Ruth Landes's account in *Ojibwa Sociology* (1937, 87–107), and on Landes's fragmentary, handwritten notes on Maggie Wilson's life also found in the RLP, box 38. Also found in the RLP were copies Landes had made of the Treaty no. 3 government annuity pay lists, which record Maggie Wilson's birth, the birth and death of her sister, Maggie Wilson's three marriages, the births of her children, and the deaths of her husbands. From Maggie Wilson's references in "The Story of My Mother" to her father's hunting partner, his cousin at Little

Forks, one surmises that his Cree missionary father had married a Rainy River Ojibwe woman. Maggie Wilson's mixed Scottish, Cree, and Ojibwe heritage was not unusual in the region. The year following her birth, she was registered on the annuity pay lists as a member of the Little Forks band of Rainy River Ojibwes. She lived her entire life in the Rainy River region, married three Ojibwe men, and raised her children as Ojibwes. That she was rooted in Ojibwe traditions is further affirmed by her descriptions of her strong personal experience with healing, naming, and dreaming and her late (1928) conversion to Christianity.

2. Farms were located at summer fishing and gardening sites. How farm animals were cared for during the fall and winter migratory activities is not clear. Waisberg (1984) describes the difficulties the people had in trying to combine the two ways of life: settled farming and the seasonal migratory economy. In the early years the people did not build fences, and the animals would eat the crops when they went away. Reciprocal arrangements may have developed with neighbors and kin to care for animals during absences. Over time women and the elderly remained behind on the reserves when men went away hunting and trapping or for wage employment.

3. Maggie Wilson is describing the Ojibwe mourning practices of wailing and the ritual cleansing of sickness and death from the home by burning items belonging to dead family members. Some grievers would also cut gashes into their skin or paint black marks on their faces. Women customarily cut their hair or wore it unbraided. Men and women wore old clothing when in mourning (Densmore 1929, 73–78).

4. It is not known why the baby was given to Maggie Wilson, but it may be that she had served as midwife at his birth and the mother knew Wilson would not reject the baby. The boy, whom Wilson called "Shaganash," meaning "little white boy," was devoted to her and she to him. For Wilson, whose legs were now weak, he became a sturdy companion and went everywhere with her. Gus Wilson (Shaganash) was seven years old the summer that Maggie

Wilson worked with Ruth Landes, and he remembered a trip they all took together to the Red Lake Reservation in Minnesota. He was much saddened by Maggie Wilson's death in 1940, after which he left Manitou Rapids. He married and worked at a pulp and paper mill in Thunder Bay, where he and his wife raised twelve children (Gus Wilson, personal communication, July 10, 1996).

5. The account of Maggie Wilson's dream and her efforts to introduce the dance to the Ojibwes is based on the narrative Ruth Landes recorded and published as "A Woman's War Vision" in *Ojibwa Religion and the Midewiwin* (1968, 207–12) and on Landes's description of the dance in *Ojibwa Sociology* (1937, 111–12).

6. Permission was required because, in the 1885 Indian Act, the Canadian government had banned the Ojibwes from congregating in groups to practice and teach ancestral traditions and beliefs— unless sanctioned by the Indian agent. Maggie Wilson's ability to organize the performance of the dance thus depended on the good will of the particular Indian agent in office in Fort Frances at the time. His granting permission likely stemmed from her description of the dance as one to bring the soldiers home safely from the war in Europe. Under this legislation storytelling too, like the ceremonial songs and dances, would have been a clandestine activity, indicating the subversiveness of Maggie Wilson's work with Ruth Landes.

7. I have not been able to learn any Ojibwe name(s) that Maggie Wilson herself may have had.

8. Densmore identified six classes of names: (1) a dream name dreamed by a namer and given ceremonially to an individual by the namer; (2) a dream name acquired by an individual in a vision, often given at puberty by a tutelary or guardian spirit; (3) a "namesake name" given a child by its parents not bestowed ceremonially and not associated with a dream; (4) a common name or nickname, often humorous; (5) a clan name; and (6) a euphonious name without any significance. There were also names produced by the translation of Ojibwe names into English, the adaptation of English names into Chippewa, and the mispronunciation in English of Ojibwe names (1929, 52–58).

9. Vizenor describes his students' outrage at the episodes of violence toward Native women in his novel *Bearheart*. He asked them, "What scenes in this novel have you not already read in your daily newspaper? . . . What is not true in this novel?" And he reports, "They could not think of anything untrue in *Bearheart*. So the descriptive scenes of violence were what troubled them, not that the scenes were not true" (1999, 110).

10. Feminist historian Luisa Passerini (1989) suggests that stories be understood as "narrative resources" deployed by women rather than as historical or biographical accounts of specific women's lives. The historical truth of events in the stories is not the primary concern of the narrator. Rather, the stories and the events they recount are metaphors of experience and lessons in living.

11. Taken together in the collective story they tell, they may be read as auto-ethnography (Eakin 1999; Reed-Danahay 1997; Smith and Watson 2001).

12. According to the archival records, it appears that a total of 119 stories were sent. Not all have survived. I have renumbered the stories according to the order in which they appear in this volume. A number, written in a handwriting that is likely Ruth Landes's, appears at the top of the first page of each of the stories in the archival collection. The numbering system is not chronological. That is, it does not follow the order of the dates the letters were sent. These numbers may indicate the order in which Landes read or reread the stories as she was indexing or cross-referencing them for the purposes of her research. At the end of the acknowledgments in this volume, I have listed the original numbers and the archival provenience for each of the stories. In my selection of stories, I have left out the handful of *adusokan* and the few stories of kings and princes that are derivative of European fairy tales. I have also omitted stories that were incomplete due to missing, damaged, or illegible pages. Maggie Wilson had also mailed a few stories written by other individuals at Manitou Rapids. In an attempt, like Wilson, to earn some money, they had asked her to send their stories to Landes. But these individuals had soon

discontinued the effort—even though they, like Wilson, needed the money. They were not gifted storytellers like Maggie Wilson. They did not have her skill at character and plot development, nor her interest in ethical dilemmas, nor the perseverance required for the labor-intensive work of narrating and overseeing the writing down of the stories. I have also left out some stories in which Wilson is clearly responding to questions from Landes asking her to compare Cree and Ojibwe practices. These stories do not have characters or narrative plots. On the other hand, I have included a few stories that show the historically close relations between the Crees and the Ojibwes inhabiting the Ontario-Manitoba border region, especially the Winnipeg River route between Kenora and Lake Winnipeg through Fort Alexander.

13. Anthropologist Julie Cruikshank has described similar storytelling practices among Yukon Athapaskan and Tlingit women. She suggests that "individual autonomy is only a means to an end for these protagonists; their goal is reconnection with the community" (Cruikshank et al. 1990, 355). Cruikshank believes that retellings of stories help to create and maintain social spaces for women. She offers a helpful perspective from which to view Maggie Wilson's stories. By telling a corpus of stories of women's lives, Maggie Wilson establishes a space for women's experience in the writing of Ojibwe history and culture.

14. Louise Erdrich's storytelling in her many books, including *Love Medicine* (1993), *The Antelope Wife* (1998), *The Last Report on the Miracles at Little No Horse* (2001b), and *The Painted Drum* (2005), can be squarely placed in the same ancient Ojibwe women's tradition as Maggie Wilson's stories, showing the great continuity and consistency in this art form.

15. Gerald Vizenor considers "survivance" an important lens through which to view Ojibwe storytelling. He writes, "Survivance, in my use of the word, means a native sense of presence, the motion of sovereignty and the will to resist dominance. Survivance is not just survival but also resistance, not heroic or tragic, but the tease of tradition, and my sense of survivance outwits dominance

and victimry. Survival is a response; survivance is a standpoint, a worldview, and a presence. . . . [T]here is a sense of dependency in the meaning of the word *survival*, a dependency on the cause of some action . . . most histories of natives are themes of dominance and victimry. My stories are about survivance, not victimry" (Vizenor and Lee 1999, 93).

16. In the endnotes I provide any additional text—greetings or postscripts—that may have accompanied the stories.

17. Randolph Lewis views the documentary films of Alanis Obomsawin as extensions of women's traditional storytelling. He sees Obomsawin as embodying the three key roles of women—teacher, visual artist, and cultural leader—in Algonquian-speaking societies (including Ojibwe society) (2006, 64, 77). In her films she tells stories that "revalue" the work and lives of Native women. Lewis describes Obomsawin as exemplifying the strong Native woman who tackles obstacles head-on by, as she puts it, "standing up in a canoe" (2006, 40). He discusses five practices in Obomsawin's work that, interestingly, parallel ways I have suggested that Maggie Wilson's storytelling may be understood. The work (1) challenges national public memory from a Native standpoint, reinscribing what has been erased from the historical record; (2) insists on the significance of individual lives especially celebrating Native women by narrating their intimate lives, giving voice to their experience; (3) depicts the political resilience and cultural creativity of Native people, complicating conventional stereotypes; (4) exposes the deceptions of governments as well as the generalized racism that supports government negligence; and (5) believes in the importance of cultural continuity and the communal rituals that surround transmission of knowledge (2006, 79–84).

1. SHE GOT IN WITH HIM AGAIN

1. A postscript reads: "Sixty-one pages. From Mrs. John Wilson. You will find the whole story in two envelopes by the numbers starting from one to sixty-two."

2. WHY DIDN'T YOU TAKE GOOD CARE OF HER?

1. A postscript reads: "Thirty pages. From Mrs. Wilson. All your namesakes are well. So, bye bye. Did you get my letter with funny picture? Ruth Landes, please try to send the pay as soon as you can. And if you want any jokes I will send you some if you want them. Everybody is well here and they all say hello to you. From your Mam, Mrs. John Wilson, and Janet. I would give the world to see you once more."

5. THE WIND TOOK THE CANOE

1. A postscript reads: "Thirty-seven pages. I hope you like it. From Mrs. John Wilson."

6. WE WILL TAKE YOU AND LOVE YOU

1. A postscript reads: "This is the end of this story. I have no more long ones to tell you, only short stories. This is twenty-five pages. Mrs. Cochrane asked me if she could send you a story about her mother when she became a *windigo*. So I told her she could. It's all right with me. Janet will write for her. Mrs. Wilson."

7. HER FATHER WAS SITTING WITH HIS HEAD DOWN

1. A postscript reads: "Thirty-two pages. Mrs. John Wilson. Please send money before September 4 for the fall fair."

8. I'LL SHOW THAT MAN THAT STOLE MY DAUGHTER

1. A postscript reads: "Thirty-three pages. Mrs. John Wilson."

9. A VERY YOUNG MAN ADOPTED THEM FOR PARENTS

1. A postscript reads: "Thirty pages. Mrs. Wilson."

11. OH, CAN'T YOU FIND A PLACE IN YOUR HEART?

1. A postscript reads: "Thirty pages. Mrs. John Wilson."

12. THEY MAKE UP THEIR MIND

1. Filed with this letter was an envelope postmarked "Barwick, Ont. Feb 22 [19]34" and addressed to "Ruth Landes, 1940 Andrews Ave. Bronx, New York City."

14. SHE LIKED HIM AS A BROTHER

1. A postscript reads: "July 9, 1934. Ruth Landes, I am sending thirty-two pages and will send some more soon. I received your postal note for $2.20 and glad to get it. Thank you. Everybody is well. Yes, Mr. Olson is still here. No, I never heard anymore of that little *manito*. Esther Iceman came to see me on the fifth just for a little while. She came with two missionary women from Ponemah. Your Mam, Mrs. Wilson."

18. LET THEM STAY SINGLE ALL THEY WANT TO

1. A postscript reads: "From Mrs. Wilson. Thirty-one pages."

20. LEAVE ME HERE TO STARVE ALONE

1. A postscript reads: "Please count this as thirty pages. We have some pages over in the other ones we already sent. From Mrs. John Wilson."

23. I HAVE A *PAWAHGUN* THAT GIVES ME THE POWER

1. The story is signed "Mrs. John Wilson."

24. IT WON'T BE HER THAT WILL KNOW

1. A postscript reads: "From Mrs. John Wilson, Emo, Ontario. Answer soon."

26. HE GAVE HER A FOLDED BIRCH-BARK MAP

1. A postscript reads: "From Mrs. John Wilson. Forty-six pages. The other part of story is in another envelope."

27. THE MOOSE WAS WISE ENOUGH

1. A note at the beginning of the story reads: "Nov. 8, 1933, Emo, Ont. Dear Madam, There are thirty pages in this story of an old man. Hope you will like it. Yours truly, Mrs. John Wilson, Emo, Ont., Canada."

28. THE BEAR WANTED HER TO GO SOMEPLACE

1. A postscript reads: "Excuse mistakes. No time to read it over. Janet." A second postscript reads: "Forty-five pages from Mrs. John Wilson, Emo, Ont. Thank you very much for the albums you sent. Also I received the money okay."

29. THIS WOMAN SHE DREAMED WAS THE BEAR

1. A postscript reads: "I would like to buy a dress for myself. As soon as you get this story, try to send me the money. We would like to buy a dress each to wear on treaty the first of June. Janet's birthday will be on twenty-eighth of May. She will be nineteen years old. Mrs. Wilson."

30. I WANT TO BE YOUR *PAWAHGUN*

1. A postscript reads: "This is the end of this story. Twenty-four pages. From Mrs. John Wilson."

I have retained Maggie and Janet Wilson's spellings of Ojibwe words. These often varied between and within stories. I have noted here in square brackets spellings in *A Concise Dictionary of Minnesota Ojibwe* (Nichols and Nyholm 1995).

adoption: Traditional social practice to replace family members lost to death, disease, or warfare or to provide care for orphans or children in need of protection. Older people or extended family members might adopt a child as a son or daughter; young people might adopt old people as grandparents.

adusokan [aadisookaan]: Traditional story, sacred narrative; characters in a sacred narrative; "ancestors," "our grandfathers" (Angel 2002).

anishinaabe: Ojibwe, Ojibwa (Canadian), Chippewa, Ojibway.

bone game: A game of dexterity played with ten deer dewclaws strung on a narrow strip of deer hide at one end of which is an oval piece of leather pierced with twenty-five holes; at the other end is a needlelike piece of bone. The needle is held in the right hand, and the other end of the hide strip of dewclaws is held taut in the left hand. The objective is to release the tension on the deer-hide strip and "catch" the dewclaws on the needle. Various scores are obtained each time depending on how many and which dewclaws a player succeeds in catching on the needle. Played in teams. Each player continues his play as long as he scores. Typically, one hundred points constitutes one game (Densmore 1929, 118).

cross-cousin: Father's sister's child or mother's brother's child.

dodem [doodem]: Totem; clan.

duhwaim [indawemaa]: My sibling of the opposite sex (brother or sister); my parallel cousin of the opposite sex (my mother's sister's child or my father's brother's child).

ginyu [giniw]: Golden eagle.

goods: Trade goods; yard goods. *See also* print.

Grand Medicine Society: *See* midewiwin.

hand game: A betting game of chance played to the accompaniment of traditional gambling songs. Two objects (customarily a flint and a gun worm) are hidden in two of four possible hiding places (two in the players' hands and two under the edge of a blanket laid on the ground). Points are made by guessing the position of either article. Score is kept by means of sharpened sticks stuck in the ground beside the players (Densmore 1929, 115).

hustler: A man who is a hard worker and a good hunter.

jisukan; jisukanun [jiisakaan; jiisakaanan]: Shaking tent.

jisuki [jiisakii; jiisakiiwinini]: To practice divination in a shaking tent; to act as an intermediary between people and the spirits; seer who uses a shaking tent.

keewainige [giiwenige]: To give away things to complete the mourning of the death of a relative, especially a spouse, after which the widowed spouse may remarry; gifts to relatives of someone deceased in completion of mourning on anniversary of death.

kiniboban: It died.

lacrosse: A game of dexterity played with a ball covered with deerskin thrown by bent sticks with pockets of netting on one end. Played by a large number of players divided into opposing sides, usually at summer gatherings (Densmore 1929, 119). A form of entertainment and an opportunity to display physical powers, also serving a ceremonial function as mock warfare or healing ritual and expression of hope for a long life (Green 1999, 37).

manito; manitou [manidoo]: Spirit; power.

manitokaso/win [manidookaazo]: To take on spiritual power by one's own authority.

medicine: Native medical practice and knowledge based on plants and inseparable from spiritual healing. A variety of medicines are used to cure and cause illness, locate game or enemy warriors, or secure the affections of the opposite sex: curing medicines, protection medicines, bad medicine, and love medicine.

Métis: Person of Cree or Ojibwe and French parentage.

midewi; midawi: To participate in the *midewiwin*; to go through the levels of training of the *midewiwin*.

midewiwin; midewiiwe: Grand Medicine Society; Medicine Dance; a spiritual society whose members, seeking a long, productive, and healthy life, adhere to a complex set of rituals and teachings involving a series of different levels or degrees (Angel 2002).

mitikogiwam: Wood wigwam.

moccasin game: A gambling game in which four bullets, one of which is marked, are hidden under four moccasins, the object being to guess which moccasin hides the marked bullet. Four men usually play the game, each "hiding" player having a partner who sings and pounds the drum while the opponent guesses the location of the marked bullet (Densmore 1929, 114–15).

moshabewicomig: A type of large wigwam.

nahdahwiiwe/a [nanaandawi'iwe]: To doctor/heal people. Spellings and usage of this term vary widely in Maggie Wilson's stories and include also *nanadawiiwa/e, nahdahwi(i)a(h), nahnahdah-wiiway, nahnahdahwia*.

namesake: Reciprocal relationship between name-giving sponsor and child (Nichols and Nyholm 1995, 217). Parents might name a child after someone for whom they have high regard—the pair would then become "namesakes." Unlike other names, this name is not dreamed for the child and does not transfer power to the child. Often a humorous nickname given because of a perceived resemblance to someone or something (Densmore 1929, 52–53).

nita [niita]: My (male's) brother-in-law.

noshis [noohzhis]: Grandchild.

nuhdoobuhni [nandobani]: To go to war; warrior.

ogima [ogimaa]: Leader; chief.

pahguk [paagak]: Skeleton.

pa(h)wahgun; pa(h)wahgahn; pawaganuh; powagunuh: Power, guardian spirit; spirit benefactor, personal *manito* who comes to a person in a dream; also referred to by Maggie Wilson as "dream visitors"; a source of assistance to individuals in daily life; "other-than-human persons" possessing great power (Hallowell 1992, 68; spelling in Hallowell: *pawagan*; pl. *pawaganak*); "tutelary spirit" (Densmore 1929, 52, 79). Individuals typically obtain a personal guardian spirit at puberty through a vision after fasting and seclusion. New guardian spirits may be obtained in dreams throughout one's adult life (Landes 1938, 1968). Offerings are given and rituals of respect are shown to one's *pawahgun*. In reciprocity a *pawahgun* promises help in hunting, war, love, or curing or protection against misfortune.

pishiw [bizhiw]: Lynx.

print: Cotton calico yard goods for clothing obtained through trade or purchase at fur trade posts. Highly valued by women.

shabodahwan [shaabodaawan]: Long lodge.

snake stick game: A game of chance played with four wooden snakes (carved ten-inch-long sticks with mouths painted red; two are unpainted, and two have an undulating red line the length of their bodies). Several shorter sticks are used as counters. Players are seated around a blanket spread on the ground. The players hold the snakes in their right hand and throw them onto the blankets. Points are scored depending on the way the snakes fall (Densmore 1929, 116).

squaw hockey: Wilson's term for the women's game described by Densmore (1929, 118–19). Each player has a pair of long, slender sticks with which she attempts to catch and carry two short, thick sticks tied together with a thong. Played in a large, open field at either end of which is a "goal stake." Only the fastest runners play this game. Players are divided into two sides, each of which has a leader. The leader of one side opens the play by tossing the pair of short sticks into the air. All players rush forward to try to get it and carry it through the opponent's line to the opposite goal. A score is made by striking the pair of sticks against a goalpost.

tobacco: Ritual offering, gift.

treaty: Annuity paid annually each summer to each adult as a provision of Treaty no. 3, signed between the Canadian government and the Rainy River Ojibwes in 1873.

wahbahno [waabano]: Member of the Waabanowiwin Society; Society of the Dawn; a healing society in which members use fire in rituals that take place at night and conclude at dawn (Angel 2002).

wasisee [awaazisii]: Bullhead.

wikab [wiigob]: Basswood inner bark fiber used to make twine.

windigo [wiindigoo]: Winter cannibal or ice monster, appearing during times of starvation; an idea that "implies all that is fear compelling, as the windigo were said to be terrible beings who craved human flesh" (Densmore 1929, 70).

Albers, Patricia. 1989. From illusion to illumination: Anthropological studies of American Indian women. In *Gender and anthropology*, ed. Sandra Morgen, 132–70. Washington DC: American Anthropological Association.

Angel, Michael. 2002. *Preserving the sacred: Historical perspectives on the Ojibwa midewiwin.* Winnipeg: University of Manitoba Press.

Berlo, Janet, and Ruth Phillips. 1998. *Native North American art.* Oxford: Oxford University Press.

Bessire, Lucas. 2003. Talking back to primitivism: Divided audiences, collective desires. *American Anthropologist* 105 (4): 832–37.

Black-Rogers, Mary. 1989. Dan Raincloud: "Keeping our Indian way." In *Being and becoming Indian: Biographical studies of North American frontiers*, ed. James A. Clifton, 226–48. Chicago: Dorsey.

Blaeser, Kimberly. 1994. *Trailing you.* New York: Greenfield Review Press.

———. 1997. Like "reeds through the ribs of a basket": Native women weaving stories. *American Indian Quarterly* 21 (4): 555–65.

Brown, Jennifer. 1986. Northern Algonquians from Lake Superior and Hudson Bay to Manitoba in the historical period. In *Native peoples: The Canadian experience*, ed. R. Bruce Morrison and C. Roderick Wilson, 208–36. Toronto: McClelland & Stewart.

———. 1989. "A place in your mind for them all": Chief William Berens. In *Being and becoming Indian: Biographical studies of North American frontiers*, ed. James A. Clifton, 204–25. Chicago: Dorsey.

Cannizzo, Jeanne. 1983. George Hunt and the invention of Kwakiutl culture. *Canadian Review of Sociology and Anthropology* 20 (1): 44–58.

Clark, Jim. 2002. *Naawigiizis: The memories of Center of the

Moon. Ed. Keller Paap, Lisa LaRonger, and Heid Erdrich. Minneapolis: Birchbark Books.

Cole, Sally. 2003. *Ruth Landes: A life in anthropology*. Lincoln: University of Nebraska Press.

Cruikshank, Julie, in collaboration with Angela Sidney, Kitty Smith, and Annie Ned. 1990. *Life lived like a story: Life stories of three Yukon Native elders*. Vancouver: University of British Columbia Press.

Darnell, Regna. 1992. The Boasian text tradition and the history of anthropology. *Culture* 12 (1): 39–47.

Densmore, Frances. 1928. *Uses of plants by the Chippewa Indians*. 44th Annual Report of the Bureau of American Ethnology. Washington DC.

———. 1929. *Chippewa customs*. Bureau of American Ethnology Bulletin 86. Washington DC.

Dorris, Michael. 1989. *The broken cord*. New York: Harper Perennial.

Eakin, Paul John. 1999. *How our lives become stories: Making selves*. Ithaca NY: Cornell University Press.

Erdrich, Louise. 1993. *Love medicine*. New York: Holt, Rinehart & Winston.

———. 1998. *The antelope wife*. New York: Harper Flamingo.

———. 2001a. An emissary of the between world. http://www.theatlantic.com/unbound/interviews/int2001-01-17.htm.

———. 2001b. *The last report on the miracles at Little No Horse*. New York: HarperCollins.

———. 2003. *Books and islands in Ojibwe country*. Washington DC: National Geographic Society.

———. 2005. *The painted drum*. New York: HarperCollins.

Ginsburg, Faye. 2002. Screen memories: Resignifying the traditional in indigenous media. In *Media worlds: Anthropology on new terrain*, ed. Lila Abu-Lughod, Faye Ginsburg, and Brian Larkin, 39–58. Berkeley: University of California Press.

Green, Rayna. 1999. *The British Museum encyclopedia of Native North America*. London: British Museum Press.

Hallowell, A. Irving. 1938. Review of *Ojibwa sociology* and *The Ojibwa woman*. *American Sociological Review* 3:892–93.

———. 1992. *The Ojibwa of Berens River, Manitoba: Ethnography into history*. Ed. Jennifer Brown. Fort Worth: Harcourt Brace Jovanovich.

Hayes, Derek. 2002. *Historical atlas of Canada: Canada's history illustrated with original maps*. Vancouver: Douglas & McIntyre.

Hickerson, Harold. 1988. *Chippewa and their neighbors: A study in ethnohistory*. Rev. ed. With foreword and critical review by Jennifer S. H. Brown and Laura Peers. Prospect Heights IL: Waveland.

Hill, Greg. 2006. *Norval Morrisseau: Shaman artist*. Ottawa: National Gallery of Canada.

Hunter, Al. 2001. *Spirit horses*. Wiarton ON: Kegedonce.

Jameson, Anna. 1923. *Winter studies and summer rambles*. Toronto: McClelland & Stewart.

Kehoe, Alice. 1996. Transcribing Insima, a Blackfoot "old lady." In *Reading beyond words: Contexts for Native history*, ed. Jennifer Brown and Elizabeth Vibert, 381–402. Peterborough ON: Broadview.

Klein, Laura, and Lillian Ackerman, eds. 1995. *Women and power in Native North America*. Norman: University of Oklahoma Press.

Landes, Ruth. 1937. *Ojibwa sociology*. New York: Columbia University Press.

———. 1938. *The Ojibwa woman*. New York: Columbia University Press. 2nd ed., W. W. Norton, 1971.

———. 1947. *City of women*. New York: Macmillan.

———. 1966. The Ojibwa and their observers. Ruth Landes Papers, box 15. National Anthropological Archives, Smithsonian Institution, Washington DC.

———. 1968. *Ojibwa religion and the midéwiwin*. Madison: University of Wisconsin Press.

Leacock, E. 1978. Women's status in egalitarian societies. *Current Anthropology* 19 (2): 247–75.

Lewis, Randolph. 2006. *Alanis Obomsawin: The vision of a Native filmmaker*. Lincoln: University of Nebraska Press.

Morrisseau, Norval, and Donald Robinson. 1997. *Norval Morrisseau: Travels to the house of invention*. Toronto: Key Porter Books.

Nichols, John, and Earl Nyholm. 1995. *A concise dictionary of Minnesota Ojibwe*. Minneapolis: University of Minnesota Press.

Noble, William C., ed. 1984. Historical synthesis of the Manitou Mounds site on the Rainy River, Ontario. Unpublished manuscript. National Library of Canada, Ottawa.

Passerini, Luisa. 1989. Women's personal narratives: Myths, experiences, and emotions. In *Interpreting women's lives: Feminist theory and personal narratives*, ed. Personal Narratives Group, 189–97. Bloomington: Indiana University Press.

Peers, Laura. 1994. *The Ojibwa of western Canada, 1780–1870*. Winnipeg: University of Manitoba Press.

Phillips, Ruth B. 2006. Morrisseau's "entrance": Negotiating primitivism, modernism and Anishnaabe tradition. In *Norval Morrisseau: Shaman artist*, by Greg Hill, 42–77. Ottawa: National Gallery of Canada.

Quimby, G. I. 1960. *Indian life in the upper Great Lakes 11,000 BC to AD 1800*. Chicago: University of Chicago Press.

———. 1966. *Indian culture and European trade goods: The archaeology of the historic period in the western region of the western Great Lakes region*. Madison: University of Wisconsin Press.

Radin, Paul. 1927. *Primitive man as philosopher*. New York: Dover.

Reed-Danahay, Deborah. 1997. *Auto/ethnography: Rewriting the social and the self*. New York: Berg.

Robinson, Harry. 1992. *Nature power: In the spirit of an Okanagan storyteller*. Comp. and ed. Wendy Wickwire. Toronto: Douglas & McIntyre.

Schenck, Theresa. 1995. Beyond gender: 19th century Ojibwa

women as leaders. Paper presented at the American Society for Ethnohistory Annual Meetings, Kalamazoo MI.

Smith, Sidonie, and Julia Watson, eds. 2001. *Reading autobiography: A guide for interpreting life narratives*. Minneapolis: University of Minnesota Press.

Vizenor, Gerald. 2000. *The everlasting sky*. St. Paul: Minnesota Historical Society.

Vizenor, Gerald, and Robert Lee. 1999. *Postindian conversations*. Lincoln: University of Nebraska Press.

Waisberg, Leo. 1984. An ethnographic and historical outline of the Rainy River Ojibway. In Historical synthesis of the Manitou Mounds site on the Rainy River, Ontario, ed. William C. Noble, 119–274. Unpublished Manuscript. National Library of Canada, Ottawa.

Waisberg, Leo, and Tim Holzkamm. 1993. "A tendency to discourage them from cultivating": Ojibwa agriculture and Indian affairs administration in northwestern Ontario. *Ethnohistory* 40 (2): 175–211.

Wolf, Eric. 1984. *Europe and the people without history*. Berkeley: University of California Press.

courtship, 3–4
cousins, 83, 88, 140–41
Cruikshank, Julie, 210n13

dance, xxxix–xl, xli, 22, 136, 139, 154–56, 163, 200
death: burials and, 79–80, 109–10, 130–31, 189–90, 201–2; of children, 15, 25–27, 62–63, 87, 129–30, 134, 184–85, 189–90, 194–95, 200; due to alcohol, 20; due to bears, 189; due to fire, 81; due to freezing, 20, 58–59; due to murder, 13–14, 32–33; due to starvation, 68–69, 129–30; due to train accidents, 102; due to wolves, 181–84; feasts and rituals related to, 136–37; ghosts and, 80–81, 148; of parents, 44–45, 97–98, 178
Densmore, Frances, xli, xlii, xlv, 205n1, 208n8
dogs, 175
dreams, xxxix–xliii, 198–201, 208n5
duck hunting, 35–36, 65
Duluth, Virginia and Rainy Lake Railway, lxv
Dumont, Gabriel, lxiii

education, lxiv, 109, 184
Erdrich, Louise, xxxi, xlii; *The Antelope Wife*, 210n14; *Books and Islands in Ojibwe Country*, lii–liii; *The Last Report on the Miracles at Little No Horse*, 210n14; *Love Medicine*, 210n14; *The Painted Drum*, 210n14

families, Ojibwe: adoption by, 47, 65, 91–92, 104–5, 140–42, 185, 204; cousins and, 83, 140–41; in-laws and, 3–6, 55–57, 67, 79–81, 90; of missing persons, 73–76; and Ojibwe society, xxix; portrayal of, in stories, xlvii; social positions and roles in, xxix–xxxi
farming, xxxv–xxxvi, xxxviii–xxxix, lvii, lxv, 72, 123, 191, 207n2
feasts, 136–37
First World War, xxxix, lxv
fishing, lxiii, lxiv, lxv, 72, 90, 119
food, 37, 38–39, 72, 85, 182
furs, 37, 38, 79, 117

gambling, 21
games and sports, 21, 30–31, 61–62, 98–102, 136, 146
ghosts, 80–81, 148
Ginsburg, Faye, liv
Glenn, James, xii–xiii
Grand Medicine, 49–50, 62–63, 64, 91, 136, 137, 200
grief, 25–27, 43–44, 50, 97–98, 108, 184–85
guns, 30–31, 56–57

Hallowell, Irving, 205n1, 206n2
healing. *See* medicine
hides, animal, 36, 37, 38, 68, 79, 113
Hill, Greg, xli, liv
Hudson's Bay Company, xxxiv, xlvi, lix–lxi, 14, 44, 51, 84, 98–101, 121, 131, 173, 184, 186, 193, 194
hunger. *See* poverty and hunger
Hungry Hall, 15, 21–22, 134, 175, 178, 195
Hunt, George, 205n1
hunting, xxix–xxxi, xxxvi, 28, 57; of bear, 15–16, 17, 59, 67,

of, lvii–lviii; and soul travel, xli;
spirituality of, xxxix–xlii; and
survivance, 210n15; as visionaries, xli–xlii; and whites, 11–12,
38, 93, 131–32, 178–79, 184;
wigwams of, *xxvii*, 6, 13, 17.
See also men, Ojibwe; women,
Ojibwe
Ontario and Rainy River Railway,
lxiv

The Painted Drum (Erdrich),
210n14
Passerini, Luisa, 209n10
pawahgun, l, 150–53, 198–99,
201
Phillips, Ruth, xliv, liv
pigeons, 198–200, 201–2
potlatch ceremonies, lxiii–lxiv
poverty and hunger, xxxviii–xxxix,
xlv, lxiii, 57–58, 118–19, 135,
192; deaths due to, 68–69,
128–29

rabbits, 124, 128, 129
railroads, lxiii, lxiv, lxv, 31, 84,
102, 124–25
Rat Portage. *See* Kenora
Riel, Louis, lxi, lxiii
ropemaking, 86–87
Ruth Landes (Cole), xiii

Schenck, Theresa, xxx
siblings, 73–81, 107
Sioux Indians, 150–57, 160–62,
168–71, 186–89
songs, war, 154–56
soul travel, xli
Spence, Benjamin, xxxiv–xxxvi
Spence, Elizabeth, xxxiv–xxxvi
Spence, Peter, xxxiv–xxxv

Spence, Thomas, xxxvii
sports. *See* games and sports
starvation. *See* poverty and hunger
stepparents, 43–48, 147–50
stories, Ojibwe: autobiographical,
xlviii; historical events and, xlvi,
xlviii–xlix, 209n10; portrayal
of families in, xlvii; telling of,
by women, xxxi–xxxiv, 205n1,
210n13, 211n17; themes and
presentation of, xlix–lii; as told
by Maggie Wilson, xxxii–xxxiv,
xlvi–xlix, l–li, liii–lv, 205n1;
truth in, xlvii–xlviii, 209n10;
violence in, xlvi–xlvii
Strong, William Duncan, xii–xiii
sugar, 44, 46, 149
suicide, 69
survivance, 210n15
sweat tents, 91

Tanner, John, xxxi
tobacco, 151
trading posts, 38, 184, 186, 193; in
Kenora, 9, 42, 78, 141
trains, lxiii, lxiv, lxv, 31, 102, 124

Union Star Dance, xxxix–xl

violence, xlvi–xlvii; between in-
laws, 56–57, 103, 135; between
men, 32–33, 115, 153–54;
between siblings, 73; between
Sioux and Ojibwes, 150–57,
160–62, 164–65; between whites
and Ojibwes, 108, 109; between
women, 21–22, 93; conjugal, 9,
13–14, 31–32, 53, 103, 120–21,
139–40, 209n9
Vizenor, Gerald, xxxi–xxxii, xlviii,
210n15; *Bearheart*, 209n9

www.ingramcontent.com/pod-product-compliance
Lightning Source LLC
Chambersburg PA
CBHW051143030726
47504CB00004B/1014